THE VESTED WAY

Five Rules For Achieving The Impossible

Kate Vitasek

THE VESTED WAY

Five Rules For Achieving The Impossible

Kate Vitasek

Praise for *The Vested Way*

"Most partnerships don't fail because of bad intentions. They fail because expectations aren't aligned. *The Vested Way* shows you how to fix that and build relationships that last."

— **Chester Elton, #1 *New York Times* bestselling author**

* * *

"Innovation requires the kind of deep collaboration Kate Vitasek maps out in *The Vested Way*. This book shows a blueprint of how to transform your most critical partnerships and win together in ways neither party could achieve alone."

— **Jayshree Seth, 3M Chief Science Advocate and author of The Heart of Science trilogy published by Society of Women Engineers.**

* * *

"If you're ready to tackle your impossible, Kate Vitasek's *The Vested Way* is the field guide to help you climb your own Mount Everest."

— **Alison Levine, team captain, American Women's Everest Expedition and author of *On the Edge***

* * *

"The Vested model redefines collaboration by shifting the focus from individual gain to shared success. The business model offers a breakthrough approach that fosters trust and alignment between partners, enabling organisations to create lasting, win-win relationships."

— **Monika Kosman, COO, Thinkers50**

Table of Contents

Author's Note

I have the coolest job on the planet.

For 20-plus years I have researched and advanced the art, science and practice of how to create (and sustain!) highly collaborative relationships. Some days I am a curious student researching how to unlock ways to improve collaboration, while other days I am a dedicated teacher helping companies and my executive education students take their most important business partnerships to next level. Sometimes that means helping organizations go from good to great. And other times it means getting partners back to the basics by repairing fractured relationships that suffer trust gaps and a deep-seated us-versus-them chasm.

Regardless of the starting point, everything I do—from researching and teaching to writing books—is about how to drive exponential results through collaboration.

Before I joined the faculty at University of Tennessee (where I lead research on strategic partnerships), I worked at fast-paced and innovative companies like P&G and Microsoft. I, like many of you, was constantly chartered to do better, faster, cheaper or safer. Often there were bonuses and stock options tied to achieving my goals. Almost always my success meant working with someone who was not in my direct control. People in other functions. Suppliers. Customers.

Most often (thankfully!) I achieved my goals and kept climbing the corporate ladder. I got my first ah-ha moment when I crossed over to what some call "the dark side" when I shifted from working for Microsoft to working for Microsoft's largest supplier. By physically sitting in the chair of the person who I had sat across from previously, I started to better understand the reason behind their questions, concerns and negotiation tactics.

Along the way I also spent nearly a decade as a consultant.

My background has offered me the precious gift of being able to view relationships from all angles: buyers, suppliers, and consultants alike.

My real ah-ha into cracking the code on collaboration came after joining the University of Tennessee where I've had the opportunity to study some of the world's most successful business partnerships. My research got a lift when the Air Force became intrigued and provided funding.

The initial research focused on complex outsourcing partnerships that demanded trading partners work together for success. That early work has evolved from research to a recognized methodology—called Vested—that involves creating highly collaborative relationships in which the parties have a committed and profound interest in each other's success. Simply put, the parties are *vested* in each other's success: they are most successful when both are successful.

In my research and practice, I've witnessed what it truly means to have the magic of collaboration, the kind of relationship where 1+1 equals 11. I've had the opportunity to unpack how that magic happens and the platform to share this message across nearly every industry and business function. It's been rewarding for me to see how Vested relationships can lead to new opportunities and mutual success across a variety of situations.

MY PROMISE

My promise to you, if you choose to read this book, is simple:

First, I promise a book that is not filled with academic jargon. Instead you'll find a book that is easy to read and clearly shows you how to get the most out of your most important relationships. I'll show you how to lay the foundation for those relationships. And equally important, I'll unpack five simple rules you can apply to improve how you collaborate for success with your partners.

Second, I promise you will find a practical book full of solutions. You will not need a billion-dollar contract to use it. You will just need a clear goal and a willingness to rethink how you are working with your partner.

I've filled the book with some of my favorite (and many awe inspiring!) case studies to show how real organizations are putting the concepts I teach into practice.

HOW TO USE THIS BOOK

Across this book's 10 chapters you will find real examples and many simple tools you can use. My hope is that you will use this book for inspiration to see the art of the possible—learning how others achieved remarkable success by consciously choosing to collaborate in a highly effective manner.

As I teach in my executive education courses, consider working through this book with your partner. I have found that those who are the most serious about improving their collaborations don't try to use collaboration tools as a one-sided effort. After all, a partnership by definitions means there is more than just you. For example, if you are trying to improve collaboration across functions in your organization, consider a weekly lunch and learn event/meetup going over a chapter each week and save two weeks at the end to develop your playbook on what you are committing to change to make your relationship better.

My second tip is to use this book as a playbook. Interact with the book. Digitally clip notes that you can review. Or, if you're old-school like me, use a highlighter to make it easy to come back for a review later as you strategize how to put the lessons into practice. I've purposefully added tools and a checklist throughout the book so you can pause and think about how you can apply Vested insights into your collaborations and take stock of perverse incentives, misalignments or suboptimal behaviors that may have slipped into your relationships.

Third, if you wish to use any of the tools and tips I share, you can download them for free at VestedWay.com/tools. Pick and choose the ones you think will help you the best or download all of them with one easy click.

Lastly, I urge you to not fall into the trap of doing nothing. I am 100% confident that you will gain at least one insight you can use to make your relationships better. Use your notes and the tools to develop your own playbook, preferably with your partner. And when (not if!) you are successful, please share on social media with #VestedWay so myself and others can learn from and be inspired by your success.

HOW THIS BOOK IS STRUCTURED

This book will help you discover and implement how the Vested way can transform your relationships.

Part 1—The Foundation of Great Partnerships

The book's first section introduces the building blocks of strong relationships: trust, transparency and cultural fit. I devote an entire chapter to each topic and share examples of how real people and real organizations are getting this right.

Part 2—The Way Forward

Part 2 builds on the heart of my research—the Vested methodology. The Vested Five Rules were originally developed as a way to guide organizations on crafting complex outsourcing partnerships. Over the years the rules have been applied by over 150 organizations across five continents in many diverse scenarios, such as how Canada's Island Health Authority and a group of specialized Hospitalist physicians used the rules to rewrite how they worked to shift their culture from toxic and adversarial to collaborative, trusting and innovative. In each chapter I also share how the rules can be applied in personal relationships. You'll also find a Tools of the Trade toolkit and see how the tools are being in applied in various scenarios.

Part 3—A Call to Action

Part 3 is short and sweet. The end of the book has just one chapter, a call to action that invites you to consider systems thinking and explore how the rules work together to deliver optimal results for you and your partner.

MY CHALLENGE TO YOU

We're constantly being bombarded with information from emails, apps, news-feeds and Netflix. And yet, you're still reading. That tells me you care about building relationships that work and you want more out of the ones in your life.

For those who want to dig in deeper and drive real change in your most precious relationships, I encourage you to join the Vested movement. While my research is steeped in complex strategic deals, the rules can be applied to any type of relationship. I encourage you to share your notes with business partners and teammates—and use what you learn to shape a healthier home life for you and your family

Or pass on your highlighted book to a local politician and encourage them to choose a better way to work that builds a better community.

1

From Me to We

Us vs. Them.
This side vs. that side.
With us or against us.

These are divided times. Distrust and conflict are tearing at the fabric of our communities, workplaces, neighborhoods and even our own dinner tables. Divisions leave us feeling isolated and separated.

We face complex challenges that require input from others, yet we fall back on self-protective habits—short-term wins, negotiation tactics and zero-sum thinking. Everyone pulls harder, but not in the same direction.

We focus on our differences instead of seeking common ground.

We double down on our positions, convinced we're right—and that everyone else is a threat.

Friction and division have left us stuck, with the sinking feeling that we could accomplish so much more if only we learned how to get along. But collaboration isn't something most of us have ever effectively learned how to do. This reality is revealed through sad statistics that show we struggle to make our most cherished business or personal relationships succeed.

Nearly 70% of business partnerships fail within the first three years, while about 40% of marriages end in divorce. Friendships are also struggling—the percentage of adults who report having no close friends has quadrupled over the course of 35 years. More and more adult children are choosing to go "no contact" with their parents, deciding to pull away because the relationship has fractured.

Poor collaboration is impacting our interpersonal relationships at work with unprecedented levels of incivility in the workplace. And when things get too difficult, individuals and organizations find themselves mired in costly court battles. Case in point, employment issues and breach of contract are the two most common types of disputes.

Our communities and broader society are also suffering as the U.S. is continuing its trend toward increased political polarization.

Simply put, we're struggling to get along.

V FORMATIONS AND VESTED RELATIONSHIPS

Even though we struggle to get on the same page, deep down, we truly do need each other. I'm sure you sense that, too. If you don't believe me, consider what driving on the road would feel like if everyone followed their own rules and didn't work together.

It would be pure chaos (even more than it already is).

Nature also offers lessons about collaboration. Picture a flock of birds flying in a V formation—an arrangement that reflects not only the power of group dynamics and sticking together, but also the efficiency of the group. The way the birds arrange themselves isn't a mistake, it's by design.

Flying in a V formation allows the trailing birds to maximize the boost from the air flow and in turn, expend about 20% less energy than if they were flying alone. Each bird rides the uplift of the bird ahead to reduce drag and save energy. When the lead bird tires, it drops back and another takes point. They go farther together because they rely on one another.

The V is more than a formation. It's an identity. When you fly in formation, you draft off shared momentum. When you lead, you carry the wind for the group. When you tire, you rotate back and keep the pace. No heroics. No drag. Just progress together.

The process of working together isn't innate and automatic for us like it is for the birds. We have to work at it.

Think about getting assigned a big project at work with someone you don't get along with. If you want to be successful, you set aside your differences and work together. Or consider the relationships in your life that aren't as strong as you want them to be.

You've likely observed these relationships are often time sucking and energy draining. They take work. But then again think about your best relationships. The ones that are working well and creating tangible benefits from the collaboration. I'd bet it's almost certain you put work into those relationships too.

Through my research and experience I discovered the secret sauce that fosters successful relationships.

My fellow researchers and I codified these lessons into the Vested methodology—a system that helps people get and stay aligned.

Why the name Vested? Because our research revealed that when collaborators have a committed and profound interest in each other's success, they are exponentially more likely to be successful. Simply put, they are *vested* in each other's success: they are most successful when both are successful.

When partners are Vested they can achieve the impossible together—like climbing Everest.

BETTER TOGETHER

Namgyal Wangdi would have understood the concept of being vested in the success of his partner even though he never attended school, let alone college. Born poor around 1914, his background is sketchy. Some historians say he ran away from home twice and was sent to a nearby monastery to be a monk. It didn't work. Perhaps he had a higher calling,

Namgyal later changed his name to Tenzing Norgay and became a porter helping climbers during their adventures exploring Mount Everest.

By 1953, he was on his seventh expedition as a sherpa on an expedition led by Colonel John Hunt. When two members of the expedition failed to reach the top, Hunt directed the next pair of climbers to conquer the summit. Edmund Hillary and Sherpa Tenzing started the climb.

On May 29, 1953, the men became the first to to summit Mount Everest—a feat once thought impossible.

People clamored to find out whose spike was the first to reach a height never before attained by any man. Both men maintained that they had ascended the top of the mountain together. Hunt would declare, "This is teamwork, actually we climbed together."

Hillary, too, brushed aside the question.

"What does it matter?" he said. "We were roped together. Neither of us could have got anywhere without the other."

Was there really a winner?

Did one man spike that first boot before another?

In his book *Tiger of the Snows*, Norgay addressed what the partnership meant to him.

"All the way up and down we helped, and were helped by, each other—and that was the way it should be. But we were not leader and led. We were partners."

He continued: "I was not thinking of 'first' and 'second.' I did not say to myself, 'There is a golden apple up there. I will push Hillary aside and run for it.' We went on slowly, steadily. And then we were there. Hillary stepped on top first. And I stepped up after him."

"If it is a discredit to me that I was a step behind Hillary, then I must live with that discredit," he wrote.

The simple fact is it did not matter who got there first; *the climbers both achieved something that had never been done.* And both men knew they could not have done it without the other. Mutual success. Mutual reward. Winning together.

FROM MOUNTAINS TO MARRIAGES AND MOPS

Winning together may work when it comes to climbing a mountain, but does it apply to the real world of business and marriages? The answer is yes.

Perhaps a classic example of a successful partnership is a healthy marriage. Being happily married brings many positive benefits versus tackling the world solo. Census Bureau statistics report married couples aged 65 and older have a median net worth of $600,000, while unmarried male householders and unmarried female householders of the same age had median net worths of $197,900 and $184,000. Young couples fare well too, with married couples between the ages of 24 and 35 having a net worth up to nine times as high as single households.

But married couples are not just wealthier, they are also happier and healthier.

Research has repeatedly shown that married people have better mental health than those who are single, widowed, separated and divorced. Did you know that married men and women outlive their single counterparts? A meta-analysis of over 90 research studies showed single women have a 48-64% higher mortality risk, depending on age group while single men have a mortality rate approximately 73% higher than married men.[15]

Winning together, similarly, proves beneficial for the economics of business relationships.

Take, for example the mega successful partnership behind Procter & Gamble's Swiffer brand of cleaning products. When Craig Wynett, Director of Corporate New Ventures, watched his wife struggling to keep their floors clean he thought there had to be a better way.

With that hunch, P&G assembled a team to find a solution. They watched people cleaning their floors and came to recognize that floor cleaning required a complex process with a system of products. It wasn't easy or simple at all. It involved sweeping and mopping—with the mop water and mop head/sponges getting progressively dirtier with usage.

P&G came up with a prototype—initially dubbed "a diaper wipe on a stick"—which was branded FastClean. The solution used disposable sheets attached to a handle.

The idea *worked*. But there was a problem.

A Japan-based company, UniCharm, had already developed a handheld dusting tool that was much better than the prototype product the P&G team developed. And to complicate the situation UniCharm was a fierce competitor in Japan across several product lines in Asia. Would it be willing to collaborate in other markets across the globe?

P&G thought it was worth a try.

UniCharm was receptive and ultimately decided that collaboration was better than competition; P&G's solution? Buy the rights to the duster outside of Japan. To speed up time to market, UniCharm made the dusters and helped start up production at a P&G plant in Canada. Both companies even used the same advertising.

The Swiffer Duster was an instant success. In the first four months the duster cleaned up $100 million in sales. Consumers loved seeing dust and debris trapped in those curly fibers. And the shared winning continues.

Who Won?

Everyone.

UniCharm didn't have the supply chain capabilities or marketing strength to take the product to other markets. If it had tried, who knows how long it would have taken. Certainly longer than the 18 months that it took P&G to launch the product under its Swiffer brand.

P&G won by having an innovative product to add to its quick-clean market. Not just one market, but 15 global markets. Add to that continual improvements and innovations, and the results are eye-opening. It is one of the leading brands in P&G's fabric and home care division.

Consumers won too. They now have a product that cleans efficiently, is reasonably priced, and makes them more effective with their home cleaning tasks.

Two competitors. Both winning. Together.

They found their Pony.

FINDING THE PONY

Former U.S. President Ronald Reagan had a favorite joke about twin boys who were five or six years old. The boys developed extreme personalities. One was an absolute pessimist, the other a cheery optimist. Their parents were so concerned, they met with a renowned psychiatrist.

The psychiatrist treated the pessimistic boy first. He took the child to a room piled to the ceiling with all types of new toys. The little boy burst into tears.

"What's the matter?" the psychiatrist asked. "Don't you want to play with any of the toys?"

"Yes," the little boy cried, "but if I did I'd only break them."

Stunned, the psychiatrist next met with the optimistic child. Here the room was completely different. In an attempt to dampen the child's outlook, the room was filled to the ceiling with horse manure. The boy yelped in delight, climbed to the top of the pile, and began digging through the manure with his bare hands.

"What on earth do you think you're doing?" the psychiatrist asked.

"With all this manure," the boy replied, beaming, "there must be a pony in here somewhere!"

"Reagan told the joke so often," Ed Meese, Reagan's former chief of staff, said, "that it got to be kind of a joke with the rest of us. Whenever something would go wrong, somebody on the staff would be sure to say, "There must be a pony in here somewhere.""

Problem or Opportunity?

How many times do we see the manure but fail to see the Pony? It all boils down to the perspective to see problems as opportunities and to recognize the art of the possible when others cannot.

Of course, some problems are relatively small and can be dealt with without too much inconvenience. They are tolerable issues with easy fixes.

And then there are those big, impossible, impractical problems—the kinds of problems that, if solved, would make a lot of people very happy.

Most of us have names for our big problems. Impossible. Impractical. P&G refers to them as "wicked problems." If you solve a wicked problem, you'll make a lot of people very happy.

Solving big problems and making the "impossible" possible offers us the potential to unlock value-creating opportunities when others cannot. There are lots of tough issues facing our communities and world. And maybe the solutions are out there, just waiting for you to uncover them.

The Little Engine That Could

James Watt had a problem. He was broke. He had spent all of his money on his invention. His partner and financial backer had gone bankrupt. His patent had expired, leaving him without any funds to continue his research.

Deep down he knew he should continue. But how?

After two years of visiting the Patent Office in London from his home in Glasgow, Watt received an extension on his patent. With it, he was able to secure funding from Matthew Boulton.

James Watt developed the concept of horsepower. The unit of measurement called the watt is named after him. Together Watt and Boulton brought a more efficient and powerful steam engine to market in England. Watt's steam engine is credited for jump-starting the Industrial Revolution. But Watt could not have done it without Boulton.

Watt and Boulton even revolutionized the way customers paid for the use of their efficient steam engine to make it more affordable. They charged an annual payment, equal to one third of the value of the coal saved by switching from older, less efficient coal-burning engines performing the same work.

James Watt had great ideas on improving the steam engine but lacked necessary resources. Matthew Boulton saw the value of improving the engine and had the financial resources to do so. Together, by sharing their respective skills and resources, they changed the world.

They both could see the potential Pony. Together, they really did create the little engine that could.

What's Your Pony?

If you are facing a problem or trying to achieve the impossible, perhaps there is a Pony in it for you by consciously choosing to work with a more collaborative win-win mindset and follow the Vested Five Rules. Your definition of "impossible" could be anything.

- Getting along with an enemy.
- Completing a demanding work project.
- Strengthening your relationships with family and friends.
- Achieving more out of a transactional, frustrating business partnership.
- Accomplishing something that's never been done before.

The process of getting and staying Vested requires a lot more than just wanting to improve your collaboration. There are reasons why your past collaborations or relationships might have fallen short. And through the Vested way, there is a pathway to strengthen and empower your most important collaborations.

Whatever your goal, this book is the field guide to help you achieve your impossible.

THE VESTED WAY

Vested is a mindset and methodology that enables people to solve seemingly impossible problems. It's a mindset that shifts from *what's-in-it-for-Me* (WIIFMe) to *what's-in-it-for-We* (WIIFWe) to harness the power of true collaboration.

But it is so much more than simply a mindset; it's a proven methodology that has been adopted by leading organizations around the world such as Intel, bp, JLL, Discovery Health, Compass, Telenet, EY, ISS, IBM, Securitas and the Canadian government.

The core of Vested is simple. Partners purposely lay a strong foundation by consciously building trust, transparency and cultural fit. They then follow five proven "rules" that align interests and harness the potential of true collaboration, unlocking value and creating healthy partnerships.

On the surface, the rules seem simple. However, in practice they are often elusive. Rob McIntosh, now the Senior Vice President in Global Operations at Dell Technologies, shared how he was originally a skeptic in an interview with Supply Chain Brain magazine.

"The Vested concept was a little bit far-reaching," McIntosh shared in the interview. "It was a cultural change more than a commercial change on how we looked at the relationship."

Implementing the Vested way enabled Rob and the reverse logistics team at Dell to reduce costs by 42%, scrap by 67%, and defective parts per million to record-low levels. Their supplier (Genco, later acquired by FedEx Supply Chain Services) increased their profit by as much as 10x in some quarters through incentives.

Why are there skeptics like Rob? Because the rules often go against human nature to use power when you have it. And to take the easy path to success which most often means short-term wins. While successful, these approaches limit our willingness to want to swing for the fences and seek out big hairy audacious goals that may seem impossible. These forces are even harder in business relationships, where many have been hard-wired to believe that winning means winning at the other partner's expense.

The sad fact is we're often conditioned to use power-based approaches to help us win at the expense of others. This fact came across loud and clear during my research when one Chief Procurement Officer of a Fortune 100 company matter-of-factly stated, "Kate, win-win is when we get to win twice."

A reliance on power to win is not new. Sun Tzu's classic treatise *The Art of War* is now more than 2,000 years old. But while muscular approaches may bring short-term benefits, research shows that using them has a damaging effect over time—especially in situations where parties have ongoing interaction. Trust erodes. Costs increase. Partners become more guarded and are drawn to deepen their collaborations with others.

THE VESTED MOVEMENT

Rob McIntosh was one of the first leaders to challenge his organization to give Vested a try. Since then, I've taught the rules to over 13,000 leaders from over 900 organizations challenging the status quo on how they collaborate for success. Many have gone on to graduate from the University of Tennessee's Certified Deal Architect program. Under their leadership, cities have solved crises, companies have saved millions, governments are improving patient care and supplier's profits are growing.

Across decades of research and real-world application, the Vested movement has grown from its university origins into a global movement practiced by organizations around the world. In 2025, Vested was selected by Thinkers50, a global resource for identifying and ranking leading management strategies, as one of the Breakthrough Ideas.

The heart of the Vested movement? A desire to move beyond us-versus-them thinking and a willingness to choose a WIIFWe mindset. When we play to win together, our mutual success creates more success. Success begets success.

Today, organizations across five continents have turned to Vested to transform how they work with some of their most strategic partners. I am honored to be able to profile leading organizations with case studies featured throughout the book. Many organizations have been openly public about how they have adopted Vested for select strategic partnerships.

And equally rewarding is that some of these leaders have shared their personal stories on how the rules they applied in the business world also helped them improve the health and harmony of their relationships on the homefront.

If Vested has been transformative for some of the world's biggest and most complex collaborations, it can certainly be transformative for your relationships and partnerships, too.

As you read the stories and lessons I share in this book, I challenge you to answer this question: Just how Vested am I in the success of my partner? If you do not have a vested interest in your partner's success, you are likely not getting the best from them. And they are likely not getting the best from you, either.

Part 1:

Laying the Foundation

Maria and Martin pursued their dream life.

Two kids. White picket fence.

They were off to a good start with two beautiful girls—Ava and Liv. Between the children and lots of work-from-home remote conferencing, things started getting cramped. They set aside quite a bit of money for a new house. But then they hit a wall.

The problems began innocently enough. Martin started golfing more frequently with his buddies, and Maria felt like she deserved her "me time," too, in the form of manicures and massages. It was for her sanity, she told herself.

The husband and wife were putting themselves first—and that me-first thinking was keeping them from accomplishing their ultimate goal of buying their new house. Not only that, but they also viewed their own actions as justified, increasing the likelihood of frustrations bubbling over. They faced an inflection point.

* * *

Kim Kerrone, Island Health's Vice President, Chief Financial Officer, Legal Services & Risk, was at her wit's end. There was a vast divide with a group of doctors who performed advanced hospitalist services at two of Island Health's main hospitals, and contract negotiations had come to a standstill.

But Kim was not the only one frustrated. Dr. Jean Maskey—the lead doctor in charge of the negotiations for the Hospitalists—referred to the contract negotiations as "the troubles." Despite attempts at negotiation, the contract expired. The parties continued to operate under the terms of the expired contract, but the environment to achieve a new contract was challenging.

Each side argued that the contract talks were not about money, but about how to perform the job and by how many doctors. The Hospitalists felt they were being micromanaged and squeezed monetarily. They wanted a more flexible workload-based contract and argued Island Health's plan included cutbacks that would jeopardize physician safety and the ability to deliver an excellent and consistent service to patients. On the other side, Island Health Administrators were concerned about the transparency of the Hospitalists scheduling and hourly billing practices. The administrators were pushing for a new model aimed at more transparent measurement and reporting. They also wanted efficiency initiatives.

With each negotiation cycle, the culture took a step backward, growing increasingly bitter as neither side seemed to be making headway in the contract negotiations. An external assessment painted a stark picture of just how bad the relationship was; 84% of the administrators and doctors described the relationship as negative, using words such as "distrustful," "toxic" and "bullying." Clearly, neither side was happy.

* * *

In 1971, the city of Durham, North Carolina found itself in a very tense situation after a federal district judge ordered Durham Schools to desegregate.

With tensions rising, Durham needed to pull together.

The idea came up to use a collaborative "charrette" process to address issues facing the community and establish a series of recommendations. The goal of the charrette? A committee of diverse community members would provide recommendations on improvements for Durham's schools. The discussions would cover all sorts of topics, including racism, student safety and teacher qualifications.

The initiative was called "Save Our Schools."

C.P. Ellis and Ann Atwater were selected to serve as co-chairs of the Save Our Schools charrette. Ellis and Atwater could not be more culturally misfit. Ellis was the president of the local Ku Klux Klan chapter and Atwater was an outspoken black community activist. Ellis and Atwater had often argued with each other at various town meetings. Needless to say, they were not enthusiastic about working together.

* * *

Writers and producers David Crane and Marta Kauffman had an idea for a TV sitcom. In 1994, they pitched a show about six young adults trying to make it in New York City. The characters included Monica, a smart, cynical chef; Rachel, Monica's spoiled and adorable best friend from high school; the new-age Phoebe, Monica's former roommate; Ross, Monica's intelligent and emotional brother; Joey, a smug wannabe actor; and Chandler, droll and sharp-witted, who sits in front of a computer all day doing something (no one quite knows what that is).

NBC liked the idea and ordered a pilot even before a script was written. The show was called *Friends Like Us* and *Six of One* before settling on its straightforward name, *Friends*.

But who would play the characters? The show's casting director took the job seriously, reviewing hundreds of glossy black-and-white photos for each role. About 75 actors read for each part.

Everything—whether the show would be well received and continue or fall by the wayside and be immediately forgotten—would come down to the cast. The friends needed to click and bond. A group of great actors who didn't gel would mean a failed show. In order for this to work, *these actors needed to actually become friends.*

* * *

As you will see in this book, each of the stories above involved having an open mind to consider at least looking at the "the other person" in terms of a person with a problem and not the competitor or the enemy on the other side with a position.

Having that open mind isn't always easy. Far too often, we stay in our own social bubble and choose sides.

Us vs. Them.

This side vs. that side.

With us or against us.

To make matters worse, our society has evolved where it's easier than ever for people to operate in their own information and social bubbles, isolated from those whose viewpoints don't align with theirs. It's easier to stay stuck focusing on our differences instead of putting in the work to lay the foundation to see if there could potentially be common ground. We double down on our positions, convinced we're right, and tell ourselves that everyone else who views it differently is a threat.

The result? At best we find ourselves in tough business negotiations. At worst we sit on the sidelines while our communities fail to tackle tough problems. And at home we fall in the trap of avoiding our partners in order to sidestep arguments.

In order to achieve your impossible, you almost certainly will need to work with "the other guy." When you are put in that position, you can go in with a closed "What's in it for Me" mindset. But doing so will almost always trigger a similar response from the other guy.

Or you can enter the situation with an inquisitive "What's in it for We" mindset. That shift may feel like an impossible task—but it is possible if you openly discuss concepts like trust, transparency and cultural fit.

Accordingly, Part 1 of the book is devoted to **Laying the Foundation**. The pages ahead detail the essential pre-conditions for a successful relationship to flourish: trust, transparency and cultural fit.

As you read the stories and lessons, challenge yourself to consider if you have used the tools and tricks as these partners have to lay the right foundation.

If you have not put in the hard work laying the foundation with your partner, you are likely not getting the best out of them.

Of course, you will likely go into the discussion thinking you don't have much in common. But if you take the time to sit down with the other side and have a rational discussion using the tools and tips used in these chapters you may find yourself surprised.

Taking the first step to sit down and have that discussion is a choice. But that choice to take the first step may just be the magic moment you need to turn your relationship around or get out of the gate with a new relationship.

2

Not Everyone Can Be Best Friends

Ride or die
Besties.
Oprah and Gayle.

No celebrities quite embody true friendship like Oprah Winfrey and Gayle King. The duo first connected in the mid-1970s when they worked at WJZ-TV in Baltimore. Winfrey was one of the TV station's on-air anchors, and King was a production assistant.

There was a snowstorm and King couldn't get home. She ended up staying at Winfrey's house, which was much closer to the TV Station. They've been inseparable ever since.

For Oprah and Gayle, their friendship is built on respect—the kind that, as Oprah stated in a 2006 interview, "comes from being with somebody you know doesn't want anything from you but you. There will never be an ulterior motive. I have to say, this would have been a much different relationship had that ever happened. Not that I wouldn't have done it, but in order to have a real friendship, you have to be equals." They practice an authentic form of candor. Gayle had no problem, during the height of her friend's TV influence and fame, placing "emergency" calls to give her two cents about Oprah's wardrobe or hair. Someone needed to say it, after all, and why not Gayle? Oprah would return the favor years later as her friend's TV career took off.

In the other they saw a kindred spirit. Both were young black women who grew up in all-white communities trying to find their way in the world. The two were never equals financially or in regard to fame. King has done quite well for herself as a trusted CBS News anchor—but Oprah is *Oprah*, after all.

"Equal in respect. I can't put myself in a position where I need you to do things for me, or expect you to do things for me with any kind of strings attached," Oprah said in the same interview.

"Yeah, I never feel lesser than or one down. Never," King added.

Equal in respect. Friendship without strings attached.

It's the kind of mutual respect we should all strive for—especially when we are seeking to find a partner to help solve our toughest personal, professional and social problems. When considering the partnerships we want to elevate most, it can be beneficial to uplift our strongest relationships. A deep bond and the desire to collaborate on a new level are great foundational elements on the path to Vested.

On the other hand, your potential Vested partner need not be your best friend. Sometimes you wind up collaborating deeply with someone out of need or mutual benefit. Whether you begin your Vested journey with a best friend or a bitter rival, there are other elements that must come into play for the partnership to be successful.

Let's explore the power of "best friends." Such relationships aren't easy to find. And when they appear, we can't help but be drawn in.

GROWING TOGETHER

Millions of us were glued to our televisions each week to watch the aptly-named TV show *Friends*. The hit show, which debuted in 1994, was centered around six 20-somethings finding their way. The core characters—Rachel, Ross, Monica, Chandler, Phoebe and Joey—captivated us as they grew together over 10 seasons and 236 episodes.

The cast shared a depiction of true friendship that would carry each other through relationships, marriages, children, jobs, moves, life experiences, fertility struggles, tragedy and triumph. As the show's iconic theme song goes, *I'll be there for you.*

Friends, while idealistic, remains a beacon of hope for the potential of friendships and highlights the importance of not just *finding* your best friends, but growing and evolving and maturing together—bringing out the best in one another.

That was reflected in the collaborative nature on the set, where the actors were given true agency, a seat at the table. As David Schwimmer, who played Ross, said, "they made it clear to me that it was going to be a collaborative effort and that I would have a voice."

The castmates fed off of one another and gave each other ideas and input. None of the actors tried to position themselves above the rest. They made the same amount of money and appeared in interviews together as a cohesive unit.

The cast's strong foundation allowed them to grow together. The ensemble nature of the show allowed the six to shine collectively. They were all on a journey, and the only other people in the world who really understood what was going on in each other's lives was the other five.

As Jennifer Aniston, who played Rachel, recalled in a 2021 series reunion special, "It kind of imprinted in our neural pathways...we are actually family."

THE TRUTH ABOUT CLOSE FRIENDS

Not everyone is your best friend. Most people aren't—and that's OK.

According to a 2023 Pew Research Center survey on friendship, just over half of U.S. adults (53%) say they have between one and four close friends. Another 38% reported having five or more.

Close friends and casual friends aren't the same. While Oprah and Gayle and the cast of *Friends* represent examples of true friendships, Facebook turned the concept of a "friend" from one of your trusted allies to one that is akin to trying to keep up with all of your sorority sisters and distant cousins. The average Facebook user has about 150-200 "friends." LinkedIn further transactionalized the concept of friendship with the easy-to-use "connect" button. Today you can connect with anyone you have met in your professional life with the hopes of someday networking with them in the future. It's nice to have friends. But from all of these "friends" and "connections," how many do you truly trust? How many can you rely on?

It's better to have a few close friends, the kind who have your back through the thick and thin of life. Best friends can bring out the best in us, keep us accountable, celebrate us in the good times and lift us up when we need it most. The discourse, vulnerability and trust you share with close friends can go so much deeper than conversations with our typical connections and acquaintances. We feel like we can be more open and honest—our true self—with our best friends. With others, we tend to hold back and stay guarded.

The more common our goals with our best friends, the stronger our bonds in enabling us to achieve a greater success.

The same can be said about great business partnerships.

It's the magic that happened when Disney brought Pixar under its wing to revolutionize the animation industry, with Pixar marrying their cutting-edge animation technology with Disney's storytelling expertise and global reach. The creative collaboration dominated the animation industry with blockbuster hits like *Toy Story*, *The Incredibles* and *Finding Nemo*. Or it's how P&G cleaned up when they partnered with Unicharm to take Unicharm's curly cleaning fiber technology and turn it into the billion dollar Swiffer brand.

But not all partnerships have a high potential. And recognizing that fact can help us prioritize the relationships that matter most and accomplish amazing things together.

TRANSACTIONAL RELATIONSHIPS

Most relationships are transactional in nature. You probably wouldn't expect to have the same level of connection with your dry cleaner or your child's school bus driver as you do with your spouse or best friend. Transactional relationships like these aren't contingent on transparency. You don't have to let them know that you had a fight with your sibling or used your debit card to get the car serviced.

Similarly, many, if not most, business relationships are transactional. There is no long-term loyalty present or desire to seek a deeper relationship. A simple sole proprietorship might work with dozens of such outside companies, while global corporations could have tens of thousands of outside business partners (P&G for example has more than 60,000 business partners).

When you work in a transactional way, there are few if any deeper ties. It's pretty simple to switch out your dry cleaner or pen supplier.

Often we want to build deeper relationships—by choice or by need. A couple may decide to get married after successfully dating. An entrepreneur and an investor by default create deeper ties because they rely on each other for their mutual success; the more successful the entrepreneur, the higher the return for the investor. Or a company may need to rely on a sole-source supplier relationship for a critical part of service. When there is more dependency either by choice or need, the rules of the relationship need to change. Why? You can't simply switch out a spouse or a strategic business partner.

Problems arise when we have a strategic relationship and don't change the underlying nature to foster the essential trust and transparency that enables our VIP relationships to flourish.

"SELL THE MAILROOM"

The journey recognize and prioritize our most important business relationships has evolved in recent decades, moving us past the days when many companies relied on vertical integration and local suppliers. As businesses became more diverse, internal support services and functional silos developed. Over the years the number of business relationships has grown as well.

In the late 1980s and 1990s scholars and leading consultants began to challenge the bureaucratic bulge of big business. One of the biggest challenges came from management consultant and educator Peter Drucker, who wrote an iconic essay, "Sell the Mailroom," that was published in the *Wall Street Journal* in 1989.

Why were companies being challenged? For most businesses, performing work that is not a core competency is not efficient or effective. Drucker and other leading academics argued in-house service and support activities are de facto monopolies with little incentive to improve their productivity. There is, after all, no competition.

Amid this background the concept of focusing on your core competencies came to the forefront. The concept is simple: if you're not the best at something, you should work with somebody else who is. Said another way, do what you do best and outsource the rest.

The result? The concept of outsourcing grew rapidly. Today, 90% of Fortune 500 companies outsource at least some logistics and over 50% of companies outsource facilities management operations.

As companies began to outsource, they also began to look at low-cost countries as a source of production and to perform low-value added tasks. Take, for example, the automotive industry. A Ford Mustang GT is assembled at the Ford's Flat Rock Assembly Plant in Flat Rock, Michigan. According to American University's 2024 Made in America auto index, 27% of the content in a Ford Mustang GT with a manual transmission has parts that hail from countries outside of the United States. Or consider the fact the global business process outsourcing market was valued at US$280 billion in 2023 and is projected to grow at a Compound Annual Growth Rate (CAGR) of 9.4 percent from 2023 to 2030.

Our business relationships are more complex than ever before. And through that complexity there's lots that can go wrong.

PERVERSE INCENTIVES

We often say our partner is "special," "strategic" or "the one" but mistakenly treat them in a transactional manner. One reason transactional relationships struggle to achieve alignment is inherent perverse incentives, which often stemming from the way organizations and individuals are measured and compensated.

Perverse incentives inflicted progress on the Transcontinental Railroad in the 1860s connecting the Central Pacific and Union Pacific railroads. Congress offered bonds for each mile of railroad completed. As a result, the two companies laid 225 miles of parallel tracks before halting efforts. Similarly, 19th-century paleontologists traveling to China used to pay peasants for dinosaur bones that they found. Much to their surprise, they discovered the peasants were breaking the bones into smaller pieces to maximize their payments.

One of my favorite examples of perverse incentives is a story involving a cheese company. The company's HR leader called after reaching their wit's end.

"We've got a problem," they said. "We established a performance management and bonus system to motivate workers, but the company's been losing money after we put the bonus system in place. Why is it not working?"

The answer was simple. Measurement and rewards were at the individual department level, creating a focus on functional silo optimization rather than cross-functional collaboration. For example procurement professionals got a bonus based on how cheaply they could buy curd. The team was highly motivated to meet their target, and to no one's surprise, hit their targets and unlocked their bonus.

The unintended consequence from the inferior cheese curd popped up downstream in manufacturing because it caused the machines that make the cheese to gum up. The downtime caused poor manufacturing throughput—the key performance metric for the manufacturing function. The team brainstormed solutions on how to improve performance and found the perfect solution: do fewer product changeovers. So once the line was set up for cheddar cheese, they made tons (literally tons) of it so they could improve their throughput rate (and yes, earn their bonus).

Of course this caused an unintended consequence further downstream for the distribution team, which was faced with out of stocks on everything except cheddar cheese.

Everybody was doing the best they could *for their functional silo* but overall performance for the company as a whole suffered.

I often use an analogy of tug-of-war. In the classic childhood game of tug-of-war, you dig in and use your force and weight to pull the other team in your direction. Team members were working really hard but they weren't all on the same team pulling the rope in the same direction.

LOOKING AT PARTNERSHIPS WITH A DIFFERENT LENS

What if we approached our more precious relationships—those we either want to go deeper with by choice or those we have to make work because of a high degree of dependency—with a different mindset? A mindset that we need to care and treat these "special" relationships differently than typical transactional partners.

Let's revisit the tug-of-war analogy. Imagine if we changed the rules of the game where the goal is to get on the same side of the rope with our partner and put our problem on the other side. Imagine the exponential power of pulling together rather than pulling in opposite directions. Imagine the tension between functional silos and trading partners fading away as team members and companies pull in harmony to achieve the broader goals of the organization.

The best strategic relationships do just that. They collaborate under a shared vision and mutually defined desired outcomes where the parties' goals are aligned.

Unfortunately it's easy to fall into the trap of having a great vision or mission statement but still falling short of your expected outcomes.

That problem is especially true for big companies where individual workers often find themselves stuck in silos and struggling to break free. Working across teams adds complexity when everybody has their functional silo hats on, whereas one person's (or an entire team's) silo metrics can conflict with another team or functional silo.

The problem grows even more complex when organizations work with external partners. Take for example the classic buyer-supplier tug-of-war of price. The procurement function in a buying company often uses a metric called purchase price variance (PPV). The goal of PPV is for procurement professionals to measure how much money they save versus the last time that item (or service) was purchased. On the surface it looks like a smart metric because it encourages procurement professionals to try to save money for their company by seeking to get the lower price.

But consider the fact that sitting across the negotiating table is a sales professional from the supplier. Salespeople are often compensated with a commission, a bonus linked on the amount of revenue they sell. This means they want higher prices and more revenue.

By default, those goals conflict. It's akin to playing tug-of-war—with each company using their power to win at the negotiations table.

When we are sitting across the table from individuals, departments and companies that should be our partners, we find ourselves with a system problem like we learned about from the cheese company. The individual parts are working hard to achieve their goal, but often end up working against each other.

Getting alignment means putting egos aside and coming together as one, focusing on eliminating friction between you and your goal. When we're all working together to move in the same direction there's no stopping what we can accomplish.

The Boys in the Boat

Rowing is a sport about alignment and synchronization. The rowers respond to the coxswain's commands. If one rower is creating too much drag with their oar or rowing at the wrong time, it creates friction as the boat moves through the water, slowing down the entire group.

A group of young men from sun-deprived Seattle didn't have a lot of rowing experience. But the University of Washington students, who hailed from humble backgrounds, had heart and determination. And UW's head coach Al Ulbrickson had a special knack for shaping and molding rowers' raw athleticism into something more.

A key part of Ulbrickson's strategy was to put together the best possible team that would set egos aside and work together. One person in the wrong position would hamper the team's chances for success.

Ulbrickson mixed and matched team members until he found the right combination. This wasn't about simply finding the best rowers, but the best *combination* of rowers. The best combination of *friends*. Their mission, together, became "rowing as one."

The perfect combination consisted of Bobby Moch at coxswain, Donald Hume at stroke, and Joe Rantz, George Hunt, Jim McMillin, Johnny White, Gordon Adam and Charles Day, with Roger Morris in the bow seat.

"This was a hardscrabble bunch, mentally and physically tough from years of manual labor and dogged perseverance," the University of Washington wrote in a reflection of the team. "Ulbrickson declared them the Washington varsity eight. They would never lose a race together."

The team was successful that season, winning the collegiate championship. Then they headed to the Olympic trials where they faced the top crews in the country. Somehow, some way, the University of Washington team won, earning them an invitation to the 1936 Olympic games which were held in Berlin.

The UW team—facing crosswinds and choppy waters—struggled in the early going of the race. But the team kept rowing with a united goal: finish first. Driving. Pushing. Outsprinting other teams in perfect harmony. In the last stretch of the race, with the crowd noise deafening, they churned past the German team and caught the Italian rowers to take a lead with just 50 meters remaining. It was a race to the finish.

The final stretch.

The rowers' oars glided through the water in unison, propelling the boat forward toward the finish line. Three boats, neck and neck.

The University of Washington team's boat crossed the finish line first. Just one second separated the medals.

The boys in the UW boat were Olympic champions. Their story was later detailed in the book and movie *The Boys in the Boat*. It's a story of resilience and what we can accomplish together when we put ego aside and come together as one, focusing on eliminating friction between you and your goal.

It's nice to achieve the storybook finish, but that's not always how things wind up. Even with the best of intentions in our relationships, problems can arise. And when they do, it's up to us to find a way forward.

THE IMPACT OF MISALIGNMENTS

We all know of romantic relationships that fall apart because of misalignments. Maybe one partner wants children and the other doesn't. Or one partner is a homebody and the other loves to go out and travel.

Misalignments are common in business relationships, too.

Misalignments reveal themselves in a number of ways: as friction, eroded trust, misunderstandings and unnecessary headaches. And a lot of times we have no idea how misaligned we truly are until it is too late.

A 2023 study of strategic alignment among organizations found that participants were "largely optimistic" and thought agreement within their companies was 82% on average.

The twist? Actual internal alignment was only 23%.

By the time we find ourselves out of alignment, whether with a personal or business relationship, it can feel as though we are stuck in a downward spiral and incapable of turning things around. You feel yourself on edge whenever you encounter the other party, digging in for an adversarial exchange or walking on eggshells trying to avoid another fight.

Or maybe you have past experience with vibrant relationships and want to see the current relationship follow suit. The relationship isn't what you want it to be, but it's not easy to uncover how to fix it.

Hugging it Out

When misalignments occur with secondary or tertiary relationships, it may not really impact us much. Maybe we try to fix them, or maybe we simply move on. It may not be worth the time to repair the relationship.

It hits differently when misalignments involve a spouse, a great friendship, or an essential business partnership. The worst thing you can do is let misunderstandings and resentments fester. Good partnerships are built on trust, and at the first sign of friction you need to promptly address the concerns rather than shuffling them under the rug.

The good news is if you have relationship bonds based on trust and transparency, you can more easily get back on the same page.

The Season 2 Episode 16 of *Friends*, "The One Where Joey Moves Out," reflects the power of friendship. Chandler (Matthew Perry) and Joey (Matt LeBlanc) bicker about their living together.

They go to a party where Joey hears that a place with "park views and high ceilings" is available. Joey is interested in taking it. Chandler is resentful.

"Alright. You want the truth? I'm thinking about it," Joey tells his friend.

"What?" Chandler is aghast.

"I'm sorry. I'm 28 years old, I've never lived alone, and I'm finally at a place where I got enough money that I don't need a roommate anymore."

Chandler, feeling rejected, acts resentful. He takes it personally. The move doesn't have as much to do with him as he thinks, but he puts himself at the center of it anyway.

After Joey's boxes are moved out there is an awkward moment between the friends.

"So … I guess this is it," Joey says, looking around the half-empty apartment.

He walks to the door.

"Listen, I don't know when I'm going to see you again," Joey says.

"I'm guessing tonight at the coffee house," Chandler responds.

"Right. Yeah. OK. Take care."

"Yeah."

Chandler closes the door and looks at the quiet apartment when Joey reenters and circles his arms around his friend's torso, hugging him tight. Nothing is said and nothing needs to be said. The friends are going to be OK.

It's a little gesture but had a big impact. This fight isn't the end of their friendship, not by any stretch. The scene represents a moment of truth about what it means to be a best friend. It means putting your own interests aside. It means hugging your friend and wishing them well when they end up moving, even if it tears you up inside.

Real Loyalty: "You Have to Do It"

When you find your partner(s) or person(s) you need to approach situations with their best interests in mind, not just your own.

Gayle King began hosting her own show for her pal Oprah Winfrey's network, OWN, in 2011. Amid the network's struggles CBS News came calling, offering to make King co-anchor of *CBS This Morning*, a major role at a major network.

"I can't do it," she told Oprah, "because if I leave, everybody's going to say, 'even your best friend has abandoned you.'" Oprah could have protected her own interests or acted selfishly. She could have pushed and pleaded for Gayle to stay. But she didn't.

"You have to do it," Oprah told her. "OWN is going to be what OWN's going to be. You love the news and if they offer (the job) to you, you better take it." Oprah encouraged Gayle to explore her dreams, even if it was detrimental to herself. *That* is true friendship—stepping outside of ourselves and celebrating the wins together.

"I WISH GAYLE COULD BE HERE TO SEE THIS"

Oprah celebrated her 40th birthday in 1994 and was surprised for an episode of *The Oprah Winfrey Show* by some of her favorite people: Gladys Knight, Patti LaBelle, Aretha Franklin and Phylicia Rashad. But Gayle was absent. Near the end of the celebration Gayle appeared. Seeing her best friend made Oprah cry.

"This is so touching to me, because when Patti was here and then Aretha came, and then everybody was coming, I thought, *gee, I wish Gayle could be here to see this.*"

"I have no song to sing," Gayle told her friend. "After coming out after those guys I went, God, do I have to go out there? I have no words of wisdom. I just wanted to be here with you today."

True friendship is hard to find and uphold. More than anything, it means *being there* for your closest friends.

It means being there for your best customers when there is a shortage of supply. It means being there for your strategic supplier to collaborate on ways to reduce costs versus hardballing them on price. And it means being there to pull your weight to work with fellow community members to solve tough problems instead of simply showing up in protest when "the other side" does something you don't like.

Being there for each other is a great first step in building a foundation for a Vested partnership. But for a potential relationship to last it also helps to be on the same page—compatible with your partner.

3

Compatibility and Cultural Fit

Peanut butter and jelly.
Milk and cookies.
Oil and water?

When collaborating with a partner it helps to have the right chemistry and be compatible. Many organizations identify cultural fit as a key ingredient in the success of their strategic business relationships.

Compatibility—often referred to as cultural fit—means the degree to which partners are compatible on philosophy, values, decision-making, communication patterns and behaviors. Cultural fit does not mean "sameness," but rather avoiding incompatibilities that can create conflict from incongruent philosophies. It means taking similar approaches, maintaining similar values, and operating in a similar manner.

When you ask people about cultural fit, they will often say, "you just know it when you have it." Simply put it just feels right. Think about your first interactions with your spouse or best friends. Did they feel different than other interactions? Did they say or do something that made you just know this was someone worth getting to know better?

The first time the *Friends* cast performed together, rehearsing at the coffee shop stage (Central Perk), they could tell there was something special brewing. "You could feel it," cast member David Schwimmer said years later. "There was something *really* special about the six different voices and the energy of the six of us. There are six pieces of a puzzle that happen to click just right because of casting and because of the particular energy of the six people." If the cultural fit with even one of the six actors wasn't right, if their commitment to cohesiveness didn't carry forward, the show might have failed.

Cultural fit often serves as the glue bonding great partners together. It represents the ability for partners to get along and to align around their similarities instead of their differences.

It empowers "best friends" forward. It also reveals misalignments that could derail a partnership. Exploring cultural fit, in a sense, is a way for partners to stress-test their relationship and ensure that they are a good match.

While cultural fit can help to strengthen a partnership, partnerships can also be forged in the absence of cultural fit if the right elements, such as aligning on shared goals, are present. A poor cultural fit isn't necessarily a deal breaker at the beginning of a partnership. But being compatible from the get-go certainly helps.

Let's dive deeper into compatibility and cultural fit to see how these vague and confusing elements can also help us recognize our best, strongest and closest partners.

WHERE DOES CULTURAL FIT "FIT" IN

Cultural fit isn't always easy to define. But when you have it you can feel it.

The importance of cultural fit emerges quickly in romantic relationships and job interviews, where both parties need to know whether they are on the same page. We've all had those connections. The conversation was going great. And then the other person said one thing that made you pull back and reconsider them. Or we said something and the other person recoiled.

What felt like a great cultural fit at first maybe wasn't after all.

Given that cultural fit is often so easily misunderstood, it can be helpful to learn from well-known examples of cultural fit.

Cultural Fit in Personal Relationships

It was known as Bennifer 2.0—the rekindled romance between Ben Affleck and Jennifer Lopez.

The entertainers had previously been engaged in the early 2000s. The first time around, they appeared in bad movies and were seen on yachts together. They were effusive in their public affection for each other, and their whirlwind romance became a media sensation before buckling under the weight of expectations and visibility. They split up and spent their time apart dating and marrying other people.

But after they both found themselves single they began dating again in 2021 and got married—with multiple ceremonies—the following year.

There was something so refreshing about the pair back together. Seeing Ben and Jen together again was a testament to the power of new beginnings, moving forward and second chances.

They were *soul mates*. This was *meant to be*. This was *forever*. There was something more grown-up and more grounded with their rekindled romance.

The media coverage fueled the desire to see the power couple back together.

Among the most aspirational Bennifer headlines:

- The public turned their backs on celebrities during the pandemic. 'Bennifer' is here to save them and us.
- Bennifer's Reappearance Is a Harbinger of Better Times to Come
- Are Jennifer Lopez and Ben Affleck rebranding middle age?
- Why Bennifer's Built to Last: Jennifer Lopez and Ben Affleck Picked Up Where They Left Off, Only Better

But despite so much optimism Bennifer 2.0 was not built to last. As quickly as the relationship blossomed, it just as quickly fell on troubled times, and Lopez filed for divorce in 2024, citing "irreconcilable differences."

While it's tough to consider what went wrong with the relationship, culture fit seems to have played a factor, with a person close to the couple blaming the split, in part, on their being "very different people." As the insider told *People*, "She's super public and is more social, and he's more of an introvert and is happy to hang out at home."

Simply put, they were a cultural misfit.

Kate Lloyd, writing for Vogue, suggested that the whirlwind nature of their relationships factored into their endings—that they hadn't spent enough time considering each other's flaws and ensuring that they were right for each other.

"I think that over the years, this idea—that our true romantic partner is not a sexy new person, it's actually a safe person from our past—has seeped into some of our brain jelly (a scientific term)," Lloyd wrote.

> I call this the "it-was-them-all-along" theory, and it hits when you're at your weakest: after you've had a couple of failed relationships or you're sick of dating apps or you're in the middle of a pandemic... You look back on past flings and old friendships with rose-tinted glasses, ignoring the (usually very good) reasons things didn't work out in the past. The rose-tinted glasses are often present in relationships, romantic or otherwise, that don't last. We want partnerships to last, but without a strong cultural fit, we can't will them to go the distance just on enthusiasm alone.

Cultural Fit in Business Relationships

Just like with personal relationships, cultural fit is often a key focus in business relationships. Take job interviews as an example. Candidates are peppered with questions trying to gauge whether they are the right fit and educated on company values. Making the wrong hire can be extremely costly and make workers more inclined to check out or leave their jobs. Research suggests that turnover from poor cultural fit can cost an organization 50-60% of an employee's salary.

It's important to celebrate companies that get it right. Patagonia is among the most environmentally-conscious—and work-life-balance-committed—companies in the world.

Company founder Yvon Chouinard regularly encourages employees to get outside and surf (thus, the name of his book *Let My People Go Surfing*). That focus on culture carries all the way to the hiring process.

The human resources team doesn't start reviewing resumes from the top down.

Instead, they start from the bottom up, reviewing the applicant's interests, hobbies and volunteer work.

Another company that stands out for its hiring approach is Southwest. Southwest prides itself on being *fun*, from flight attendant quips and jokes to toilet paper birthday cakes for passengers celebrating their big day. And it has attracted new talent with the mantra "hire for attitude, train for skill."

As Julie Weber, vice president of people, described it, "The mentality isn't 'We'll know it when we see it.' It's 'Does this person already live the way we do?'" Southwest gauges cultural fit through behavioral interview questions, asking candidates to answer prompts such as describing a time when they went above and beyond to help a candidate succeed.

And employees are measured not just on results but how they get those results.

Southwest has consistently earned the No. 1 ranking for Customer Service metrics 26 times in 34 years.

While Patagonia and Southwest have cracked the code on hiring for cultural fit, many organizations struggle. It's easy enough for a job candidate to say the right things, only to find out later that there isn't actually a strong cultural fit at all. One trap hiring managers easily fall into relying on their unconscious biases—hiring people who remind them of themselves instead of hiring the most qualified or for the best fit. They choose someone with a shared alma mater or pick the person they could see themselves golfing with.

Harvard Business School Professor Youngme Moon explains how easy this trap is. "There are so many industries that have a history of relying on the 'soft stuff,' and the soft stuff has worked in the favor of a particular kind of individual. The truth is the soft stuff is often a euphemism, in many cases, for bias; for people being able to use their discretion to hire people who are just like them, that they are comfortable with, that look like them, that act like them, and talk like them."

Experts suggest organizations create a hiring process that encourages a wider range of applicants where job candidates experience a series of touchpoints involving multiple people in the company as a way to prevent biases.

Patience is also important. Some of our biggest hiring decisions are rash. As the saying goes, "hire slow, fire fast." Lots of companies hire fast then find themselves with the wrong workers and a massive headache to boot. Better to take your time and be more selective.

Cultural Fit in Business Partnerships

While compatibility is important for job candidates and their hiring companies, it's especially crucial for business relationships. In that sense, business partnerships, B2B relationships, mergers and acquisitions represent the need for cultural fit on steroids.

How important is cultural fit? Research shows that poor cultural fit between business partners results in lower productivity, lower financial performance outcomes, lower relationship satisfaction, and higher levels of conflict.

Cultural fit can also make or break mergers and acquisitions between companies, with studies reporting failure rates between 70-80%.

If cultural fit is so important why is it that companies often get it wrong? A key reason why organizations don't find partners with a good cultural fit is because they don't put the time and work into finding the right partners.

Serial entrepreneur and venture capitalist Mike Lazerow shares an interesting perspective about cultural fit when it comes to business relationships: you often don't understand the importance of this lesson until you make the mistake of not getting it right.

Mike recalled teaming with visionary artist Jonathan Cramer. Mike and Cramer were friends outside of business and Mike was excited to support his friend's business venture. Jonathan and Mike teamed up to bring Jonathan's concept, known as Shape Matrix, to market. But despite the momentum and investors, the commercial applications they'd developed never took off.

Mike believes that the relationship between the co-founders and their different visions for the partnership hampered the startup's success.

Mike is a serial entrepreneur and Jonathan is a gifted artist.

"Let's just say we were not the most compatible co-founders, and the company suffered because of it," he said. They didn't have a shared vision on what success looked like, and as Mike now recognizes, they should have talked more deeply to ensure that they were both on the same page.

The good news is they recognized this and were able to part ways amicably, something that does not always happen.

Another example involves a medical device company that outsourced its workplace services and maintenance operations to a culturally incongruent supplier.

The medical device company's operating culture valued collaborative decision-making, flexibility, and innovation, while the supplier's culture was hierarchical and process-oriented. Employees of the medical device company often joked they suffered from attention deficit disorder because they needed dozens of people in every meeting to make a decision. In contrast, the service provider—noted for their high quality and reasonable pricing—had an operational culture that valued standardization and frowned on flexibility. Contrary to the medical device company, excessive meetings were considered a waste of time. The service provider had a hard time keeping people on the "high maintenance and schizophrenic" medical device company's account. The A team turned into the C team, service levels dropped, and the parties found themselves in back-and-forth tit-for-tat actions of petty claims. Ultimately, the medical device company chose to terminate the contract early, something that was costly and frustrating for both parties.

CULTURAL FIT TAKES TIME AND WORK

Making sure you have a partner with a good fit takes time and work. While strong cultural fit seems like a *lucky* occurrence it often isn't lucky at all, but a reflection of a very strategic and thoughtful process of aligning partners to succeed together.

A McKinsey and Company study on cultural fit in business relationships found most business leaders believe forging a strong cultural fit between companies will be relatively easy just because they get along well. The study shares that most organizations underestimate the challenges different management practices create for most employees: they use satisfaction surveys and focus groups to try and strengthen cultural fit between firms. But while easy, these simple mechanisms fail to truly understand the underlying elements that make partnerships successful. And when this happens, company cultures remain detached and disjointed.

Finding the Perfect Six

Let's return to the TV show *Friends*, the bastion of sitcom fellowship. The six main characters of the show operated as one.

While it may appear that picking the perfect set of friends was effortless, it wasn't effortless at all. When the show was being cast, the casting director received hundreds of glossy black-and-white photos for each role and about 75 actors read for each part.

For the role of Chandler, the show's creators liked the witty, self-deprecating actor Matthew Perry. But he was already signed up for another show, *LAX*

2194, about baggage handlers at the airport of the future. Since Perry wasn't available, "the producers wanted to go with Craig Bierko," according to casting director Lori Openden. Bierko was offered the part but passed, which was a sigh of relief for the producers. And when *LAX 2194* was destined to bomb, the show had its Chandler.

Courteney Cox—the biggest name of the bunch due to her stint in Bruce Springsteen's "Dancing in the Dark" music video and turn on *Family Ties*—was considered to play Rachel. But Cox wanted to play Monica instead. She wound up getting the part over Nancy McKeon, who'd been a star on *The Facts of Life*.

For the character of macho Joey, Matt LeBlanc quickly became a favorite. Before his audition, he was practicing lines with another actor, who suggested that since the show was all about a group of friends, "we should go out tonight and get drunk, as though we were friends," LeBlanc recalled. He did—and wound up falling down and skinning his nose. LeBlanc showed up for his audition with a scab on his face. But there was something funny, something warm, about him.

The producers and NBC had a tough time casting for Rachel, a character who was pampered and spoiled. With the wrong actress, Rachel could easily come across as unlikable. The actress needed to be someone the audience could relate to. Jami Gertz was offered the part but turned it down. Jennifer Aniston—who'd struggled to land a breakout role with other projects—was a favorite, but she was already committed to a show, *Muddling Through*, that was airing on CBS. But NBC wanted her. As a result, the network aired Danielle Steel movies opposite *Muddling Through* to undermine its female viewership. With *Muddling Through* fading away, NBC had its Rachel.

Lisa Kudrow was already a known commodity due to her role on NBC's *Mad About You*, and she had experience auditioning, too. She played *quirky*. The show needed quirky. It was an easy choice to cast her as Phoebe.

The producers liked David Schwimmer, who had auditioned for a previous pilot they'd developed. But the actor was burned out from TV. He wanted to stick to theater. His agent talked to him about *Friends*. So did famed TV director James Burrows, who would direct the show's pilot. Schwimmer decided to have a meeting. Soon enough, the show had its Ross.

What if one of the cast members decided they should make more money or get more screen time than the other actors? What if one of the cast members isolated themselves from the rest of the group?

"If any one of those people had been different, what would the show be? It's a totally different show," co-creator David Crane said about said in an interview about the show's success.

P&G and JLL: A Partnership Grounded by Cultural Fit

Putting the time and work into finding a business partner with the right cultural fit can pay off as well. It is something that P&G practiced when searching for a supplier to manage the company's global facilities management operations.

Since its founding in 1837, P&G has been laser-focused on customer needs and innovation.

P&G—known for iconic consumer products like Ivory soap, Gillette razors, Tide laundry detergent, Crest toothpaste, Swiffer sweepers, and Dawn Power-wash dish spray—is just as committed to innovating in how it operates as it is to developing superior products.

One area that was suitable for transformation was facilities management.

Over the years, P&G had built, leased, or inherited facilities on a country-by-country basis across five continents. It occupied 150+ office and re-search facilities spanning more than 17 million square feet in 86 countries. An in-house crew of several hundred people were augmented with a hodgepodge of local and regional suppliers around the world.

P&G tapped William Reeves, an Alabama native who had been with the company for more than 30 years, to help P&G lead the transformation effort. The company—under Reeves' guidance—sought to reinvent their approach to facilities management.

A key part of the transformation effort? Creating an outsourcing solution with a world-class global supplier to focus on transformation and not simply on performing transactions. A key part of the initiative? Picking the right partner.

The team narrowed in on a small list of potential partners. In their pursuit to pick the perfect partner, P&G added a unique next step: it asked suppliers to conduct weeklong site visits at three locations around the world to study the sites, understand the P&G business, and develop a five-year action plan outlining how they would manage the business.

An obvious advantage to this approach was the immediate weeding out of suppliers without global capabilities. Some suppliers held necessary visas, passports and general wherewithal about how to deal on a worldwide basis. Those suppliers who had limited international knowledge and ability to travel clearly did not meet P&G standards of being able to manage a global business.

More importantly, the process delivered critical insight into the supplier's competency. Reeves explains, "Some suppliers have good chase teams for sales, but not operations. Our process gave us a lens to see beyond a supplier's sales team. The five-year action plans each of the suppliers created allowed us to see who really understood our business and the challenges we faced. We had already streamlined significantly and, to get to the next level, we required true transformation. It was easy to see which suppliers did deep dives based on how insightful their observations were. The supplier report-outs showed if they could manage our processes in a better way—something that was key for P&G."

Another thing stood out to Reeves: cultural fit. One of the suppliers—JLL—had no discernible culture differences in the working meetings. Reeves recalled it was hard to tell who worked for which company. "Both companies had impressive histories and records of performance excellence, but P&G and JLL shared something even more important—similar corporate ethics and commitments."

In the end, the P&G team decided to move forward with JLL.

Reeves summed it up when he met with Bill Thummel to let him know that P&G had decided to go with JLL as the service provider of choice. Thummel was the JLL Global Account Executive and would go on to become Reeves' counterpart in the partnership. Reeves shook hands with Thummel to symbolically seal the deal, stating, "We know that you (JLL) and the other suppliers we evaluated have never done this before; and neither have we. But JLL has a culture that is much like P&G's. We think we have the best chance of being successful with you because you are so much like us."

In essence, Reeves and Thummel set the tone of the relationship that day. Their handshake set the precedent with P&G vowing to respect and honor JLL's role as P&G's expert in facilities management and JLL accepting the challenge to jointly move into uncharted territory—together.

At the time, the P&G-JLL outsourcing effort was the largest facilities outsourcing deal in history.

That was 2003.

The P&G-JLL relationship is just one of many I had a chance to study as part of my research. I went on to profile their relationship and its success in the book *Vested: How P&G, McDonald's and Microsoft are Redefining Winning in Business Relationships*.

Decades later, P&G and JLL's relationship is still going strong, with JLL earning P&G's prestigious *Supplier of the Year* award three times. And in 2024, JLL received P&G's first *Supplier Impact Award*, which recognizes external business partners who champion environmental sustainability, equality and inclusion, no small feat when you consider P&G has more than 60,000 business partners.

Best Enemies

You've probably been asked at some point to work together with someone you don't agree with. Someone you get along with like oil and water.

Maybe it was someone on the board of your condo association you don't see eye-to-eye with and you have to find a way to fund a much-needed roof replacement. Or your 7-year-old daughter insists you help plan the end-of-year school party with another parent who gets under your skin. Or worse—you've been voluntold by your boss to work on a high-priority project and you find out your teammate is someone you constantly clash with like oil and water.

Whatever the situation, it likely can't be as thorny as the situation C.P. Ellis and Ann Atwater faced when they were asked to co-lead a community initiative to come up with recommendations for how the Durham, North Carolina schools would desegregate following a judge's order in 1970.

With tensions flaring, AFL-CIO secured funding through a federal grant meant to aid desegregation efforts. The grant funding was used to hold a series of focused discussions known as a "charrette" to address issues facing the community and establish a series of recommendations.

The goal of the charrette? A diverse committee of community members would provide recommendations on improvements for Durham's schools. The discussions would cover all sorts of topics–including racism, student safety and teacher qualifications.

The initiative was called "Save Our Schools."

Bill Riddick, a consultant specializing in facilitating charrette processes, was tapped to manage the project. Riddick's first task? Select co-chairs and committee members. He chose Ellis and Atwater to serve as co-chairs of the Save Our Schools charrette.

Ellis and Atwater could not be more culturally misfit. Ellis was the local Ku Klux Klan leader and Atwater was an outspoken black community activist. The pair had often argued with each other at various town meetings. Needless to say, they were not enthusiastic about working together.

As Ellis recalled later, "It was impossible. How could I work with her?" Atwater similarly wished to avoid working with her adversary, but she didn't want to look bad or attract negative attention by backing out.

For the first few days of the charrette, Atwater and Ellis weren't seeing eye to eye and didn't want anything to do with one another. But from one meeting to the next, they started recognizing they had a lot more in common than they initially realized.

Working together with a common goal and clear set of rules and guidance of the charette process forced them to have difficult conversations with the mandate to find a solution.

Years later, Ellis recalled putting the elephant in the room.

"Ann, you and I should have a lot of differences and we got 'em now. But there's somethin' laid out here before us, and if it's gonna be a success, you and I are gonna have to make it one. Can we lay aside some of these feelin's?" he said.

"I'm willing if you are," she responded.

"Let's do it."

Despite their differences, Atwater and Ellis were able to recognize the need to work together. While Ellis and Atwater didn't start with a great cultural fit, the collaborative and structured process helped them come together in a way they never would have imagined.

They learned how to transform their us-versus-them mindset to a what's-in-it-for-we mindset which helped them put their differences behind them and move forward. The result? The two longtime rivals were able to bring forward the committee's recommendations to the school board.

C.P. Ellis and Ann Atwater show how even staunch opponents—given the right process and guidance—can collaborate to achieve successful outcomes. The two continued to collaborate on regional issues and became lifelong friends. But the collaboration process didn't just help them with the task at hand, it transformed them. When Ellis died in 2005, Atwater delivered his eulogy.

"God had a plan for both of us, for us to get together," she said at his funeral.

What can the lessons of P&G-JLL, hiring the cast for *Friends* and C.P. Ellis and Ann Atwater teach us? Time and work made all the difference.

SAYING I DO

A major challenge for finding a partner with good cultural fit? Defining a good fit is not always obvious. Case in point is C.P. Ellis and Ann Atwater. On the surface they were oil and water. The charrette process helped them see beneath the surface; the more time they spent together working on a common goal to integrate the Durham schools the more they found they had in common.

I often hear people complain they don't have time to go through a process to find a partner. That's when I became fascinated with researching if there was a way to fast-track helping individuals and organizations find cultural fit.

Preventing Bennifer

Recall the cultural fit mismatch between Ben Affleck and Jennifer Lopez. Could they have prevented their situation? The answer is likely yes.

In my research to study cultural fit I discovered the pioneering work of John Gottman. Gottman, a longtime professor at the University of Washington, has made a career out of studying and anticipating a couple's potential for a successful partnership by observing their behaviors. He uses video recordings of couples discussing difficult topics and studies their interactions to predict the likelihood of a marriage's success. Gottman has found success predicting a couple's outcomes six years later to the tune of 90% accuracy.

Gottman's research stands out because it involves studying couples in a natural setting discussing realistic topics, typically across an entire weekend—and studying everything from their facial reactions and body language to heart rate. He focuses on "The Four Horsemen" that can undermine a relationship:

- Criticism
- Contempt
- Defensiveness
- Stonewalling

Of those four, Gottman has classified contempt as the worst. He considers it "sulfuric acid for love." Contempt spills out in the subtlest of ways. The way someone rolls their eyes, biting sarcasm, fixing whatever your partner does *because whatever they do isn't good enough*. It represents a personal slight coupled with an insult.

Gottman's method reflects an important truth about compatibility: the clues or gaps to strong cultural fit are often present if you step back and put the partnership to the test. And sometimes the best way for gauging the strength of cultural fit is stepping back and putting the partnership to the test.

Measuring Cultural Fit For Businesses

A major challenge for finding a business partner with good cultural fit is that it is not always obvious. In most cases organizations tend to pick a potential partner based on gut feel. But some organizations (especially government organizations) want to have something more tangible and quantifiable to point to. This is one reason I started to collaborate with academic colleagues Karl Manrodt and Jerry Ledlow on what we call the Compatibility and Trust (CaT) Assessment.

> **Your Toolkit: *Compatibility and Trust (CAT) Assessment***
>
> A diagnostic tool for business relationships that reveals the true state of a relationship by measuring both cultural compatibility and trust levels. The CaT Assessment uncovers perception gaps and identifies specific areas for improvement.

The CaT assessment seeks to help companies identify cultural fit across five dimensions:

1. **Focus** is the ability to combine individual roles into a corporate direction to benefit all stakeholders. There is a common purpose and direction and clarity around that direction.
2. **Communication** is the efficient and effective transfer of meaning through words and actions to achieve and grow mutually beneficial outcomes. It includes open and timely sharing of relevant information to a partner's decision-making ability.
3. **Team Orientation** is the ability to focus and direct individual goals and objectives into a cohesive group strategy. Team orientation is a key indicator of how well trading partners work together.
4. **Innovation** is an organization's ability to dynamically deal with change and its tolerance for risk and trying out new ideas and solutions. Strong and trusting relationships allow the parties to share risks and rewards, invest in each other's capabilities and embrace continuous improvement and transformation efforts.
5. **Trust** is the consistency of performing to promise and meeting commitments. Without performance, trust cannot exist.

Think of the CaT assessment as a DNA footprint of two organizations with the goal to identify how much overlap there is between the partner's inherent DNA across each of the five dimensions. The assessment offers a chance to gauge cultural fit and choose "best friends" in a clear and empowering way.

Let's take a look at how Newfoundland and Labrador Health Services used a CaT Assessment as part of their quest to find the right partner to provide support services across their network of healthcare facilities.

Finding the Right Fit

Newfoundland and Labrador Health Services (NLHS) provides community, hospital and long-term health care in Newfoundland and Labrador, Canada, as part of the Canadian government's public health care services. Support services are critical and extensive—including patient/resident food, retail food, environmental services/housekeeping, laundry, portering and call center services.

NLHS had historically split its support services work between two suppliers. When these contracts began to expire, NLHS executives felt if they could shift to working with only one supplier it could drive efficiencies. However, putting all of NLHS's eggs in one basket with a sole source support services supplier seemed too risky. But that was before Ron Johnson (Chief Operating Officer and Vice President of Innovation and Research at NLHS) heard about my research at the University of Tennessee on Vested partnerships.

Johnson is passionate about innovation. In fact, helping NLHS innovate is actually part of his job description. So learning about innovative approaches was something that intrigued him.

NLHS ultimately decided to pilot UT's Request for Partner process, a collaborating bidding process used to identify a best fit strategic partner, to seek a partner who would work under a more strategic Vested business model. The bid document stated NLHS was "interested in receiving Proposals from Qualified Suppliers that are capable of delivering the scope of the opportunity; providing creative, innovative, effective and best value Solutions."

A key part of the Request for Partner Process was to determine which supplier had the best cultural fit. To do this, NLHS and each supplier assessed their baseline compatibility and trust levels using the CaT assessment.

The graphic below is a summary of the CaT assessment results comparing the relationship health across five dimensions for both Compass (the winning supplier) and Supplier B (NHLS's second supplier which wound up not being selected as the partner of choice in the bid process). As the graphic illustrates, the Compass relationship had three of the five dimensions falling into a "healthy" relationship, while Supplier B did not have any of the five dimensions as being "healthy."

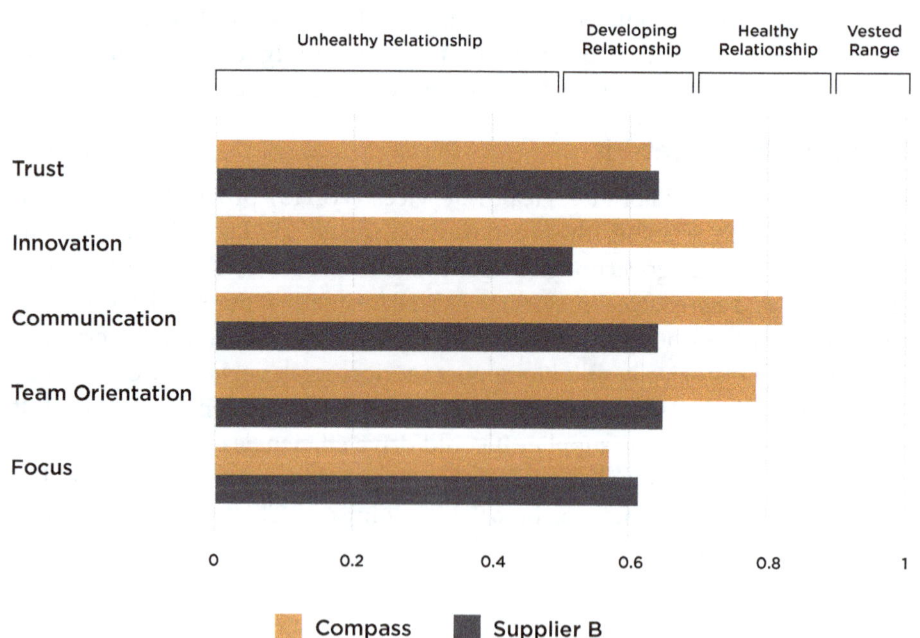

A key part of the CaT assessment is looking behind the summary and seeing the actual gaps in each of the dimensions across trading partner relationships. The figures below illustrate a sample of the results from the CaT assessment for each supplier. The top figure shows a tight alignment with Compass (the winning supplier). The bottom figure indicates a cultural gap between NLHS and Supplier B (the losing supplier).

A SAMPLE OF THE RESULTS FROM THE CAT ASSESSMENT

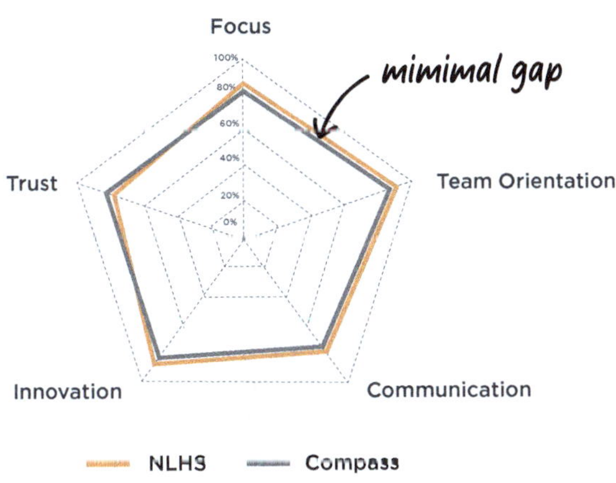

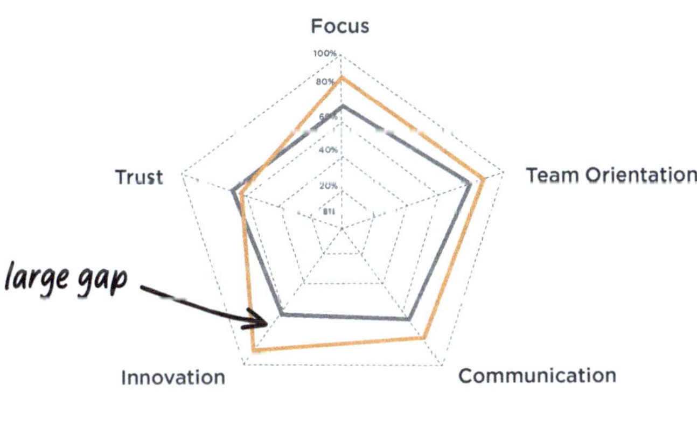

A tell-tale sign of cultural fit is when the parties are closely aligned on self-assessments with small gaps across various dimensions. For example, take a closer look at the Innovation dimension. NLHS (noted in the orange line in the graphics) scores its organization as innovative, while Supplier B scores its organization as much less innovative. The difference creates a significant gap in how the parties view innovation.

A second analysis of the CaT assessment is for team members to score each company based on their *perception* of their partner. This analysis is particularly applicable when assessing preexisting business relationships, such as those in the NLHS scenario. Once again, the assessment revealed a much healthier business relationship based on their existing working relationship.

As part of the bid process, NLHS used the assessment data as the foundation for dialogues with each supplier. The dialogue workshops challenged the suppliers to address how they would close gaps in their cultural fit by addressing the cultural fit criteria in the scoring rubric. Based on these discussions and other criteria, NLHS ultimately picked Compass as their provider of choice.

After the contract was awarded, UT researchers interviewed both. The potential partners both loved the collaborative bid process and expressed that selecting the winning supplier based on a combination of best value and cultural fit was a superior way to run a bid process. NLHS got a better solution and Compass appreciated how the focusing on cultural fit enabled them to feel more comfortable being transparent, which was especially important in developing a win-win pricing model. And the losing supplier did not protest, something that is common in large public procurement initiatives.

ONGOING COMMITMENT TO CULTURAL FIT

Cultural fit is an important element for partners. Good cultural fit is a force multiplier that helps to strengthen relationships. In the case of the TV show *Friends* it was the secret weapon fueling the show's success. But as Ann Atwater and C.P. Ellis show us, you can still represent oil and water on the surface as long as you take the time and go beyond the surface and align around common goals.

The next chapter addresses the third ingredient for laying the foundation for a successful partnership: leading with trust and transparency.

TOOLKIT QUICK REFERENCE GUIDE

Compatability and Trust Assessment

- **Purpose:** To diagnose the cultural fit and trust gaps in a relationship
- **When to use:** Ideally in the early stages of a partnership or at a pivot point when you are exploring if you want to take your relationship to the next level. However, it can be used at any point in a relationship.
- **Output:** Overall relationship health index with a deeper dive into potential compatibility and perception gaps. Also provides a sentiment analysis with percentages of positive, neutral, and negative descriptors for the relationship.

4

Trust and Transparency

Yin and yang.
Sun and moon.
Push and pull.

Trust and transparency are akin to the yin and yang of a relationship. They represent the interplay between two forces working in balance—feeding off of each other. The more parties trust the more comfortable they feel sharing information. And more transparency helps build more trust.

Together, trust and transparency create a virtuous cycle that lifts up relationships. But the opposite effect can happen as well. Without trust or transparency, relationships tend to get strained. Trust and transparency are like the bursts of wind uplifting the birds in the V formation. You can sense when they are present. And everything gets so much harder when they are missing. Without trust and transparency, partnerships can feel downright impossible.

Our strongest relationships require trust and transparency. Oprah and Gayle's friendship wouldn't be nearly as strong without them. The same goes for long-term business relationships.

Trust and transparency are more than shallow buzzwords. If you have ever been in a high-performing relationship, you know the difference between "saying" trust and transparency and actually understanding what they mean in practice. When you have it, good things happen; you can operate in confidence without worrying about micromanagement or the nagging sense that you are constantly looking over your shoulder with worry. And if trust and transparency are lacking, it's a reminder that there is work to be done—or that you might have to choose a different partner.

TRUST: THE ULTIMATE LEAP OF FAITH

Trust is at the center of any great relationship. It's the confidence we hold in someone else's character, ability or truth. Having total trust in someone means fully believing they will follow through; low trust means we don't anticipate it at all.

Trust is built on consistency. We start to gain trust when someone consistently does what they say. When someone doesn't do what they say, trust can easily erode.

Every interaction we have with others, from ordering at a restaurant to working with colleagues to getting married, is built on trust. If you have low trust that your food order will be made to your liking, how likely will you be to visit that restaurant again? If your co-worker has previously sabotaged you, you'll approach interactions cautiously. And if trust is lost in your personal relationships it can be ruinous or lead you to withdraw, to pull back and to open up less of our heart.

Although we might have every intention of completing a certain action, others can easily recognize when we don't. Think of the empty promises you or someone you know makes. Your husband will remember to start the dishwasher when it is full. Your teenager will come home when they say they will. You'll make sure to be home in time for dinner. Or telling a subordinate month after month that you will consider them for a promotion that you know is likely not to come. The slights and misalignments pile up over time, chipping away at trust each time it happens.

It's easy for people to look for reasons not to trust each other—and breaking out of this vicious circle isn't easy.

But it is possible.

Choosing to Trust

To trust or not trust is a choice, just as the clothes you wear or what you eat for lunch. Parties choose to trust each other and act in a trustworthy manner … or not. It's as simple as that.

Choosing to trust is the ultimate leap of faith because it requires us to put our faith in someone that they will do what we hope or they say they will do.

It's imperative each partner purposely sets a tone that trust is crucial to the mutual success of the relationship. Why? Think about the trajectory of a relationship that starts off by choosing to trust and acting with trusting behaviors versus entering into a partnership with a shadow of distrust. This is why the power of choosing to trust is so powerful. Think about it. And if you act distrustfully, your partner will likely act distrustfully. And vice versa.

Simply put, trust is the result of actions; it does not increase or decrease by coincidence. Since actions are the result of human thought and willpower, individuals and organizations can make choices to take actions that increase or decrease trust.

Try as we might, it is impossible to force others to be trustworthy.

It's easy to believe the "other guy" is to blame when there is a lack of trust.

And maybe they are. But there is almost always two versions of the truth. The next time you blame your partner for being untrustworthy, stop and ask yourself if you played a role in the equation. Your partner's distrusting behavior may be a reaction to one of your actions. Only when partners seek the root causes of distrust can they improve.

Psychologist Forrest Talley pointed this out in a 2024 *Psychology Today* essay stating, "The importance of being someone others can trust is so obvious that it can easily be overlooked. This is a mistake." Pop superstar Michael Jackson also understood this message with his timeless hit, "Man in the Mirror."

The bottom line on trust? Trust starts with you. We must be able to ask ourselves, "Do I, based on how I have acted in the past, deserve to be trusted?"

Before going any further, ask yourself this question: How trustworthy am I?

The Cost of Lost Trust

The hidden cost of lost trust can pile up quickly. In business relationships friction in a trading partner relationship has a name: Transaction Cost Economics (TCE).

When you have trust, it can speed business up. But when trust is lost, it can slow business down. When you have a partner that is frustrating to deal with, the time and cost associated with dealing with that partner go up. This friction is added transaction costs.

Stephen M.R. Covey's book *Speed of Trust* outlines seven "organizational taxes" that are directly related to low trust. They are:

1. Redundancy is unnecessary duplication. Redundancy stems from the mindset that people cannot be trusted unless they are closely watched.
2. Bureaucracy is when too many rules and regulations are in place such as when too many people must "sign off" on something.
3. Politics is when people use strategy to gain power. Sadly, too much time is wasted interpreting other people's motives and trying to read hidden agendas.
4. Disengagement is when people are still getting paid even though they "clocked out." Simply put, team members put in the minimal effort required to get their paycheck.
5. Turnover results when the best performers in an organization leave to pursue a job where they are seen as trusted and value-added contributors.
6. Churn is the effort and costs associated with constantly finding new customers, suppliers, distributors and investors because of a lack of loyalty.

7. Fraud is flat-out dishonesty. Fraud is a circular tax; when companies tighten the reigns to prevent fraud, they reduce their fraud-related losses, but they inevitably see an increase in the other six areas.

While most people don't doubt there is a cost associated with lost trust, they struggle to understand the hard costs associated with lost trust. Fortunately, the value of trust in business relationships has been studied for decades by dozens of leading academics and organizations across different aspects of trust.

One of the most widely publicized studies is the Edelman Trust Barometer report, which tracks trust levels in societies across the world with regard to how well individuals trust government, businesses, media and NGOs. Their findings? We are facing a "retreat into insularity." Trust levels are on the decline with a whopping 57% of individuals having a moderate or high sense of grievance, which is defined by a belief that government and business make their lives harder and serve narrow interests, and wealthy people benefit unfairly.

But can you quantify the benefits of trusting relationships?

This is a question Accenture set out to answer in a study tracking more than 7,000 companies over two-plus years. More than half of the companies studied experienced a material drop in trust during that time, losing a combined $180 billion in revenue. For context, the report estimates a $30 billion retail company experiencing a material drop in trust, the retailer should expect to have a $4 billion loss in future revenue.

Trust is not only essential between consumers and organizations; it is also essential in internal relationships between managers and their employees. Tony Simmons and Judi McLean Parks looked at how 6,500 employees across 76 U.S. and Canadian Holiday Inn hotels graded their managers' trust levels in terms of how closely their managers' words and actions were aligned using questions such "My manager delivers on promises" and "My manager practices what he preaches."

The researchers then correlated the trust levels with the hotels' customer satisfaction surveys, personnel records, and financial records. The results were stunning. Hotels where employees strongly believed their managers followed through on promises and demonstrated the values they preached were substantially more profitable than those whose managers scored average or lower. Simmons wrote about the findings in a *Harvard Business Review* article. "So strong was the link, in fact, that a one-eighth point improvement in a hotel's score on the five-point scale could be expected to increase the hotel's profitability by 2.5% of revenues—in this study, that translates to a profit increase of more than $250,000 per year per hotel. No other single aspect of manager behavior that we measured had as large an impact on profits."

Mind the Trust Gap

"Mind the gap" is a popular warning for rail passengers when moving between platforms—but it should also be a warning sign in your relationships. When trust has eroded in personal or business relationships, partners can find themselves worlds—and words—apart. The gap can feel insurmountable, as though you're stretching and stepping beyond your comfort zone to maintain the relationship.

Think of this as your final warning before taking the step yourself.

But is there an early warning sign to help you see trust gaps in a relationship? That's a question Karl Manrodt and Jerry Ledlow set out to answer. Let's revisit my work on the Compatibility and Trust assessment which measures trust levels in trading partner relationships. There is a massive difference between "good" and "typical" relationships with partners. One early warning sign of trust gaps is the words we use to describe our partner.

Think of your cherished and respected partners, and words like "Collaborative" and "Trustworthy" might come to mind. A more demanding trading partner, one whose emails or calls make your blood pressure rise, might bring up words like "Frustrating" and "Difficult."

Take a study of buyer-supplier relationships in the energy industry. Buying companies were asked to pick a "good" relationship and a "typical" relationship.

Good relationships used mostly positive adjectives (85%) such as Aligned, Collaborative and Trustworthy to describe their relationship. But when team members were describing "typical" relationships, they used positive words much less frequently, only 63% of the time. Instead, they used words like Frustrating, Restrictive and Distant. And, in 9% of cases, people in these typical relationships used really negative words such as Difficult, Strained and even Dysfunctional.

It's far too easy for partners to find themselves misaligned and the trust gap to widen.

One reason for the misalignment is the illusory superiority bias. The phenomenon is also commonly referred to as the "above-average effect" because typically well over fifty percent of respondents in surveys rate themselves above average in the perception of their own behaviors. For example, one study showed 93% of Americans rate themselves as above average for driving skills.

Of course that is statistically impossible.

Trust (or Lack of it) in Trading Partner Relationships

Our research on trading partner trust shows the illusory superiority bias is alive and strong when it comes to business relationships. How? Trading partners almost always view themselves as having a high degree of trust while perceiving their partner is operating with a lower level of trust.

Such biases intensify trust gaps between organizations because trading partners often act in ways that are not advantageous for the partnership. For example a lack of trust (or even a perceived lack of trust) may cause a buyer to increase quality checks, micromanage production outputs, or add buffer stock to inventory.

Let's return to look at perceived trust gaps in "typical" relationships. In our study, team members were lukewarm to negative about their typical trading partner almost 40% of the time, a figure that represents a major warning sign.

When you stop and realize that companies have hundreds, if not thousands, of trading partner relationships the impact of trust gaps is huge. Think about it. If almost 30% of "typical" relationships are considered frustrating, restrictive and distant and another 9% of these typical relationships are described as combative, difficult, dysfunctional and strained, what does that mean for a "bad" relationship? Just imagine what words are being used in those cases.

The X-factor

Trust isn't an endless chocolate fondue tower that will cover all of our relationships in sweet goodness. Rather it is something that takes time and attention to purposefully foster.

The good news? There are things that we can do to make others more trusting of us—steps that we can take to reduce second-guessing in how trusting we are.

That X-factor, the yang to trust's yin, is transparency.

TRANSPARENCY: A LEAP OF FAITH LIFT

If trust requires a leap of faith, transparency is the lift we need to make the jump. It makes the leap feel smaller. It helps us take the leap with confidence instead of fear.

If someone is fully transparent and not trying to hide anything, it gives us more reason to trust them. We still need to "trust but verify" of course. This isn't a suggestion to trust blindly. But transparency can take away some of our caution and reticence to trust.

In fact, a Deloitte study reveals 86% of leaders believe the more transparent an organization is, the greater the trust.

If someone is fully open and honest, whether in revealing financial details, business dealings or true feelings, it gives us reasons to believe them. Over time, if their disclosures turn out to be accurate, it makes it easier to believe them. And on the other hand, if someone isn't open and honest—if they aren't transparent—it makes it a lot more difficult to trust them. Of course, sometimes there are legitimate reasons, such as legal or confidentiality, why someone can't be fully transparent.

Think of trust and transparency in the form of a simple 2x2 matrix with trust on one axis and transparency on the other.

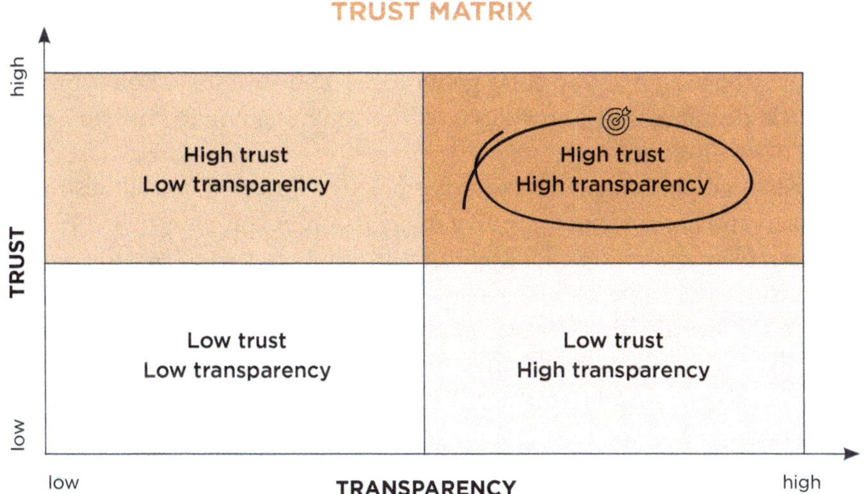

The sweet spot is having high levels of both trust and transparency. But, any increase in either dimension is better than the alternative—low trust and low transparency. And as organizations lean into being more transparent, more trust typically follows.

Choosing Transparency

Just as we need to choose to trust, transparency is also a choice.

The more trusting we are, the more transparent we are with others. It means we have nothing to hide—a complete open book. Trust and transparency go hand in hand. And transparency can lead to stronger relationships.

Transparency requires that parties share relevant information to ensure they will make good decisions for themselves and for the relationship. It also includes personal openness, which is the degree of comfort people have about sharing their concerns, motivations, wants, and needs.

By being open and sharing information in a timely manner, parties have a chance to consider relevant information and make wise decisions—both for themselves and the partnership.

The Cost of Lost Transparency

Transparency is more than a buzzword; it's one of the foundational elements of a strong partnership. Transparency is necessary when solving dynamic business problems. It can keep all parties on the same page and foster deeper connections between partners.

A lack of transparency, meanwhile, can fuel mistrust and deepen the divisions between team members, departments and companies. Think of a time when someone wasn't transparent with you and how it made you feel. If you and your spouse agreed you were going to try and save for a house but they keep buying expensive shoes without telling you, it's going to have an impact, and not a positive one.

Transparency isn't just about sharing positive information, but also about being open and honest about negative information. A company owner discussing a difficult economic outlook with their employees can help the workers both consider the impacts and discuss possible solutions. Such transparency can leave the team with a deeper measure of commitment. It's a smarter approach than trying to hide negative information away and telling mistruths when asked about it. And it can help company leaders avoid the dreaded rumor mill as employees fill the information gaps with negativity.

It is important to recognize that while transparency can bring significant benefits, it can also be taken too far. For example, having the ability to monitor every employee's keystrokes and actions could make workers feel like they're being micromanaged. In some cases, TMI—"Too Much Information"—such as sharing other employees' pay and performance levels can also overwhelm workers and backfire.

Information Is Power

When people say information is power, what they often mean is that the unequal access to information creates a power imbalance. In a world in which unequal access to information is power, people tend to hide, hoard and misrepresent information and use it as a battering ram to get their way.

Take for example the popular concept in negotiations known as a BATNA (Best Alternative to a Negotiated Agreement). The concept of a BATNA was introduced by negotiation researchers Roger Fisher and William Ury in their 1981 book, *Getting to Yes: Negotiating Agreement Without Giving In*. A BATNA is a party's alternative if negotiations are unsuccessful. Think of it as the walkaway point when negotiating—your bottom line position before stopping negotiations.

For decades it's been engrained to not only have your BATNA, but that you should not reveal your BATNA. Why? Doing so can significantly weaken your negotiating position by allowing the other party to offer you just enough to keep you from walking away, potentially limiting your ability to achieve a better deal; essentially, giving away valuable leverage in the negotiation process.

It's no wonder that people succumb to the temptation to share only information that bolsters their position or that undermines their counterpart's position, while concealing information that exposes a weakness.

But when you stop and think about it, keeping that information hidden can impact the nature of a relationship. For starters, withholding information skews other people's ability to make good decisions and it reinforces people's beliefs that they cannot trust anyone at the bargaining table. And all too often it can sow seeds of deeper mistrust and make partners feel less connected.

Shared Information is Exponential Power

If information is power, information shared is exponential power.

Instead of simply seeing information as a battering ram and hoarding it, consider the power it can have when we share information with partners. Consider the trust it can build. Consider your ability to collaborate with your partner to make better decisions, increase the size of the pie, and reduce risks for both parties when you share information. Simply put, *effective* information flow promotes better solutions and better agreements.

But information sharing is not just what is done during a negotiation. It should become common practice. Why? When people complain about "poor communication" they're often really complaining about lack of transparency— about poor communication regarding the things that matter most.

People who want greater collaboration have to start by being open, and that means sharing. Doing so can help both parties leverage the power of information.

What Should You Share?

There is no correct answer to the question regarding what information to share.

James Tamm and Ronald Luyet, the authors of the book *Radical Collaboration*, suggest having a strong bias for openness and transparency, stating "Problem solving and relationship building almost always benefit from increased openness." I agree and have seen first-hand the power of sharing information.

With some of our partners, conversations about what information to share come easily. With others, it's a struggle to dig deeper.

It can be helpful to have a test of sorts to gauge our own desire to go deeper with a partner. Scott Schroeder, the owner of RelianceCM, a small business specializing in contract manufacturing, uses what he calls the "dinner test" to determine client compatibility. There is no formal analysis, just a simple judgment call that ends with "would you bring this person home for dinner?" Schroeder first started the dinner test when he would meet with clients to talk about their relationship.

While the dinner test can work, one approach I teach is to have a "transparency discussion." It works like this. Before sharing any information, partners discuss the benefits of transparency and work through a what I call a *transparency commitment matrix*.

Your Toolkit:
Transparency Commitment Matrix
An easy to use brainstorming matrix to help partners align on what types of things they beleive are important to be transparent about.

Download the transparency commitment matrix toolkit to help you have a productive conversation about how you and your partners can leverage the benefits of being more transparent in your relationship.

Type of Information	Today	Going Forward
Money Matters		
Trust Factors		
XXX		
YYY		

Think of a transparency commitment matrix as a brainstorming tool to help you and your partner think through the types of things you feel can help you build trust through improved transparency.

The transparency commitment matrix has three columns. The first column is the type of information that would be beneficial for the partnership to help improve decision-making or reduce risk. For each item, the parties note what information they will share.

A good rule of thumb as you work through the transparency committee matrix is to assume the request is being made with good intentions. Rather than feel uncomfortable, pause and have a dialogue about why your partner wants certain information, how they will use it and what the benefits can be.

The bottom line on sharing information? If information is power, information shared is exponential power. A free flow of information can help to create a common pool of knowledge that increases the ability to arrive at better solutions and lower risks in the collective best interests of the partnership.

Let's take a look at a real example (on the following page) of how two partners completed a transparency commitment matrix for a strategic healthcare partnership.

A good rule of thumb as you work through the transparency committee matrix is to assume the request is being made with good intentions. Rather than feel uncomfortable, pause and have a dialogue about why your partner wants certain information, how they will use it and what the benefits can be.

The bottom line on sharing information? To reiterate, information is power, information shared is exponential power. A free flow of information can help to create a common pool of knowledge that increases the ability to arrive at better solutions and lower risks in the collective best interests of the partnership.

TRUST AND TRANSPARENCY IN ACTION

When individuals and organizations choose to trust and be transparent, they improve their relationships. Good relationships have the power to go from good to great. And even toxic and turbulent relationships can have a trust turnaround.

From Good to Great: NLHS and Compass

Recall how Newfoundland and Labrador Health Services (NLHS) used the CaT assessment to help pick a partner to manage their support services. NLHS intentionally set the tone that trust and transparency were essential in the bidding process by having each of the suppliers complete an assessment and participate in a series of dialogues—working meetings where NLHS could get to know each supplier on a deeper level. As part of the first dialogue workshop NLHS and the potential suppliers aligned on their core values, guiding principles and to what extent the parties were willing to be more transparent.

Compass agreed to do something unprecedented—be fully transparent with their cost structure, including profit margins. NLHS and Compass agreed on a fully transparent "cost-is-the-cost" mantra.

EXAMPLE TRANSPARENCY COMMITMENT MATRIX

	Focus Area	Today	Going Forward
Money	**Cost (with focus on Total Cost of Ownership)**	Budget level costs shared, but detail not provided	100% transparency at leadership level
	Margins	Margin are only disclosed by calculating from balance sheet Individual cost center margins not disclosed	100% transparency at leadership level
	Budgets	High-level budgets are available by cost center only, not by functional areas	100% transparency at budget level
Performance	**Overall Performance (Dashboard)**	Performance is focused at departmental level, causing some decisions that increase overall costs	ONE view of performance using ONE dashboard Focus on end-to-end performance (e.g., includes CERNA)
	Associate Performance	Strong focus on individual performance against goals	Focus on cohesive management of human capital in the partnership 100% transparent on recruiting, retention and onboarding What does it mean to live into our Statement of Intent
	Breakdowns	Breakdowns are only available by functional area, and distribution is restricted to internal company upper management	100% transparent at all levels • No blame culture; "One" root cause analysis vs "SLA" you did not do • Name the breakdown • Share the learnings to focus on fixing root cause
	Trust/Relationship Health Levels	Trust is improving, but lack of transparency causes rumors on underlying root causes for certain decisions	100% transparent at 2-in-a-Box levels 100% transparent at aggregate relationship level
Building Trust	**Roles/ Accountabilities**	Accountability is focused on individuals, not on group or team performance	100% transparent at market level Bakes into governance framework
	Company Strategies	Only the overall company strategy as published in the annual reports is widely communicated Individual department strategies are sometimes in conflict with each other	M&A visibility at the leadership level General strategies communicated at as part of the governance framework (TBD which levels)
	Elephants	In general, there are certain topics considered "off limits" for discussion	Always put an elephant in the room at all levels.

The logic? Full transparency would enable the parties to identify the true cost drivers for both organizations and create a pricing model where the parties would collaborate to streamline work processes and reduce costs.

NLHS went on to select Compass as their partner of choice and create a highly collaborative win-win Vested relationship where the parties jointly work to create value well beyond the transactional contracts NLHS had in the past.

Team members share that the shift to being fully transparent was a game changer.

Scott Bishop (Vice President of Corporate Services and Chief Financial Officer for NLHS) reflects on the power a transparent approach brought to the relationships. "The transparent approach allowed both NLHS and Compass to see the complete financial perspective of the partnership. For NLHS we could unpack the cost drivers at Compass. We got to see that Compass was not trying to take advantage of us to create more profit for themselves. But it also allowed Compass to unpack NLHS's internal cost drivers which helped make the shift from focus on price to collaborating in cost drivers which would reduce our TCO (total cost of ownership)."

For Greg Bayne, Regional Vice President for Compass, the transparency increased trust. "Prior to making the shift to a Vested relationship with NLHS there were trust issues around how we were billing and what we were billing because there wasn't full transparency. But having complete transparency and open books eliminates those questions, which is absolutely fantastic. It is so well received by the audit teams which creates a higher level of trust and confidence because nothing's hidden."

As part of designing the relationship, the parties also agreed to continue to use the CaT assessment to monitor the trust levels in their relationship health. As the graph shows on the following page, the parties have seen consistent improvements in all of the dimensions of the CAT assessment, including the "trust" dimension.

A key indicator of the cultural shift is the adjectives team members use to describe the relationship. In the NLHS/Compass baseline CaT assessment only 66.7% of the words team members used to describe the relationship were positive in nature despite the fact they had been working together for several years. But magic happened to the relationships when NLHS set the strategic direction to purposefully close the gaps in compatibility and trust. Each year the partners worked to close their gaps, and each years the percent of positive adjectives increased. By 2024, the CaT assessment showed team members were overwhelming happy with the relationship with the percent of positive adjectives increasing to 83%.

IMPROVEMENTS IN RELATIONSHIP HEALTH

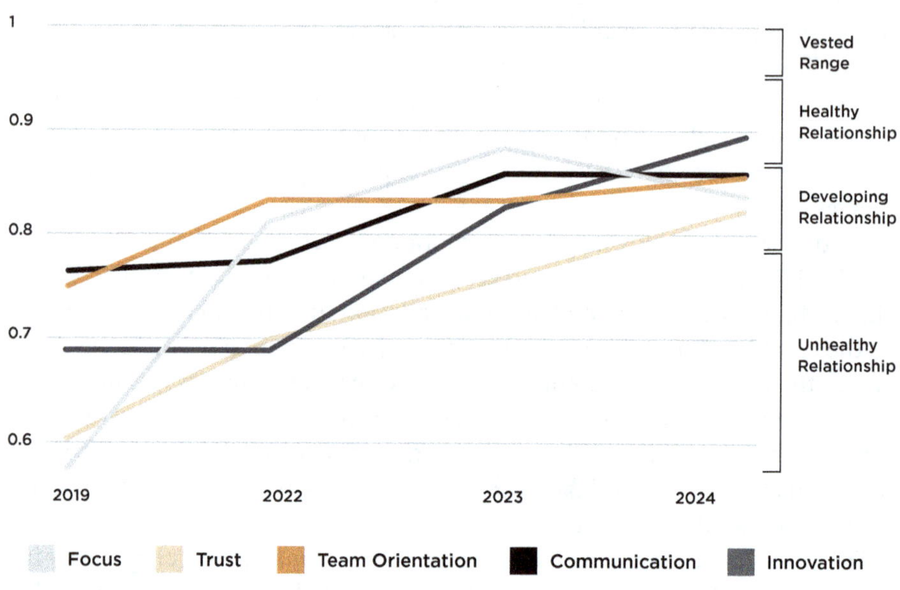

But more important, the negative energy in the relationship virtually disappeared, with the percent of negative words decreasing from 9.5% to only 1.2%.

The following Word Cloud summarizes team member sentiment in how the culture has changed over the four years.

THREE ADJECTIVES TO DESCRIBE YOUR RELATIONSHIP

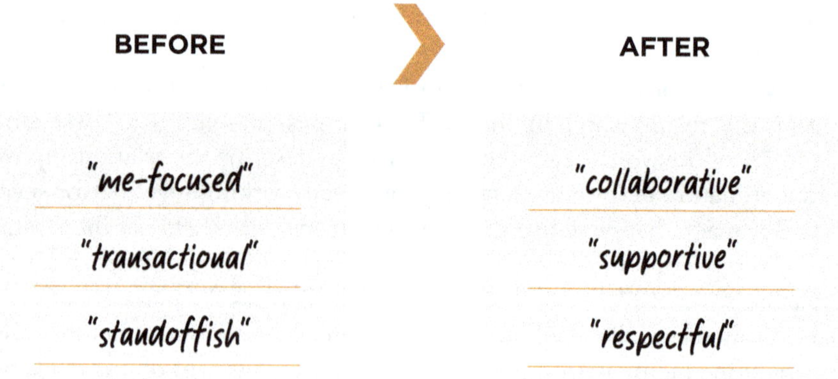

A Total Trust Turnaround: Island Health Authority

Island Health is one of Canada's health authorities and South Island Health is a group of doctors who provide hospitalist services (Hospitalists). Dr. Jean Maskey joined Island Health as a Hospitalist in 2006 and was the site chief between 2009 and 2013. To Maskey, the relationship between the Administrators and the Hospitalists was worlds apart.

> The chasm between the Administrators and physicians had always been wide. There was a running joke that we were separated by a rhododendron forest because some Hospitalists work in the Royal Jubilee Hospital and the Administrators work in offices on the same campus in a separate building called Begbie Hall. I remember early in my Hospitalist career the first time I tried to meet with someone in Begbie Hall. It was June and rhododendrons were in full bloom. I left the hospital and walked through this canopy of amazingly beautiful rhododendrons. And at the end was Begbie Hall—an old nursing building. I went to enter but the door was locked. The rhododendron forest became symbolic for me about our relationship with the Administrators because it was like there was this great divide between us and them. Instead of going on a wonderful stroll through the rhododendron canopy, it was more like you were going through a scary and evil forest. And when the Hospitalists did make the effort, it always seemed you were shut out.

By July 2014, the trust gap had widened so much the parties' contract expired when they failed to agree on new contract terms. The parties agreed to continue to operate under the terms of the expired contract with the hopes they could sign a contract in the fall. But the environment to achieve a new contract was challenging.

Many refer to this period of time as "the troubles." There was a vast divide and widening of the rhododendron forest. By 2016, the parties were at a crossroad; contract negotiations were at a standstill.

The Island Health administrators and the Hospitalists turned to a neutral review of their relationship, which included a CaT assessment. While they knew there was distrust, what surprised them was just how bad the relationship was. A whopping 84% of the words team members used to describe the relationships were negative. Words like distrustful, broken, strained, untrusting, adversarial, suspicious, toxic and even bullying made the list.

Clearly, this was not a healthy relationship.

The CaT assessment highlighted what neither party could bring themselves to admit. The Island Health administrators and Hospitalists needed a trust reset if they were going to have any hope of getting through contract negotiations. The parties made a strategic choice to turn their troubled relationship into a trusting and collaborative one, adopting the mantra "A New Day, A New Way." That new way? Choosing to lead with trust and transparency as they approached their contract negotiation. The conscious decision helped them consider their contract negotiations through a new lens, enabling them to put in the hard work needed to eliminate the root causes of distrust.

The Island Health administrators and the Hospitalists went on to not just settle their contract, but to use the Vested methodology to achieve a total trust turnaround. A follow-up CaT assessment completed two years later—showed the percentage of adjectives shifted from 84% negative in 2016 to 86% positive in 2018 and continued to climb.

THE JOURNEY FORWARD

This marks the end of Part 1 of the book.

If you are in a great partnership, you likely have the sentiment of "Ok... what you are saying is radical common sense." But for those who may be in relationships where there is tension, the tips and tools I share my be insightful or even revolutionary.

Whatever your starting point, when we choose to consciously elevate our best friends, align on cultural fit, and work to build and maintain trust and transparency, you and your partner will increase your chances of having a strong foundation for a successful partnership.

If all you want out of your partnership is a better relationships, consistently applying the lessons from Part 1 will take you leaps and bounds ahead. But for those who want more, perhaps your missing link is that you might not be playing by the right set of rules that enables your partnerships to achieve extraordinary results. Part 2 of this book details a framework of Five Rules to help increase your chances of achieving your impossible.

Part 2 is all about the way forward.

TOOLKIT QUICK REFERENCE GUIDE

Transparency Commitment Matrix

- **Purpose:** To help partners brainstorm how they can benefit from more transparency in their relationships
- **When to use:** Ideally in the early stages of a partnership or at a pivot point when you are exploring if you want to take your relationship to the next level. However, it can be used at any point in a relationship.
- **Output:** A simple table aligning partners on what information they will be transparent about

Part 2:

The Way Forward

In Part 1 of this book, we explored the foundational elements needed for a successful partnership—a purposeful intent to foster trust, transparency and cultural fit in your most important relationships. Investing the time to cultivate each of these elements can help strengthen our bonds with partners where it matters the most.

But all of the trust or transparency in the world or a strong cultural fit in isolation won't guarantee a successful partnership. Why? Because at the core of unsuccessful partnerships are misaligned interests and measurement systems that pit partners against each other. As part of the quest to unpack what makes successful partnerships work, our research at the University of Tennessee has found five core elements that, when applied, help partners help partners get and stay aligned over the long term.

The elements are so important for successful partnerships my fellow researchers and I refer to them as "rules." Combined, these rules create the Vested way of working, a set of shared rules that build atop the purposeful intent for a strong foundation.

THE IMPORTANCE OF RULES

The rules of a game, whether they are laws, business norms, corporate policies or simple instructions, impact the outcome.

Think about the importance of rules in simple card games and sporting events. The games are regulated by clear sets of rules that define the games themselves. The rules are fixed and communicated in advance.

Take baseball. There is no point in a batter arguing that he or she should be allowed to swing and miss 15 times. The rule is three strikes and you are out. Period. If you want to play, you have to abide by the rules. Running directly to third base without going to first or second base may indeed be shorter, but such shortcuts only add confusion on the field of play.

In a conventional outsourcing agreement, rules are not always so clear-cut. Consider my research on outsourcing relationships. In a conventional business agreement, businesses come together and strike a deal where the service provider gets paid for performing transactions. Companies rarely establish and keep track of the rules of their game outside of conventional contracting terms, which are almost always transactional in nature, such as the statement of work, the price list, and legal terms.

Without clear-cut rules, companies often bend and change the rules of the relationship in order to "win."

Or, consider a Fortune 50 company that reported less-than-stellar profits due in part to the declining economy. They hired a highbrow consulting firm who had a great answer—milk cash out of the business through extended payment terms with suppliers The solution? Issue a corporate policy that effective immediately the new payment terms would extend from 30 days to 120 days per the new "best practice" benchmarks. If suppliers didn't comply with the new price terms they would not be issued any new purchase orders.

It did not matter that contracts were in place; the company changed the rules to suit its needs.

Changing the rules to help you win can result in frustration and even chaos. Do tariffs come to mind? And flouting the rules makes everyone want to quit the game and go home. This can take the form of diminished performance, slower results, fewer resources or self-focused behavior. Unfortunately, changing the rules is not only tolerated, it is often expected. Many simply call it "business" and others might even call it a "strategy."

Let's look at the consequences when people don't play by the rules. Oliver Hart, a Nobel Prize-winning economic theorist who popularized the concept of "shading." When organizations change the rules to benefit their own situation at the expense of their partner, it leads to shady behavior which can easily lead to a downward cycle of tit-for-tat behaviors that often get met with subtle (and not-so-subtle) forms of retaliation.

THE RULES OF THE GAME

Vested is a game worth playing. It even has rules: Five Rules, to be precise.

Part 2, **The Way Forward**, is centered on the Five Rules that partners need to follow in order to get and stay Vested:

- Rule 1: Focus on Outcomes, Not Transactions
- Rule 2: Focus on the What, Not the How
- Rule 3: Agree on Clearly Defined and Measurable Outcomes
- Rule 4: Focus on Gains, Not Games
- Rule 5: Stay Aligned

These are the rules that collaborators have used to accomplish the seemingly impossible together.

Each of the chapters in Part 2 explores a different rule. The chapters start with an overview of the why behind the rule, sharing research supporting why the rule is essential. Each chapter also clearly links common perverse incentives of what often goes wrong when the rule is not followed. My favorite part of each chapter is real stories from real people and real organizations that are using the rules to strengthen their partnerships, often with awe-inspiring results.

PLAYING BY THE RULES

Throughout Part 2, I use an example of climbing Mount Everest. Why the analogy? Climbing up Mt. Everest is a perfect representation of the Vested framework in action because the climbers are reliant on each other for success. On Everest, me-first thinking is a path to failure—and potentially death. For that reason, we open each of the Rules chapters with a story about mountain climbing.

The challenges in your world, whether literal or figurative mountains, might feel insurmountable. They might involve family strife or friction with neighbors. Or perhaps you are faced with a major project at work or an unthinkably challenging task. Whatever those obstacles, the Vested Five Rules guide you on the way forward when you are in a situation where you need to rely on others for your success.

Want to play?

Turn the page to learn how to play by the rules.

5

Rule 1: Focus on Outcomes, Not Transactions

"Efforts and courage are not enough without purpose and direction." - John F. Kennedy

Climbing Mount Everest is the ultimate challenge—29,032 feet of struggle. About 7,000 people have reached the top of the world's tallest mountain in the past 70 years. Most of the climbers who've summited have accomplished the task in groups, with sherpas guiding their journey. Only a handful have summited solo.

Climbing mountains as a team requires a Shared Vision to summit and descend safely. Doing a difficult task like summitting Everest demands that each person move beyond transactional relationships. Can you imagine members of climbing teams being compensated for each footstep they take up the mountain and deciding to slack off because they hit their goal? Or walking extra steps in order to boost their pay?

Successful relationships aren't just trying to have an exchange, they aim for something more. And partners realize they can accomplish something better from working with the right partner.

One insightful study of groups that climbed Everest found that collectivism thinking that prioritizes group efforts over individuals increased success rates. Why? Working together caused group members to "blur" their differences and look to their similarities, which helped the individuals come together in pursuit of their common goal.

We all have our own Mount Everest in our lives: starting businesses, building families, writing books, beating cancer or buying a new house. And, if you want to accomplish something big, it's often far easier to be successful when you are working with a partner who has your back.

However, if you are working with a partner who's transactional, you're likely not going to do amazing things together unless you elevate the relationship to something deeper.

Achieving more and climbing your Mt. Everest requires partners to agree on what outcomes they want to accomplish together. That is why Vested Rule 1 starts by aligning the parters on the intent of their relationship. That goes for business and personal relationships.

FOUNDATIONAL THEORIES

Rule 1 is focused on outcomes, not transactions.

It may sound easy until you stop and realize much of the society has been focused on perfecting transactional ways of working even since Adam Smith penned his famous book *The Wealth of Nations* in 1776.

Smith, an eccentric Scottish academician at Glasgow University, is often lauded as the "Father of Modern Economics." He argued that the core of economic success was a free market where individuals and businesses could operate under an "invisible hand." The way Smith saw it, humans have a propensity for self-interest and seek what is best for themselves. Smith felt that society as a whole would benefit from free market competition, which would drive fairness and honesty.

Smith's early work led to the rise of free trade and capitalism. As the demand for global trade grew—fueled by the industrial revolution—demand for repeat transactions led to transaction-based business models. Today, transactional-based thinking dominates how we work and interact. In fact, it is so ubiquitous that most law firms have "transaction attorneys" who work on "transactions."

Short-term transactional thinking has also crept into the way businesses operate internally. Recall the functional silo thinking from the cheese company explored in Chapter 2 where each function was so focused on their own success rather than the success of the overall company. Or consider how the employer-employee relationship has changed over the years. My Dad—as I am sure many of your parents—had very few jobs in his life. Once he landed a "good" job he settled in and worked for years with the promise of good benefits and a pension. Employees worked hard and the company had their backs when they got sick and aged. But today the average job tenure is just 3.9 years.

Personal relationships are not immune from transactional thinking. Musician Sam Smith made that point clear in a 2023 hit song, proclaiming "I'm not here to make friends, I need a lover." Facebook has made having hundreds of distant friends as easy as a click of a button. And with an equally easy click, you can unfriend someone.

If transaction-based thinking is so prevalent and makes things easier because there are no strings attached, should we even fight it?

Yes and no. Transaction-based models are perfectly fine where the exchange is a simple commodity or service with an abundant supply and low complexity.

But transaction-based thinking will only take a relationship so far. There is sound research showing why it is important to make the shift to outcome-based approaches for relationships that focus on longer-term shared goals.

Shared Goals

By the early 1960s no one had landed and walked on the Moon before. The Space Race was intensifying, and the United States faced pressure to keep up with Russia, which had gotten early gains in space exploration.

President John F. Kennedy wanted to do something big and bold. Something that would require lots of commitment and collaboration. In an address to Congress on May 25, 1961, he outlined an ambitious plan. "I believe that this nation should commit itself to achieving the goal, before this decade is out, of landing a man on the moon and returning him safely to the earth."

It was a goal that Kennedy sadly would not live to see achieved. But the goal was, in fact, accomplished in July 1969.

The concept of shared goals is an important one for teams aiming to align. And it goes hand in hand with psychological safety and team learning.

As Amy Edmondson, author and Professor of Leadership at Harvard Business School, sees it, psychological safety is needed in order to drive innovation. Consider what could happen—and how innovation could be stifled—if team members aren't allowed or motivated to speak up?

Think of everything that could go wrong if a nurse doesn't feel safe in challenging a patient's dosage. Or a young pilot noticing that a senior officer made a crucial misjudgment.

"Every time we withhold, we rob ourselves and our colleagues of small moments of learning. And we don't innovate. We don't come up with new ideas. We are so busy unconsciously, for the most part, managing impressions that we don't contribute to creating a better organization," Edmondson said in a TEDx speech.

Notably for Edmondson, psychological safety is not the same as cohesiveness. Our ability to get along with each other isn't the most important factor to group success. And too much cohesiveness could make it difficult for team members to speak up.

Another pioneering voice on the concept of shared goals is longtime Stanford professor and author Kathleen Eisenhardt. As she wrote, strategic alliances are often the result of many factors. "Alliances form ... because they are competing in emergent or highly competitive industries or because they are at tempting pioneering technical strategies." In fact, many alliances involve strong social positions, strategic needs and social opportunities. Where multiple parties must share objectives, goal alignment is crucial.

This effort of shared goals calls back to the early reference to the game of tug-of-war. With shared goals, we are all effectively pulling the rope in the same direction.

Transaction Costs Economics

Oliver Williamson, the economist, professor and Nobel Laureate, devoted his career to exploring "transaction cost economics," or TCE. Those entering a business partnership often get hung up on legalese and covering every possible scenario in a contract framework, but as Williamson wrote, "all complex contracts will be incomplete—there will be gaps, errors, omissions and the like." Contracts with a flexible framework can allow and encourage partners to revisit the contract terms over time as a means of keeping the relationship fair for both parties.

The way Williamson viewed it, having an overly rigid contract leads to higher, not lower, transaction costs. And it can backfire on partners who try to "flex their muscles" or strong-arm collaborators to gain an advantage. Think of how worrisome it could be to deal with friction and negativity. Or how frustrating and time-consuming it can be to find a new partner if an earlier partnership didn't pan out.

As Williamson stated, "the muscular approach to buying goods and service is myopic and inefficient." His advice? Leaving money on the table can build long-term trust and signal an intent to work cooperatively.

P&G: FROM TRANSACTIONS TO TRANSFORMATION

Let's revisit the story of P&G teaming up with JLL to transform its facilities management operations. P&G had a Mt. Everest they were hoping to climb (transform their facilities management operations) and they had selected their sherpa with a good cultural fit, JLL.

Just how big was the P&G-JLL Mt. Everest? It was the largest facilities outsourcing deal in history at the time, spanning 60 countries and over 100 locations. The challenge was even harder because JLL would need to expand its global footprint in countries such as Egypt and Greece, where it had not operated before.

The scope was also multidisciplinary in nature, being one of the first "Integrated Facilities Management" deals. Rather than out-tasking work to different supplier specialists (such as an elevator repair supplier or a landscaping contractor), the contract bundled over 40 separate service areas such as cleaning, dining, energy management, security, landscaping, event management and project management services.

JLL was happy to accept the challenge as a true partner. As part of the collaboration P&G and JLL developed five Desired Outcomes:

- Provide services of equal or better quality at a lower cost.
- Enjoy world-class supplier support, dedicated account management.
- Build a global relationship to support P&G business objectives.
- Have a supplier that guarantees the availability of resources.
- Allow P&G to satisfy the facilities management needs of a world-class global corporation.

On paper, these desired outcomes may not seem like lofty goals. But when you think about them in terms of the Mt. Everest analogy, P&G was at the bottom of their Mt. Everest because they were not achieving these desired outcomes doing things the way they had always been done.

JLL relished the challenge to be a true partner in helping P&G—achieve transformation. However, Bill Thummel, the JLL Global Account Executive, recognized that the ambitious assignment to deliver the desired outcomes could easily overwhelm JLL managers, who were accustomed to working in a transactional manner. "We had to keep in mind P&G bought transformation—not just workers to do the job. If we simply just delivered on keeping the lights on, JLL (and P&G) would fail," explained Thummel.

Early on, JLL spent three entire days creating a project plan based on the commitments outlined in the contract. The plan was complete with phases and a timeline. Thummel explains the power of this approach. "The project plan distilled transformation into something that was doable and had a timeline associated with it. It was all clear. And, most importantly, it helped both P&G and JLL see the end game."

The approach became known as the Glidepath because, as results were generated, P&G expected to see costs graphed out in a downward sloping line depicting lower costs over time—in essence, gliding downward. Thummel knew the real test would be for JLL to deliver on the Glidepath, and that could only happen by working through the project plan and challenging existing ways that work was done. As JLL delivered, the results were clearly visible on the Glidepath as well as other critical performance indicators established by P&G. The Glidepath ensured JLL was optimizing for cost and service performance, not just slashing service to drive down costs.

GETTING IT WRONG: PERVERSE INCENTIVES IN PRACTICE

It's easy to jump into a relationship without putting much thought into it, especially when you have not discussed the purpose of your relationship. Think about country music legend Kenny Chesney and actress Rene Zellweger, whose 2005 marriage was annulled after four months. Or Kim Kardashian's 72-day marriage with NBA star Kris Humphries. One of most famous short-lived Hollywood marriages, between Ernest Borgnine and Ethel Merman, lasted only 38 days. Years later, Merman wrote a chapter in her memoir titled "My Marriage to Ernest Borgnine." The ensuing page was left blank.

You probably have friends or family members who you wish would have slowed down before jumping into a relationship too fast. With luck, your friend's marriage worked out well. But maybe all of the early momentum wasn't sustainable and in the end, the relationship didn't last.

If partners can't align on the intent for their relationship they shouldn't move forward—simple as that. In context to a personal relationship, this is akin to a potential romantic partner suggesting you should just remain friends instead of entering a relationship. Or having the discussion about your future together on topics like marriage and having children.

It's difficult to hear when someone doesn't feel the same way about us as we feel about them, but it's better to recognize that upfront to ensure that there aren't any misunderstandings. Why invest the time and energy with a potential partner who's not interested in helping you achieve your goals and only wants to focus on their goals?

Unfortunately, one (or both) partners often fail to recognize the importance of having an open and honest dialogue about where they want to go with their partner. For example, it can seem awkward to have a conversation about whether you are seeing each other casually or monogamously. If you want to be exclusive and the other person wants to date other people, it represents a moment of truth—you can either agree to the arrangement or walk away. Or if one person wants to get married and the other does not, there may be an ongoing conversation until the person with cold feet agrees to get married—or decides to bail—or vice versa.

The same logic can be applied to business relationships. Businesses often say they want a "strategic partner," but when it comes time to ink the deal, the lawyers jump in with a standard contract template where the party with the most power uses the terms and conditions that benefit them the most.

Failing to have a conversation about aligning on your intent can cause frustration and lost trust. At a minimum it wastes precious time with partners second guessing each other over time.

Vested Rule 1 is devoted to getting clear on the intent of your relationship. It's about candidly discussing your goals and aligning on what you want to get out of the partnership. And, if needed, agreeing you are not aligned, and either parting ways or agreeing to keep the relationship transactional. After all, it's OK to be friendly even if you are not best friends.

Let's look at the perverse incentives that can happen when you don't align with where you are going before you get going.

The Abilene Paradox

It was a Hades-hot day in Texas and Jerry B. Harvey was content with staying at his in-law's house with the fan on the back porch. But then his father-in-law suggested driving to Abilene. His wife agreed. Jerry, not wanting to upset the others, said yes, as did his mother-in-law.

It was an awful trip.

"Here we were, four reasonably sensible people who, of our own volition, had just taken a 106-mile trip across a godforsaken desert in a furnace-like temperature through a cloud-like dust storm to eat unpalatable food at a hole-in-the-wall cafeteria in Abilene, when none of us had really wanted to go. In fact, to be more accurate, we'd done just the opposite of what we wanted to do."

Harvey, a management consultant, wrote about his experience in an article to highlight just how easy it is to find yourself going down an undesirable path because people fail to properly communicate their needs. Failing to communicate your wants and desires effectively can lead to groupthink—taking collective action contrary to one's personal goals. And when things don't work out the way you want them to, it's easy to blame others.

One of the biggest issues facing the "Abilene-bound" group? According to Harvey, "The lack of a map—theory or model—that provides rationality to the paradox." Without the proper destination or GPS you're a lot more liable to wind up in Abilene or some other misguided destination.

The Activity Trap

One of the biggest perverse incentives stemming from traditional transactional agreements is the Activity Trap found in business relationships. Under a transactional approach, service providers are paid for every transaction (per hour, per unit, per mile, per shipment, etc.) The more transactions performed, the more money the supplier makes. There is no incentive to reduce the number of non-value-added transactions, because such a reduction would result in lower revenue.

The Activity Trap can manifest itself in a variety of ways. One of my favorite examples involves a site visit to a warehouse when I asked the general manager of a logistics service provider about a large area full of orange-tagged pallets. She replied, "That's some of our customer's old inventory we need to move to an outside storage facility." When I dug further I found out it was product that was well over five years old—and at the rate it was moving, it would last 123 years. (This is not a typo!) When I pressed further, asking why she did not work with the customer to scrap the material, the answer was "Why? I charge $18 a pallet per month to store it. I'd lose revenue if I did that!"

The Honeymoon Effect

At the beginning of any relationship the parties go through a honeymoon stage: your partner can do no wrong. But that stage often makes way for frustration and disappointment. One study involving 395 couples from one month prior through 2.5 years after marriage found that the Honeymoon Effect is experienced by 14% of the men and 10% of the women.

The Honeymoon Effect happens in business relationships too. One employee engagement survey involving nearly 850,000 responses found that 57% of workers were disengaged, lacking a feeling of promise and optimism by the two-year mark, with that early promise and optimism quickly fading.

Or consider trading partner relationships. Suppliers often jump through hoops as they ramp up and begin to collect revenue from their new client … but over time, the relationship cools. Things happen that make the buying organization question the supplier. The supplier may be meeting contractual requirements but they lack a proactive mindset. Or the supplier seems to always be coming up with surcharges claiming, "scope creep." Rather than focus on fixing the root cause, the typical response is to simply go to market and switch suppliers.

Whatever the reason, when the Honeymoon Effect kicks in, it is frustrating because you are often left wishing you could get the magic back.

ON THE HOME FRONT: BUILDING A LIFE TOGETHER

Martin and Maria met through a mutual friend and the sparks immediately flew.

They found themselves finishing each other's sentences. With the two of them, things just made sense. They shared a lot of the same interests and passions and hobbies. They started seeing each other and chose to date exclusively—boyfriend and girlfriend. Pretty soon, they were talking about their dreams for the future.

They discussed their openness to marriage (yes … someday), favorite foods, deal-breakers (dishonesty and arrogance) and past relationships.

Before long the topic turned to children and if they wished to be parents someday.

"I'd like kids. I came from a big family, and I'd like to start a family, too," Maria said. "What about you?"

Martin rubbed the back of his neck. "I don't know. I'm close to my nieces and nephews and get to spend quality time with them. My ex didn't want kids, and as a result, I told myself that I didn't want them, either. I'm still not sure if I want to raise a child of my own. Or maybe I'm not ready yet. I've never been in a relationship before where I envisioned myself having children," he said.

It wasn't the answer Maria had hoped for but it left the door open for the conversation to continue. She saw herself building a future with Martin. But if he didn't want to have kids … that would represent a deal-breaker. Maria knew couples that tried to rush forward without resolving this issue, only to break up or get divorced. It would be foolish to think long-term if her goals didn't align with Martin's. But she tried not to pressure him or twist his arm into thinking the way she did, just as Martin didn't try to pressure her.

Their relationship continued to build and grow and deepen. But they would need to come to a resolution on their long-term goals that both of them agreed to before they even considered getting married.

THE VESTED WAY

In order for personal or business partners to succeed together they need to be on the same page—pulling on the rope in the same direction versus playing tug-of-war. This starts with aligning on the intent and goals for the relationship.

The tool in the Vested toolkit for getting this alignment is a Statement of Intent.

> **Your Toolkit: *Statement of Intent***
> A co-created GPS for your relationship that aligns partners on intent and goals. This foundational tool prevents the 'Abilene Paradox' and ensures both partners are pulling the rope in the same direction.

Think of a Statement of Intent as the GPS for a relationship. It is the raison d'etre. A good Shared Vision points the direction to the future destination of the partnership, giving the partners a purpose beyond a series of transactions that happen as the partners act on a day-to-day basis. But equally important, partners who revisit their Statement of Intent when making decisions can prevent going to Abilene.

The Statement of Intent should be mutually developed and ideally written down. In a business relationship the Statement of Intent should be embedded into the partners' actual agreement (e.g., the contract) making the contract a *formal relational contract* and committing each party to long-term success of the relationship.

Download the Statement of Intent toolkit to help you jump start the discussions around the future of your partnership. As you work through co-creating your Statement of Intent you will develop a Shared Vision, high-level Desired Outcomes and Guiding Principles for your partnership.

Our Shared Vision:

DESIRED OUTCOMES:

GUIDING PRINCIPLES:

| Reciprocity | Autonomy | Honesty | Loyalty | Equity | Integrity |

Let's take a look at each of the components in more detail.

Shared Vision and Desired Outcomes

A Statement of Intent starts by getting aligned on the highest-level fundamentals about what the partners want to get out of the relationship. An easy way to do this is to mutually define a Shared Vision and a few high-level Desired Outcomes.

The Shared Vision is the long-term destination, or end game, for the relationship. Think of the Shared Vision as the ultimate destination you want for your partnership. Do you want to climb Mt. Everest? Or are you happy to ski the bunny hill at the closest ski resort?

Desired Outcomes represent more tangible goals and objectives the partners want to get out of the relationship. Let's break this concept of Desired Outcomes down further.

A desire is something both parties want—but something they don't have. And an outcome is a result that can be achieved only by both parties working together. In short, Desired Outcomes represent the critical few things you and your partner agree you want to work towards.

In regard to the GPS, Desired Outcomes represent the route or stops you will take along the way. You plug in your Shared Vision as the destination and as you progress through your journey in life or business, you will strive to accomplish the Desired Outcomes which are indicators you are staying on the right path.

In a personal relationship the Shared Vision for two couples may be to "get married and live happily ever after." But their Desired Outcomes could be very different. For example, couple one has the Desired Outcomes to have two kids, buy a house in Suburbia and save enough money to retire by the age of 60 and move to the beach. The second couple may think couple one is so conventional and BORING. This second couple may have the same Shared Vision but have a totally different set of Desired Outcomes such as not wanting kids, renting a modest condo in the city center, and a buying vacation home at the beach they can drive to for frequent long weekends. And their desired retirement plan? Move to their beach house and take trips around the world to exotic locations twice a year.

Getting to a Shared Vision and Desired Outcomes requires openness and honesty. Unfortunately—and more often than should be—one or both partners aren't candid enough and begrudgingly go along with their partner's suggestions. When this happens, it's easy to find yourself eating that bad lunch in Abilene.

Guiding Principles

If Shared Vision and Desired Outcomes provide clarity on the partner's journey, Guiding Principles are the guardrails for the relationship. Guiding Principles are the relationship's values and norms and a commitment from the partners to uphold them. Establishing and committing to Guiding Principles for the partnership provides the commitment you are there to support your partner on your journey—versus simply being a free rider. Guiding Principles prevent opportunism and competitive tit-for-tat moves because partners agree to follow proven behavioral norms.

Think of how often people agree to terms—sometimes for the sake of reaching a deal—only to renege or backtrack. Guiding Principles such as Honesty, Reciprocity, Autonomy, Integrity, Loyalty and Equity can help partners ensure that they remained aligned around the same common fundamentals.

Contracts between parties can't always map out every single possible scenario and Guiding Principles provide guidance for the parties to move past those gaps and to remain on the same page throughout their partnership. Establishing these Guiding Principles allows each partner to keep each other honest and ensure the partnership continues to flourish.

David Frydlinger (a Swedish attorney) and Oliver Hart (Harvard University Professor and winner of the 2016 Nobel Prize in Economics) expand on the power of using Guiding Principles in contracts—which includes incorporating expressed intentions around upholding the Guiding Principles in contracts. As the authors wrote, Guiding Principles can "be thought of as a simple mechanism... based on norms that are familiar in most if not all societies." Guiding Principles act like a contractual conscience for the partners, helping keep business partners from opportunistic behavior. And when business happens, the partners are obligated to discuss the best way to move forward that is aligned with the stated Guiding Principles. It's easy to want to skip aligning on those principles, but failing to do so can lead to problems.

When working with a partner it's easy to want to skip this process. You might think it's silly or trivial to have to agree to operate with honesty and integrity. But not agreeing to Guiding Principles can easily lead to massive problems when one or both partners are tempted to behave with self-interest rather than in the mutual interest to the partnership. As Frydlinger and Hart describe, formally agreeing to Guiding Principles helps partners lay a behavioral foundation and commitment for a trusting and productive relationship, guiding partners to act in accordance with their intentions.

Unfortunately, people often don't take the time to establish Guiding Principles for their relationship. They believe it takes too much time and isn't worth the effort. Instead, they focus on negotiating the substance the deal. Creating a Statement of Intent with Guiding Principles flips the concept of negotiating on its head because the relationship *is* the substance.

Partners that jointly commit to the Statement of Intent for their relationship establish a solid foundation that can help them navigate when it snows on their Mt. Everest because the Statement of Intent acts as a beacon, guiding them to not be tempted by short-term opportunistic behaviors that can easily trigger shading. By recognizing and acting in accordance with the Guiding Principles, partners show that they care more for the relationship than short-term interest. In turn, this creates and maintains trust and ultimately reduces misalignment, friction and even disputes.

FROM THEORY TO PRACTICE

Taking time to establish (and write down and commit to!) your Statement of Intent is the starting point of a great relationship. In fact, it is so essential I wrote about this with David Frydlinger and Oliver Hart in a *Harvard Business Review* article titled "A New Approach to Contracts: How to Build Better Long Term Strategic Partnerships" where we argue for the need to have formal relational contracts that put the purpose of the relationship above the transactional elements of the contract.

But even with a formal agreement (your GPS for the relationship agreed and turned on), it's not enough. Partners need to actively review where they are going and make course corrections as necessary when business or life happens (more on this in Rule 5). For now let's return to the example of Island Health and the Hospitalists to see how they got on the same page by creating a Statement of Intent for their relationship.

Island Health: Getting On The Same Page

With contract negotiations at a standstill, both Island Health and the Hospitalists were at their wits' end. Continuing with their us-versus-them negotiations was getting nowhere and distrust from the failed negotiations had deepened their divide. Something had to be done.

Could the Vested way help them get unstuck?

The Island Health and Hospitalist leadership teams agreed to send their key leaders—augmented with a cross-functional group from their teams—to spend three days in an Alignment Workshop learning about Vested and going through Rule 1 to see how the Vested methodology could help them.

Of course there were skeptics. The resentments and hostilities were spilling over. Why would this work?

Skepticism aside, what mattered was that the parties agreed to at least give the Vested methodology a try. And if they didn't want to proceed after the three days, they didn't have to move forward. Nothing ventured, nothing gained. And definitely nothing to lose.

Ahead of the workshop, the parties' Vested coach conducted a formal review of the relationship consisting of a contract review and a Compatibility and Trust assessment. The actual workshop was held offsite at the University of

Victoria—symbolic the parties were both there to learn. But it also set the tone as a "neutral" location that allowed the participants to focus on the relationship discussions without being distracted by day-to-day circumstances.

Courtney Peereboom, the Director of Special Projects for Island Health, was skeptical at the onset. But she was not alone. "Most people went into that room with folded arms and negative body language. The feeling of the room was uncomfortable and not very open," Peereboom said.

Putting the Trust Elephant in the Room

The workshop started with an ice-breaker exercise where each person introduced themselves and their role and gave a short story about the first car they owned. It was a chance for each person to see others on the opposite side of the divide in a light-hearted manner.

The workshop then turned serious—putting the state of the relationship front and center. The Vested coach kicked off the relationship review with the Compatibility and Trust (CaT) assessment. The CaT assessment revealed just how broken the relationship was. A whopping 84% of the adjectives team members used to describe the relationship were negative, with responses such as "distrustful," "strained," "broken," "toxic" and "bullying." The CaT Assessment also revealed several ah-ha's. For example, despite the friction, the parties actually had a high degree of cultural fit with the shared goal of patient care. The CaT pointed to a classic case of the illusory superiority bias: each party felt they were not the ones causing the problem—it was "the other guy."

Dr. Kenneth Smith—one of the Hospitalists—summed up the cause of the perception gaps. "Simply put, neither side knew what the other was doing: the Hospitalists had no idea what the Island Health budget was for them, and Island Health Administrators did not know how the Hospitalists scheduled patient care. It was easy to see how there were such huge perception gaps."

The problem was not the other guy, but everyone. Collectively they had created an opaque and adversarial culture that bred distrust.

To further bring down the walls, the Vested coach introduced a "buddy system" for lunch. The Island Health administrators and the Hospitalists were asked to find a buddy (someone they did not know well and wanted to know better) and go to lunch. The only rule? They could not talk about work. Vacations. Hobbies. Kids. All fair game. But discussing work was off-limits.

It was a simple exercise, but one that struck a chord with many of the team members. The exercise not only got them talking, but it gave them a chance to see "the other guy" as human beings and discover just how much commonality they had.

The second agenda item was the contract review. The Vested coach showed how the parties' existing transactional contract was full of structural flaws that created perverse incentives. The contract review pointed to hope. It illustrated how it was hard for the parties to be aligned in their behaviors when they were contractually obligated by transactional ways of work that put Island Health and the Hospitalists on opposites sides of the table. The result? The parties were playing a virtual game of tug-of-war in how they worked.

Developing the Statement of Intent

The second day of the Alignment Workshop focused not on the past, but on the future of the relationship. The Vested way does this by having partners work through developing a Statement of Intent—something their current relationship did not have formally or informally. For the first time in a long time, the sides started to have candid discussions about how to create an avenue for mutual success. They also sat side-by-side co-creating the foundational aspects of their relationship working through each part in a Statement of Intent.

A Shared Vision emerged and was refined in a series of collaborative workshop sprints.

> *Together, we are a team that celebrates and advances excellence in care for our patients and ourselves through shared responsibility, collaborative innovation, mutual understanding, and the courage to act, in a safe and supportive environment. We will be recognized leaders in healthcare. (later the team added the statement: We will achieve this vision by building relationships grounded in trust and respect and anchored in the following Guiding Principles and Intended Behaviors).*

The parties then tackled identifying the Desired Outcomes for their partnership. Four Desired Outcomes emerged as the cross-organizational/cross-functional teams collaborated.

- A Sustainable and Resilient Hospitalist Service
- Excellence in Patient Care
- Relationship Health Excellence
- A Best Value Hospitalist Service

Next up on the agenda? Adopting Guiding Principles for the partnership that would guide the parties in their decision-making process, "especially during times of adversity." Together, they agreed on the exact wording of the Guiding Principles that not only went on to become the foundation for the negotiations of their contract—but became foundational in the contract itself.

The process helped the partners discover how the Guiding Principles could help them: by committing to behavioral norms they could prevent virtually all of the issues that had evolved over the years. The partners developed the following six guiding principles.

Reciprocity: We conduct ourselves in the spirit of achieving mutual benefit and understanding. We recognize this requires ongoing give and take. We each will bring unique strengths and resources that will enable us to overcome our challenges and celebrate our successes

Autonomy: We give each other the freedom to manage and make decisions within the framework of our unique skills, training and professional responsibilities. We individually commit to make decisions and take actions that respect and strengthen the collective interest to achieve our Shared Vision.

Honesty: We will be truthful and authentic even when that makes us vulnerable or uncomfortable. This includes honesty about facts, unknowns, feelings, intentions, perceptions, and preferred outcomes.

Loyalty: We are committed to our relationship. We will value each other's interests as we value our own. Standing together through adversity, we will achieve our Shared Vision.

Equity: We are committed to fairness, which does not always mean equality. We will make decisions based on a balanced assessment of needs, risks and available resources.

Integrity: Our actions will be intentionally consistent with our words and agreements. Decisions will not be made arbitrarily, but will align with our Shared Vision and Guiding Principles. Our collective words and actions will be for the greater good of the relationship and the provision of patient-centered care.

With the Guiding Principles as the foundation, Island Health and the Hospitalists also drafted a series of "Intended Behaviors" that would help them jointly build a "positive culture that will enable us to achieve our Shared Vision and extraordinary results." The Intended Behaviors are:

- Patient-Centered
- Honesty
- Collaboration
- Empathy
- Forward Focus
- Communication
- Accountability

All of those efforts—the Shared Vision, Desired Outcomes, Guiding Principles and Intended Behaviors—formed the parties' Statement of Intent. After years of being at each other's throats, the sides were finally speaking the same language. They were finally aligned.

Over the next months a smaller subset of the Island Health administrators and Hospitalist went on not only to successfully negotiate their contract following the other four Vested rules, but to transform their relationship from toxic and distrustful to one of being collaborative, trusting and even innovative. And at the heart of the relationship? Their Statement of Intent was formally embedded into the first three pages of their contract.

> **Pro Tip:** I teach to also include "Intended Behaviors" for strategic business partnerships. While Guiding Principles are proven social norms, intended behaviors are optional and include behaviors the partners want to promote. For example, flexibility, courage, patient-centered.

SUCCESS ON THE HOME FRONT

When Maria first asked Martin about having kids a few months earlier, Martin was conflicted. He wanted to travel at a moment's notice. He wanted freedom! Having a child is definitely not that. And it can be expensive to raise a child.

Martin was relieved Maria hadn't forced the issue on him... even if she dropped a few not-so-subtle hints from time to time, like looking at baby clothes whenever they went shopping or oohing and ahhing whenever Maria's best friend texted a new picture of her baby. They gave each other space to figure out the topic.

But after seeing Maria play with his nieces and nephews, Martin began to realize there are so many awesome, rewarding things that can occur from having children. Their relationship had been progressing nicely and Martin was saving up to buy a ring. But the topic of kids had been a sticking point that they needed to resolve first.

Martin decided to have the kid discussion during a weekend getaway trip. They were deep into one of their favorite bottles of cabernet sauvignon when Martin broached the kid topic.

"You know, I've been thinking about kids, and whether I'd like to have them someday. I know a few months ago when we talked about it, I wasn't committed to the idea of having kids. But seeing you around kids, and deepening our relationship... I'm coming around to it," he said. "It would be an adventure, but one I think I'd want to take someday."

This time Maria was one the one taken aback.

"That's amazing to hear," she said. "I think you'd be an awesome dad."

"Thanks. That means a lot. You'd be an awesome mom. I know you come from a big family... but I think one or two kids would be perfect for me. Especially if we were to spend more time together, just the two of us, before starting a family. I'd want to save up some money and get a little more established in my career before we bring someone else into the mix. And that way if I'm a little more established, I could have more flexibility in my schedule and work from home to help with the baby. I want to be able to save up to afford a house, too. I want to raise our family in a good location."

"That could work. But the timing matters. I don't want to wait too long to start a family. If we get married in the next couple years, then we try to have a baby when we're around 30 or so and see how that goes. We could start with one baby and keep an open mind about having another."

They were having fun envisioning their future life together when Maria jumped up and grabbed a pen and a piece of paper. "Martin, for fun let's create a little vision board for our life together!" By the time the bottle of wine was empty the pair had a Statement of Intent scribbled out on the paper.

> **Our Shared Vision:**
> *To get married and live happily ever after.*

DESIRED OUTCOMES:

Get married in the next two years

1-2 kids by before we turn 33

Set money aside to buy a house in a good neighborhood

Maria and Martin were excited. It was a great start to a new beginning. They toasted each other as they took the last sip of wine in their glasses, vowing to always put family first and make decisions with their bigger-picture goals in mind.

TOOLKIT QUICK REFERENCE GUIDE

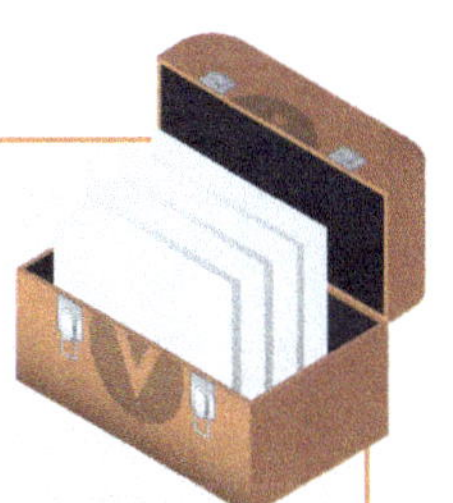

Statement of Intent

- **Purpose:** To align partners on the intent and goals of their relationship.
- **When to Use:** When you want to take a relationship to the next level. If you have not created a Statement of Intent, you can start at any time.
- **Components:** Shared vision, Desired Outcomes and Guiding Principles. Intended behaviors are optional, but recommended.
- **Guidelines:** The formality of your Statement of Intent depends on the formality of your relationship. For example, strategic business relationships should embed their Statement of Intent into their contract to create a formal relational contract.
- **Output:** Typically a one page document, but can be as long as you need it to be to feel comfortable with the strategic direction of your partnership.
- **Perverse Incentives it Prevents:** Abilene Paradox, The Activity Trap, The Honeymoon Effect.

6

Rule 2: Focus on the What, Not the How

"It doesn't make sense to hire smart people and then tell them what to do. We hire smart people so they can tell us what to do." - Steve Jobs

Climbers from all over the world hire sherpas to help them conquer one of the world's biggest challenges. The sherpas of Everest are elite climbers who understand the terrain and whose bodies are well prepared for high altitudes. When preparing to climb Mount Everest, you don't write a job description for your sherpa—you hire them for their expertise and rely on their guidance.

It's easy to think of the challenge of Everest and quickly fall in line in trusting a sherpa's guidance. But when people face their own everyday mountains— far too often they hire a sherpa and then turn around and question, challenge or even reject their every move. In short, they hire an expert to do the work only to turn around and micromanage them!

Being micromanaged—whether you're a sherpa or the worker in the third cubicle on the left—can snuff out enthusiasm and cause people to give up and check out. Lots of workers disengage and pull back in the act of silent defiance often referred to as "quiet quitting."

When people think of micromanaging it is often in context to being micromanaged by their boss. But micromanagement is common in lots of relationships.

With clients.

With children.

With spouses.

Micromanaging is frustrating and disempowering and inefficient. It's an insidious weed drawing nourishment and sunlight and resources in our relationship garden. And we need to be vigilant to encourage the beautiful flowers to take root and grow.

The research organization Gallup suggests you can spot micromanagement in business relationships with one simple question: Is a team customer-obsessed or boss-obsessed? Customer-obsessed teams are focused on outcomes (what); boss-obsessed teams are focused on orders (how). "Micromanaging creates a transactional relationship in which the manager fixates on minor mistakes and focuses on a person's weaknesses and work style. Great coaching, on the other hand, is an ongoing relationship of support and trust that emerges out of a rhythm of collaborative conversations, leading to teamwork and shared accountability."

Micromanagement also happens in personal relationships ranging from mundane tasks like how to cook dinner to criticisms about how to parent the kids.

In order to achieve a Vested relationship we need to be able to move past micromanaging and rely on each partner for their expertise. That's why Rule 2 is Focus on the What, not the How.

FOUNDATIONAL THEORIES

While Rule 1 explored the importance of establishing a partnership and aligning on mutually defined desired outcomes, Rule 2 is about looking at the work that needs to be done to climb your Mt. Everest and finding the optimal way to do the work.

Under Vested Rule 2, relationships flourish when partners embrace autonomy and use a challenger mindset where partners are focused on problem-solving, adaptability and continuous improvement.

The Power of Autonomy

Think of the best boss you've ever had. How did they allow you to shine? How much freedom did they give you to explore and test?

Daniel Pink popularized the concept of using autonomy to achieve better results in his successful book *Drive: The Surprising Truth About What Motivates Us*. He described how a ROWE, a Results-Only Work Environment, encourages employees to get their work done without dictating how. "How they do it, when they do it, and where they do it is up to them."

But how does a workplace perform without a manager, well, *managing*?

Multiple research papers reflect the fact that when workers are given autonomy they tend to have stronger job performance, higher job satisfaction and greater commitment to the organization. One such study links increased job autonomy with a 12% increase in worker satisfaction. And evidence indicates that autonomy is a key factor for the most satisfied employees.

Practicing autonomy by consciously avoiding micromanagement is a key theme Stephen Covey addressed in his iconic book *7 Habits of Highly Effective People*.

Covey was a master at teaching the power of autonomy, often using a story from his own life. When Covey started traveling more frequently for work, he asked family members to step up and help out with household chores. Covey's son, 7-year-old Stephen M.R. Covey, volunteered to take care of the family's yard.

The elder Covey set the expectation for a what-not-how mantra: *green and clean*. "You're free to do it any way you want, except paint it." While giving Stephen autonomy to do the work, he did offer help.

The young Covey was eager to learn.

"How would you do it, Dad?"

"I'd turn on the sprinklers. But you may want to use buckets or a hose. It makes no difference to me. All we care about is the color green. Okay?"

"Okay."

Covey spent about two weeks teaching and coaching young Stephen before turning the job over to his son. Covey made a point to tell Stephen that by taking the job of doing the yard it would be his job. He would trust young Stephen to keep the yard *green and clean*. And little Stephen's boss would be himself—not Dad. But if little Stephen needed help he could ask his dad.

A few days passed... and the young Stephen Covey was doing what boys do—playing instead of doing his chores. Simply put, the yard was not staying *green and clean*. But Covey resisted the urge to jump in and start barking orders. Instead, Covey recommended they walk around the yard together, as they'd agreed, to check on Stephen's progress. Young Stephen grew upset as they began to walk outside and evaluated how well he had done.

Busted.

The dad gently referred back to their agreement; he would help if he had the time.

After a long pause, little Stephen timidly did ask his father for help. They got to work getting the lawn *green and clean*.

By giving his son freedom to care for the lawn whichever way he saw fit, Covey found a way to motivate his son to truly take ownership and embrace the work of maintaining the lawn. If Covey had drilled his son on how to do the work and mandated it be done a certain way, his son son could easily become resentful about the task and less likely to make it his own.

Covey's "green and clean" lesson may seem quaint but the spirit of it is just as relevant to big business as it is your backyard, and a "what-not-how" approach has helped transform lots of business relationships.

Years later, Stephen M.R. Covey reflected on his version of the story in an interview. "I was a 7-year-old boy. I didn't know what those words meant [win-win agreements and stewardship delegation], but here's what I knew as a 7-year-old: I felt trusted. I felt my father trusted me. I didn't want to let him down."

The Challenger Mindset

According to the old saying, the only person who likes change is a wet baby. It's likely you have people in your organization who are change-averse. Worse, your entire organization may not be open to change. General Electric's former CEO and management guru Jack Welch pointed to inertia as one of the worst traits undermining organizations. "When I try to summarize what I've learned since 1981, one of the big lessons is that change has no constituency. People like the status quo."

Challenging the status quo isn't about putting someone in a box and telling them to think outside of it. Instead, you're challenging them to use their expertise to build a better box. You're empowering them to achieve their best effort in furtherance of the greater good.

Challenging the status quo is how Toyota workers come to work every day. The Toyota Production System aims to "thoroughly eliminate waste and shorten lead times to deliver vehicles to customers quickly, at a low cost, and with high quality." Workers on the Toyota assembly line don't simply show up to build a car, they show up to figure out how to build a car better, faster, cheaper, safer, smarter, and more sustainably.

The simple truth is that challenging the how—the status quo—is the only way to achieve progress.

Challenging the status quo of how existing mops work leads to new products like the Swiffer.

Challenging the status quo of how people negotiate is what led Island Health and the Hospitalists to get past their deadlock and get to a new contract.

And challenging the status quo is what helped the state of Minnesota rebuild the I-35 bridge in just 13 months after it collapsed—while being under budget and winning nearly two dozen quality awards.

MINNESOTA DOT: FROM TRAGEDY TO TRIUMPH

It was a scorching summer evening just after 6 p.m. on August 1, 2007. Rush hour.

Kim Dahl was driving a busload of students participating in a summer program back from a field trip at Bunker Beach Water Park. Many of the children were still in their swimsuits and sang songs as the bus rolled along.

As Dahl drove her yellow school bus across the I-35W Bridge, she noticed the bridge start swaying. Then she heard a loud clank.

That clank? It wasn't a prank from one of the kids. Nor was it a collision. Or even an explosion. Rather, it was a sign that the I-35 bridge Dahl was crossing was about the collapse. Seconds later a gusset plate supporting the eight-lane bridge buckled and gave way. The roadway beneath the bus fell 30 feet.

"The next thing you know, we were slammed down, and we went up again, and we slammed down again, and there was this big dust cloud."

Dahl gripped the steering wheel, slammed her foot on the brake and set the parking brake as windshield glass rained down on her.

Kim's yellow school bus was perched precariously on the edge of the bridge guardrail, just feet from a burning semi-truck. Dazed and in pain, all she could think about was making sure all of the children were brought to safety. Two of her own kids were among the students, but after driving the bus for five years, she thought of all of the children as her own. Thankfully a staff aide kicked out the back door and Kim and all of the passengers were able to make their way off the bus.

Kim was one of the lucky ones. Thirteen people died that day.

A replacement bridge was needed—and fast. Normally, an extensive bridge replacement project takes five years or more. One thing was certain: a different approach was needed that would challenge the status quo processes and dogmas of how bridges were typically built.

Governor Tim Pawlenty knew with the right people and vision, the state of Minnesota could find triumph amid the tragedy. Governor Pawlenty had a Mt. Everest. A big, audacious goal to replace the bridge within 18 months.

Everyone understood why speed was important. The interstate is a critical artery connecting two sides of Minneapolis, with between 100,000-200,000 vehicles passing over the bridge on a daily basis. Every day the bridge remained closed the average economic loss was mounting. The Minnesota Department of Transportation (MnDOT) Office of Investment Management estimated the daily cost to motorists at $400,000. And the State Department of Economic Development Impact Analysis believed the average net economic impact incurred an additional $113,000 daily reduction in the State's economic output. The Minneapolis Regional Chamber of Commerce claimed the daily cost to business exceeded half a million dollars.

While no one could agree on an exact magnitude of impact, everyone agreed that a long delay was not an option. Governor Pawlenty and other lawmakers got to work securing funding. Within days of the collapse, President George W. Bush signed legislation authorizing $250 million in funding for the bridge replacement, far from a hefty budget one might expect or want for a project so large.

One of the status quo processes that would need to be challenged was procurement. Historically, the state used a competitive bid process where the contractor with the lowest price would win the contract. On the surface, it was a smart measure used to curtail unnecessary government spending. However, over the years, grandma's old adage that "you get what you pay for" often proved out, with large construction projects often suffering from long delays and cost overruns.

The MnDOT team, led by project manager Jon Chiglo, brainstormed ideas. Two came to mind. First, a relatively new—yet rarely used—policy allowed for a best value approach that would balance cost, quality and timeliness in choosing a contractor to rebuild the bridge. Second, they challenged the conventional "design-bid-build" approach in which MnDOT would design the project then put the plans and specifications out for bidding. Instead they would use a "design-build" approach that bundled the design and construction into one contract. Such an approach would streamline the contracting process, save time, and allow bidders more freedom to come up with creative solutions for building the bridge that would meet the aggressive timeline.

The foundations were in motion for MnDOT to follow Vested Rule 2.

The MnDOT team got to work, and on August 4, 2007—only three days after the bridge collapse—and issued a Request for Qualifications (RFQs) from interested bidders. Five contractors were downselected as qualified suppliers to move into a second Request for Proposal (RFP) phase of the bid process. The RFP described six primary desired outcomes on less than one page that potential bidders needed to solve:

- Safety
- Quality
- Schedule
- Environmental Compliance
- Budget
- Aesthetics

What was missing? The typical nauseating detail of a government procurement bid document. Instead of detailing specifications and tasks in a traditional Statement of Work, the six desired outcomes outlined the "what" while giving the potential contractors the autonomy to develop innovative and efficient solutions to meet expectations. It gave contractors an overview of the problems that needed to be solved while giving them the flexibility to come up with solutions. The bid process allowed the contractors to bring forward their most innovative solutions instead of simply responding to pre-defined specifications with a price.

By following Rule 2, MnDOT focused on the what not how, and by default created autonomy for suppliers. They weren't simply aiming to find a contractor to build a bridge, they sought a strategic partner—a sherpa—to collaborate with to reimagine bridge building.

British-born Peter Sanderson was excited about the possibility of working on the I-35 Bridge replacement. Sanderson learned of the bridge collapse while he was in Mumbai, India, working on a bridge over the Arabian Sea. Sanderson had long worried about the United States' aging infrastructure. Watching the footage of crumbling pavement and smoke-filled skies in Minnesota, he immediately knew the project would be a big deal. "I believed, surely, there would be a lot of work to do. And I wanted to be part of bringing credibility back to bridge building," he said.

One of the things that excited him was the flexibility of the bid approach that would truly allow a great contractor to shine.

Sanderson flew to the U.S to help develop the proposal from Flatiron-Manson, a joint venture between Flatiron Constructors, Inc. and Manson Construction Company. Both firms had lots of experience with bridge work. Flatiron is a leader in the construction and civil engineering industry, while Manson Construction specializes in foundations, bridges and piers and has a professional workforce—many of them second-, third- and fourth-generation workers.

The Flatiron Manson proposal called the design for the I-35 bridge replacement to be a "high-tech, high-performance smart bridge of the future." Their proposal set out to minimize life cycle costs and provided a low maintenance schedule. Structural enhancements offered in the proposal included added protection from high-performance concrete, multiple levels of redundancy, superior deck durability, an integrated wearing surface, and even the ability to accommodate the future addition of a 12-foot-wide suspended pedestrian bridge underneath.

There was one gap that Sanderson and his team needed to solve for in their proposal. Recall one of the I-35 Bridge desired outcomes outlined in the bid document was aesthetics. While Flatiron-Manson was an expert in many ways, they knew they needed their own sherpa to help them with world-class architectural elements. Here they turned to Linda Figg, the owner of FIGG Engineering. Figg is well known for her architectural skill in designing "Bridges As Art." For the replacement of the I-35W bridge, she focused on the theme of "Arches, Water, Reflection." Arches were reflected by graceful proportions and elegant simplicity, connecting the bridge elements with refinement. Water represented the Mississippi River. Reflection was a spiritual reflection of the bridge site as a memorial as well as the literal reflection captured by the shapes, natural light and water.

Within 60 days of the bridge collapse, MnDOT signed a contract with Flatiron-Manson to rebuild the I-35W Bridge with the plan of reopening to traffic by Christmas Eve, 2008—less than 16 months away.

It was a big goal, something never done before. It would demand MnDOT and Flatiron-Manson continued to follow Rule 2 and challenge the status quo.

Like with concrete casting.

Dr. Kevin A. MacDonald, vice president for engineering services of the Cemstone Products Company, served as a sherpa for the project's concrete production, from providing creative, environmentally-focused mixes that created a stronger bridge to devising a way to continue concrete casting regardless of the temperature.

Remember, the bridge was being built through the winter. A Minnesota winter. Typically that would mean delays, delays, delays. Concrete does not set well in the cold, and Minnesota winters are colder than cold: frigid and windy and unrelenting.

But this project wasn't like most other projects.

MacDonald used mathematical modeling techniques instead of a time-intensive process of creating trial mixes and testing them over time to develop the bridge's mix designs. Instead of waiting around, hoping for the weather to turn and the snow to stop falling, work crews built large hut-type structures where they placed forms. The structures included fans that provided heat directly into the forms. This gave the team a chance to monitor and control temperatures so concrete could be poured and cured safely, with quality specifications ensured. The workers even installed ground heaters to prevent the ground from freezing.

But they also had to protect the concrete from heat damage. A chemical reaction within fresh concrete creates heat, and that heat could compromise the integrity of the structure as it cured. The solution? The workers streamed river water through narrow plastic PVC tubes into the poured concrete, dropping the temperature of the wet concrete and allowing optimum curing.

But speed was only one component of the project. Safety was another. MacDonald ensured the concrete far exceeded strength tests.

Another innovation involved how the concrete forms were set. Contractors usually buy one set of bridge pier forms and construct one pier at a time, but Flatiron-Manson bought forms to construct all the substructure elements simultaneously. The backspan sections were cast in place, and casting beds on the construction site produced precast segments for the main spans that were moved into place using "Bohemian Blue," a large river crane.

The first segments of the new bridge were lifted into place on May 25, 2008, less than 10 months after the bridge collapse.

The innovations didn't stop with the concrete. The bridge was one of the first to use sensors to monitor the bridge's performance. Two hundred and forty sensors evaluate surface wear and tear, the pressure on expansion joints and bearings, as well as other metrics. The data gathered by sensors helps reduce costs and maintenance of the bridge. The innovative approach has aided future bridge projects around the world.

Another design innovation? The sculptures at each end of the bridge. On the surface the sculptures simply look like a nice design feature. But behind the scenes the columns eat air pollution! A special photocatalytic concrete called TX Active reacts with ultraviolet light and pulls pollutant particles like carbon monoxide out of the air and converts them to less harmful substances.

The results of following Vested Rule 2 are impressive—and helped MnDOT achieve the impossible: replace the bridge in just 13 months, under budget and with quality levels than won almost two dozen awards. If MnDOT had focused on the how—outlining the specifics of the project—such innovation wouldn't have been possible.

GETTING IT WRONG: PERVERSE INCENTIVES IN PRACTICE

Think about what would have happened if MnDOT came up with a long list of specifications and tasks for the bridge project. Or what if Stephen Covey had detailed a long list of rules and restrictions his son needed to follow in order to keep the yard "green and clean." How effective do you think those efforts would have been?

Consider a contract for dining services. It is not uncommon for a typical statement of work document to stretch across 50-plus pages. I've even seen a dining contract that included a complete list of approved recipes. Trust me when I say the best talent in food services feel henpecked and restricted and do not like to work these accounts.

Focusing too much on the how can lead to a host of perverse incentives, leading to frustration, duplication of effort, and lost opportunities to find better, faster, cheaper, safer and more sustainable ways to get work done.

Let's look at a few of the things that happen when you don't follow Vested Rule 2.

A Unicorn Is Not Just a Typical Horse

Making the right hire can be a long, costly process. When companies seek to find candidates to fill job openings, they often work with employment search firms to find the *perfect* candidate, a true unicorn. The process can average nearly $5,000 but can cost three to four times the position's salary.

When that perfect person finally begins their new job, they often have to confront layers of bureaucracy and dogmas: *This is how we do things here.* The new hire is crestfallen. Why bother going through all the effort when you're just going to set parameters and restrictions around the role? Why treat a unicorn like just a typical horse? Or worse, treating them like a pack mule who is just there to do the heavy lifting of a job.

Now sometimes you just need a pack mule or a typical horse. But when you do want to find that perfect unicorn to do amazing things, don't put them in a box and ask them to think outside of the box.

Some companies are known for their ability to hire and support their unicorns in their organization. One of the most well-known is 3M, which promotes a "15% Culture" approach in which scientists and engineers are encouraged to explore ideas beyond their day-to-day roles.

For 3M, 15% isn't just a metric, it's a mindset made possible by lots of collaboration. "Many of our most impactful customer-focused solutions start with the curiosity sparked by our 15% Culture," says John Banovetz, Chief Technology Officer and Executive Vice President for R&D at 3M.

One recent example of 15% culture innovation is the Scotch Cushion Lock, an alternative to plastic bubble wrap that was inspired by a 3Mer working on Kirigami, the Japanese art of cutting and folding paper. A Kirigami structure provides the product's interlocking honeycomb design. "It's not just practical, it's 100% recycled paper and curbside recyclable, reducing plastic waste," Banovetz said.

Jayshree Seth, a corporate scientist and 3M's Chief Science Advocate, is proud of the company's innovation efforts. Seth's years of experience and analysis has led her to describe 3M's innovation culture as being made up of six critical components, with each component meant to help drive ideas forward. They are Expectation, Risk-taking, Resources, Opportunity, Reward and Socialization, which appropriately form the acronym ERRORS. "These elements also reinforce the mindset that true progress can emerge when we have the safety to explore and make mistakes and try new things. And all the elements are critical. If you skip any, you don't get the desired results," Seth said.

The Outsourcing Paradox

The Outsourcing Paradox happens when an organization hires a supplier as the expert and then tells them how to do the work. This happens when the organization that is outsourcing the work develops the set of tasks, frequencies and measures into the "perfect" statement of work (SOW) or specification dictating how the supplier needs to perform the work. Paradoxically, the SOW then contractually obligates the supplier to perform the work as told, effectively locking the buying organization into the status quo way of working.

A classic example of the outsourcing paradox comes from a logistics service provider that runs a spare parts warehouse. During a site visit, there were eight team members servicing a facility that on average had fewer than 75 orders per day. I asked: Why all the resources for so few orders? The answer? "That is what the company that is outsourcing requires per our statement of work. So we have to staff at that level to meet the contract requirements."

An overly prescriptive SOW acts like handcuffs that restrain the supplier to the boundaries of the SOW. This locks the supplier into the status quo process and preventing innovation. An interesting twist? Typically companies that outsource are doing so because they desperately want the supplier's expertise and innovation and they fail to realize they are the ones that are constraining progress.

The Junkyard Dog Factor

The Junkyard Dog Factor occurs when one of the partners hunkers down and draws a line in the sand, claiming that certain processes simply "must" be done the way they have always been done.

Junkyard Dogs are often known for being "anal retentive" or "micromanagers," which almost always leads to duplication of effort. Consider the relationship between David (a project manager at a marketing firm) and his team members. Jordan works on the team and is responsible for drafting client proposals. After Jordan submits a draft, David doesn't provide guidance or ask questions. Rather, he simply rewrites large portions of it himself, line by line. David then sends the updated version back to Jordan with comments like, "I fixed the structure for clarity." Over time, Jordan puts in less effort, knowing David will just redo her work. She stops offering new ideas and avoids ownership of the work. Worse, her performance slips—not because she lacks skill, but because she's lost the motivation to try. Eventually, she starts looking for another job where her contributions will be trusted.

TROUBLE ON THE HOME FRONT

Perverse incentives from not following the Vested Rule 2's what-not-how mantra can happen in personal relationships as well.

Martin and Maria ended up getting married and having two girls: Ava (a family name) and Liv (named in honor of Maria's grandmother Olivia, who had a spirit for living life to the fullest).

The couple struggled to juggle parenting and work duties with household tasks. Early in their marriage they took a divide-and-conquer approach to chores. One person cooks, the other person does the dishes. Typically, Maria cooks. She enjoys testing out healthy, tasty recipes she finds online and in recipe books. Her favorite dish to cook is eggplant parm. She has the process down to a science. She finds ripe eggplant at the store, slices it up and dries it, breads the pieces, bakes them, then adds the sauce and cheese and puts the dish in the oven, and *voila.*

With Maria handling the cooking, Martin tackles dishes. Martin doesn't enjoy doing the dishes, and that shows in the way he approaches the task. He often puts off doing dishes in pursuit of watching his favorite sports team on TV after dinner. It drives Maria up a wall when sauce hardens on her bakeware and she lets Martin hear it whenever it happens.

"This isn't the right way to do the dishes," she says.

"But this is the way I do the dishes," he responds.

Dishes became a sticking point, something on which they were never going to agree.

Maria's micromanagement was getting under Martin's skin. Martin knew he had to do something to address this. There was a solution to be found, he just couldn't figure out what it was.

THE VESTED WAY

Not every project requires mountain climbing, doing the unthinkable or innovating.

If you already have a clear grasp on what you are trying to accomplish it's perfectly all right to simply hire a helping hand and tell them how to do the work you would like them to do. Like when you are a startup on a budget and you choose someone on Fiverr to design your company logo. It's OK for the relationship to be transactional in nature because you are simply paying someone to do a specific task. You pay $90 and in exchange, Bob develops a new logo for your company. It's a simple transaction. Bob does the work and you pay Bob. Bob is a pack mule, not a unicorn—and that is OK.

In a Vested relationship, the goal changes. You are not just simply plugging somebody into a role to perform a task, but are collaborating to achieve greatness together. Vested Rule 2 keeps everyone centered on their role and how they are adding value to achieve the desired outcomes. Done right, Rule 2 helps partners avoid the micromanaging trap during the climb up that Mt. Everest.

Micromanaging can emerge due to numerous reasons, but a lack of trust is a big component.

Think of a relationship where you have complete trust. You don't need to tell your partner how to do their part of work; rather, you trust they know the how and do what they say. And more importantly, you don't have to micromanage them. Instead, you can put your focus and energy on collaborating to achieve your desired outcomes rather than checking up on their progress. Each party is working to deliver—or exceed—expectations.

The tool in the Vested toolkit for helping partners focus on the what not how is a taxonomy and workload allocation.

> ## Your Toolkit:
> ### *Taxonomy and Workload Allocation*
> A co-created inventory of all processes and sub-processes in scope, regardless of who does the work. Once the taxonomy is defined, partners assign accountabiity for each process. This foundational tool provides clarity on how partners will interact as they work. This privides end-to-end visibilkity and ensures partners know who owns what so they can focus on outcomes instead of oversight.

In biology, taxonomy (from Ancient Greek τάξις (taxis) "arrangement" and -νομία (-nomia) "method") is the scientific study of naming, defining and classifying groups of biological organisms based on shared characteristics. My fellow researchers and I leveraged this concept as a way to help companies that outsource complex goods and services to follow Rule 2.

First, collaborators list all of the work that needs to be done—regardless of who does the work. Let's go back to our mountain climbing example in context to a buyer-supplier relationship. The climber is the buyer and the supplier is the sherpa. Both have things that need to be done to successfully summit and descend from their collaboration to conquer Mt. Everest. Think of a taxonomy as an inventory of all of the work—the processes and sub-processes within the work scope—that needs to be performed, with a brief identification of each process. The goal is to develop a catalog of the work to be done regardless of who is doing it.

Workload allocation, on the other hand, is meant to identify who is accountable for each of the processes identified in the taxonomy. A workload allocation builds on the partners' taxonomy.

A good way to understand how to put a taxonomy and workload allocation in practice is to visualize it as a simple table. Each row in the table is the work that needs to be done—the taxonomy. The columns of the table are who is doing what work—the workload allocation.

Using a taxonomy and workload allocation is a powerful tool because it helps partners learn how to let go by "seeing" how the parties will interact and work together on their journey. Whether you are climbing Mt. Everest, finding a better way to build a bridge, collaborating to provide outsourced IT support or finding the best way to align on chores at home; a taxonomy and workload allocation creates clarity and commitment of responsibilities.

To get started, download the Taxonomy and Workload Allocation toolkit (see next page for example).

TAXONOMY AND WORKLOAD ALLOCATION TOOLKIT

Process Level 1	Process Level 2	Process Level 3	Accountability		Opportunity to Change Existing Process	Exceptions
			Me	You		

Start by listing all of the processes/tasks that are needed for your partnership. Think end-to-end if the work (e.g., to get to the top of Mt. Everest the climber and the sherpa both have to do work). If needed, break down a process/task into subprocesses by adding rows and columns to the table.

Once you have a draft of the taxonomy, begin to fill in the columns on the right side and note who is responsible for each process/task. The general rule of thumb is the partner who can do the work better, faster or cheaper should take the ownership for that part of the work. Hint! If there is more than one company/person responsible for the same process/task, break the process/task into smaller chunks where only one company/person is responsible. Having duplication creates confusion and can easily lead to micromanagement and create frustration.

As you work through your Taxonomy and Workload allocation, feel free to modify the toolkit as needed to provide additional insights that may be helpful for your partnership. For example, if you are struggling with a broken or inefficient processes add a column with a note you will address this process as part of your collaboration. Or note any exceptions.

> **Pro Tip:** If you are find yourself micromanaging (or being micromanaged) after you have completed your taxonomy and workload allocation, talk to your partner and work out a way to ramp up/train your partner or ask them what they need to trust you to "let go."
> Hint: Remember how Stephen Covey ramped up his son for taking care of the yard?

FROM THEORY TO PRACTICE

In practice, partners use the taxonomy and workload allocation to clearly align on their roles and responsibilities. In a personal relationship this might mean who does what chores or how siblings will share responsibilities when taking care of an aging parent. It does not mean the work has to be 50/50 (I do dishes 50% of the time and you do dishes 50% of the time), but rather how you divide the roles and responsibilities to best leverage the skillset and resources of each partner. In a business relationship this takes the place of a traditional statement of work.

A Taxonomy and Workload Allocation shifts partners from a transactional way of working to turning on the power of autonomy and embracing a challenger mindset. When done right, you are not just dividing and conquering for the work that has to be done, but looking to see how you are collaborating to invest the needed time and energy into work that often gets overlooked.

Let's look at how Newfoundland Labrador Health Services and Compass used a taxonomy and workload allocation to help them not only define the scope and roles for the partnership, but to identify areas for potential efficiencies. From there we will look at how focusing on the what and not the how unlocked the power of autonomy and the challenger mindset for the Department of Energy in driving innovation in the cleanup and closure of the Rocky Flats Plant.

NLHS and Compass: Clarity in Collaborating

Support services are a critical and extensive part of operating a health system. Prior to their Vested journey, Newfoundland Labrador Health Services (NLHS) worked with two primary suppliers, Compass being one of them. After a collaborative bid process NLHS selected Compass as their partner of choice to help them drive transformation of their support services operations. The two partners then set out to craft a Vested partnership that followed the Vested Five Rules. One of the biggest things that changed between how the partners worked was exactly that—how the partners worked.

A cross-company/cross-functional team worked through the Taxonomy and documented all of the work needed to achieve the parties' shared vision and desired outcomes, regardless of which company would perform the work. The work scope included patient/resident food, retail food, environmental services/housekeeping, laundry, portering and call center services. Each high-level category of work was broken down by up to three levels, as shown in the figure below, which shares a small sample of the comprehensive acute care program scope of work.

With the high-level taxonomy complete, the team worked through the Workload Allocation portion of Rule 2. The workload allocation helped the partners identify if there was any overlap in the work or if any balls were being dropped. For every line item in the taxonomy, the team noted who was accountable with a simple "YES" under the name of the company. Either NLHS or Compass was accountable. If the team identified an overlap in the work, it signaled a potential improvement opportunity to streamline the work and reduce potential redundancies. Lastly, developing the taxonomy and workload allocation helped NLHS and Compass openly discuss how the work had been done (the status quo) and identify additional opportunities for improvement. As the figure illustrates, there were several items that were flagged as having potential to change (noted in the column "opportunity to change existing process."

EXAMPLE EXCERPT TAXONOMY/WORKLOAD ALLOCATION

Housekeeping Services Example

Process Level 1	Process Level 2	Process Level 3	Accountability		Opportunity to Change Existing Process	Exceptions
			NL Health	Compass		
Comprensive Cleaning Acute Care Program	Operating Rooms (OR) cleaning			Yes	Yes	HSC Labor & Delivery OR rooms
	Regular Discharge Room Cleaning			Yes		
	Isolation/Precaution Cleans - Patient Room Cleaning			Yes	Yes	Refer to Orphan Item project
	Routine Cleaning of All spaces			Yes		Mechanical Room space (to be confirmed as part of sq meters review project)
	Enhanced Cleaning	Requests and approval of requests to perform Enhanced cleaning	Yes			
		Execute Enhanced Cleaning		Yes		
	Patient Room Furniture					
	Orphan Items		Yes		Yes	
	Linen Handling	Stripping of beds	Yes		Yes	
		Removal from patient room to a soiled utility room	Yes		Yes	Compass at HSC and LTC in Rural
		Moving linen from Soiled Utility to a pick-up location for Central Laundry		Yes		Compass at HSC
		Making of beds after discharge		Yes		
	Grounds around buildings and parking lots		Yes		Yes	

HSC = Health Science Centre, LTC = Long Term Care, OR = Operation Room

Completing these two steps differed greatly from the traditional approach NLHS used to define a supplier statement of work. It outlined each party's accountability and also helped NLHS see their role as not to manage Compass, but rather to support them.

Notably, the taxonomy and workload allocation does not go into detail telling Compass "how" to do the work, which in turn gave Compass the flexibility to make changes to processes that could benefit from automation or streamlining.

The result was exceptional clarity—something that was missing in the past. It also gave the partners a roadmap of potential improvement opportunities.

Recall in the Vested methodology, innovation projects are called Ponies. One of the Ponies in the NLHS-Compass partnership was an overhauled safety program measured by Lost Time Injury (LTI) rate.

An LTI is an injury or illness that results in an associate being unable to perform their regular work duties and requiring time off from work. It occurs when an injury or work-related illness is severe enough to prevent an associate from returning to their job for at least one scheduled workday or shift after the day of the incident.

The LTI rate reflects the high-risk nature of health care work. Musculoskeletal injuries—often caused from manual handling tasks such as lifting and transferring patients—accounted for approximately 50% of the workplace injuries. In addition, violence and aggression from patients or residents in health care settings has become an increasing concern, particularly in emergency rooms and psychiatric wards.

The financial impact of these injuries is substantial, with millions of dollars in compensation paid out annually and additional indirect costs affecting productivity, staffing, and the overall efficiency of health care operations. According to WorkplaceNL, the average compensation per LTI claim in health care is around $35,000 to $50,000 depending on the severity of the injury. In addition, there are substantial indirect costs such as lost productivity, overtime for replacement staff, retraining and administrative expenses, which can be up to four times higher than direct costs. This means that for every LTI, the total cost to health care employers could be upwards of $140,000 to $200,000 per claim.

Vested's "Focus on the What, not the How" rule has been game changing in terms of challenging the status quo in things like managing employee safety. Under the NLHS-Compass partnership, the partners have collaborated to implement many new safety initiatives, leading to a decrease of LTIs from 13.90 to 9.03 per 100 workers. That whopping reduction reflects not only a much safer workplace but also millions of dollars in cost savings.

Rocky Flats: The Ultimate Clean-Up

The Atomic Energy Commission's Rocky Flats Plant was nestled on a mile-high mountain shelf where gold prospectors once roamed. The place earned its nickname because it is both rocky and flat. From 1952 to 1992, the Rocky Flats Plant produced the plutonium pit, or "trigger," for nuclear weapons to fuel America's nuclear arsenal.

From its inception, Rocky Flats was shrouded in secrecy. After all, when you are making nuclear weapons you don't just want anyone dropping by to see what you are up to. The secrecy eventually led to the Environmental Protection Agency (EPA) and the Federal Bureau of Investigation (FBI) raiding Rocky Flats in 1989 in an investigation code-named "Operation Desert Glow." As a result of the raid, the Rocky Flats plant was designated a hazardous waste site. In 1992, President George H. W. Bush ordered the Rocky Flats site to be permanently closed and cleaned up.

The problem? How to clean it up. Rocky Flats was not just one facility. Rather it was a compound of 800-plus buildings spanning 6,240 acres in the foothills of Colorado's Rocky Mountains. The soil, sediment, groundwater and surface water were contaminated with hazardous chemicals and radioactive constituents from 40 years of work. A cleanup of a nuclear production facility had never been accomplished before. Many deemed success impossible. Studies suggested that the project could take 75 years and cost $37 billion. One could argue the Rocky Flats cleanup project was its own Mt. Everest.

A General Accounting Office (GAO) report to Congress described the Rocky Flats plant like this:

> *The site's weapons production activities left high-risk radioactive and hazardous materials and wastes, severely contaminated buildings, and large areas of contaminated soil—all in close proximity to the 2.5 million residents of Denver and its surrounding communities. The job at hand is huge. For example, the total amount of radioactive waste that the contractor is required to package and ship off-site is enough to fill a 19 story building the size of a football field. The first challenge was to get the necessary government agencies coming together and getting alignment. The result was the Final Rocky Flats Cleanup Agreement signed by the State of Colorado, the Environmental Protection Agency and Department of Energy in 1996.*

The agreement established a regulatory framework for achieving the cleanup of the site and defined the following shared vision:

- To achieve accelerated cleanup and closure of Rocky Flats in a safe, environmentally protective manner and in compliance with applicable state and federal environmental laws;
- To ensure that Rocky Flats does not pose an unacceptable risk to the citizens of Colorado or to the site's workers from either contamination or an accident; and
- To work toward the disposition of contamination, wastes, buildings, facilities and infrastructure from Rocky Flats consistent with community preference and national goals.

The agreement granted DOE the authority to work with a commercial contractor. Kaiser-Hill (a joint venture of CH2M Hill and Kaiser Engineers) was selected as the partner of choice, the DOE's sherpa. An added challenge? Kaiser-Hill would work with the existing government workforce, almost 4,500 union workers.

While the government—and workers—had lots of experience producing nuclear chemicals manufactured at Rocky Flats, no one had ever done the kind of work needed to clean up and close a nuclear chemical facility. There was no statement of work. There was no precedent.

DOE leaders such as Project Managers Mark Silverman and Jesse Roberson fought to get language included in the agreement to allow for flexibility and innovation. For example:

> *Seek ways to accelerate cleanup actions and eliminate unnecessary tasks and reviews, by requiring that the Parties to the Agreement work together. Provide the flexibility to modify the work scope and schedules, recognizing that priorities of specific tasks and schedules may change as the cleanup progresses due to emerging information on Site conditions, risk priorities, and available resources.*

While there were specific requirements and risk rankings, Kaiser-Hill had flexibility in how they met requirements. For example, the Kaiser-Hill leadership team chose to remove the Administration Building first. While it was a lower-priority project, it sent a message to the union workforce that "we're all in this together," because it forced senior management to work out of a shared workspace in the middle of the action.

Using a what-not-how mantra also opened up the door for much needed innovation. A cleanup like this had never been done before, and as a result, some tasks had to be invented, such as how to decontaminate two "infinity rooms" (the areas were so contaminated with plutonium, the radioactivity levels couldn't be measured with standard monitoring equipment, thus the nickname "infinity rooms").

In the spirit of "what, not how," workers began exploring ways to clean up these highly toxic rooms. Workers first started to explore using pressurized hot water spray, but that was not working. They kept tinkering. The solution? Workers collaborated to create a colored aerosol sugar fog to clean some of the most contaminated areas.

That process was detailed in summary written by the teams involved in the cleanup. "An aerosol sugar fog called Capture Coating was dispersed with a machine that used sound waves to make the droplets very small. After the radioactive particles in the air were fixed to the surfaces by the fog as it settled, up to a ¼-inch layer of poly-urea coating called Insta-Cote would then be sprayed on to permanently seal the contamination in place."

The contaminated surfaces could then be removed.

Adopting Rule 2—Focus on the What, not the How—paid off in spades. Kaiser-Hill was allowed lots of flexibility to experiment and find solutions as long as they followed the law. It empowered the workers to focus on innovative ways to accomplish the DOE's Mt. Everest. The result is that workers—most of whom were former government union workers—created more than 200 innovations, which enabled the Department of Energy to close Rocky Flats 55 years ahead of schedule and $30 billion under budget.

If someone had tried to micromanage them, how many innovations do you think they would have developed? And how long would the project have taken?

SUCCESS ON THE HOME FRONT

Martin was still thinking about his conflicts with Maria as he and his buddy Cal played their weekly Saturday morning golf game. Golfing gave Martin the chance to take his frustrations out on the ball and move around for a few hours.

Martin was growling as they approached Tee Box #4.

"We really need to figure out a better way," Martin said.

Cal offered a suggestion. Why not list all of the chores and whoever is best at a chore will do it?

Martin instantly liked the idea. Maria was better at doing the dishes and it was a no-brainer for her take on that chore. And Martin was better at washing their cars and he didn't mind tackling messy garbage and hauling the heavy garbage bags out to their apartment's dumpster.

Martin couldn't wait to get home after swinging clubs with Cal.

"I think I may have a solution to our battle about chores. Cal and his wife have devised this great approach where they allocate chores based on who is the most capable to do that chore."

Maria was intrigued.

Martin got out a blank piece of paper and created a simple table with three columns. The first column was the chore. The second and third columns had Maria and Martin's name as the header for the column. Together they began to list all of the chores in the first column. From there they turned to allocate who would do which chore.

LIST OF CHORES

Chore	Martin	Maria	Exceptions
Dishes		✓	Martin handles when Maria on girls night out/weekends
Garbage	✓		
Recycling	✓		
Cooking		✓	
Vacuuming	✓	✓	Trade off each weekend

Martin started. "I know you hate to deal with the garbage because it can get messy and the bags can get heavy."

"Yes!" chimed in Maria. "I dread dragging those heavy bags down our apartment stairs. And it seems like the dumpster is about a half a mile away. I especially hate it in the winter because I have to bundle up when I'd rather be sitting by the fireplace."

Maria slyly added, "Does doing the garbage include the recycling? I hate breaking down all the Amazon and Costco boxes from the kids' supplies and toys because it makes my hands dry and I seem to always be breaking a nail."

"Done!" said Martin. "I promise you will never ever have to do garbage or recycle ever again. I'll take that on as my responsibility."

Martin continued. "I was thinking about the dishes. You know I don't mind in spirit helping out with the dishes. But since I can never seem to do the dishes right, it's always frustrating you, which in turn frustrates me. Since you care so much more about how the dishes are done than I do, why don't you handle them? That way, you can do the dishes your way."

Maria agreed—with two caveats. "If am cooking and doing the dishes I think it is only fair that you make sure the girls stay out of the kitchen so I can get through everything efficiently. And, if I am away for one of my girls' weekends, please don't make me come home to a sink full of dirty dishes."

Martin spit out the words "No problem!" as fast as he could. No more getting nagged about the dishes!

They continued down the list of chores until they got to a couple that neither one liked to do—vacuuming and cleaning the bathrooms.

The solution? They would trade off each week.

Without realizing it, the pair had completed a taxonomy and workload allocation.

The simple exercise made them reflect: wasn't it silly for us to spend so much time bickering over the dishes?

Taking a different approach to household tasks allowed Martin and Maria to tackle the tasks they were most particular about, which in turn diminished their micromanaging and improved their marriage.

TOOLKIT QUICK REFERENCE GUIDE

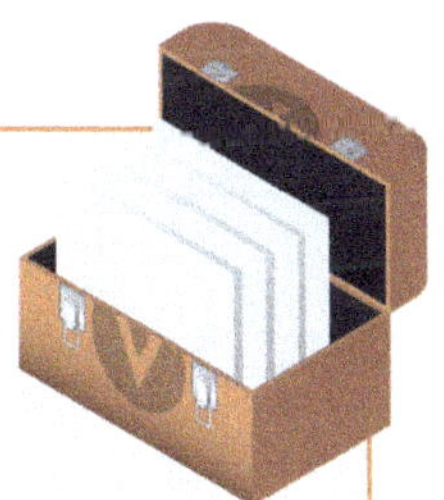

Taxonomy and Workload Allocation

- **Purpose:** To define the complete body of work required to achieve the desired outcomes and assign accountability for each process/task identified in the taxonomy.
- **When to Use:** Anytime you want to get clarity about roles/accountabilities in a relationship. For strategic business partnerships this should be done at the onset of a relationship and be embedded into the contract in the place of a Statement of Work.
- **Components:** Taxonomy (inventory of all work needed regardless of who is doing it) and a Workload Allocation (noting who is responsible for each process/task in the taxonomy).
- **Guideline:** The general rule of thumb is the partner who can do the work better, faster or cheaper should take the ownership for that part of the work.
- **Output:** A simple table providing a clear line understanding on who is doing what work that is needed for a successful collaboration.
- **Perverse Incentives it Prevents:** A Unicorn is Not Just a Typical Horse; The Outsourcing Paradox; The Junkyard Dog Factor.

7

Rule 3: Agree on Clearly Defined and Measurable Outcomes

"If you don't know where you're going, you might never get there."
-Yogi Berra

A 2020 study led by researchers at the University of Washington and the University of California, UC-Davis, sought to quantify climbing outcomes. The researchers found the success rate of summiting Everest has doubled in three decades—yet death rates have stayed close to 1% despite the fact that more climbers are attempting to scale Everest and crowding along the summit route is a concern.

For example, between 1990 and 2005 success rates for summitting Mt. Everest were 31.3% for women and 32.3% for men. In recent years the number of climbers has skyrocketed. Between 2006 and 2019, 2,860 men attempted to climb Everest with 63.9% doing so successfully. And of the 548 women who made the attempt, 68.1% were successful. It's interesting to consider how there hasn't been a big difference in climbing success rates based on gender, but overall success rates have more than doubled.

With so many climbers and so much crowding on the summit route, it's easy to assume that success probabilities would decrease. The study's authors noted, "Crowding almost certainly will slow climbers, but any negative effects of crowding may be masked by the benefits waiting at high camp and then making a summit bid only when conditions appear suitable (weather, snow)."

While summiting and survival are the ultimate desired outcomes, there are literally dozens of different metrics that climbing teams and outsiders can track to monitor climbing success.

Take age for example. Researchers noted a drop-off starting above age 40 (a decline of 1.1% per year). Climbers older than 59 summited about half as often as younger climbers.

Lots of factors—including team size and commercial versus non-commercial expeditions—didn't have a significant impact on the results. Surprisingly, climbing experience wasn't even a factor! As the study's authors wrote, the statistics "inform prospective climbers as to their current odds of success and of death, as well as inform governments of Nepal and China of the safety consequences and economic impacts of periodically debated restrictions based on climber age and experience."

But there are also success like oxygen supply, weather reports and health that help climbers approach their summit attempts with clarity and stay aligned with fellow climbers. Team members can use this information to help them make decisions like when to call off a summit attempt if conditions become an issue.

The challenge is to identify the metrics that matter and make sure those are the ones that you are actively using. And those metrics should be defined and agreed upon up front. For example, if one team member falls ill, does the whole team abort the summit? What about two members? How bad does the weather have to be before you decide not to climb?

A group of climbers can't spend precious time and energy fighting with each other in the moment. They need to be able to track and measure high-value metrics and disregard the noise. Staying on the same page can mean the difference between life and death for Everest climbers. Likewise, it also can mean the difference between business partners and personal relationships staying healthy and productive or falling apart.

Relationships often suffer because partners don't align on and use the right metrics for monitoring their progress. Or they find themselves drowning in data trying to measure everything that moves. I studied one outsourcing contract that had over 500 "key performance indicators" for the supplier!

The ever-connected Internet of Things using smart devices and sensors—combined with AI—has made capturing, slicing and dicing data easier than ever before. But that same ease also makes it easy to get lost in information overload. And ironically, despite having vast data, some companies still find themselves driving blind because they are not actively monitoring the right things.

FOUNDATIONAL THEORIES

Recall from Rule 1, one of the first things partners need to do is develop a Statement of Intent for their relationship which includes identifying the Shared Vision and high-level Desired Outcome for their relationship. The Desired Outcomes represent where the partners are going—the future desired state the partners want to achieve as a result of their partnership. Vested Rule 3 is where partners determine how they will measure and monitor success against the Desired Outcomes.

Using metrics to define and track success is not new. Peter Drucker was one of the first management gurus to emphasize the use of metrics in his 1954 book *The Practice of Management* where he introduced the term "management by objectives" (or MBOs for short). If you've ever worked on yearly performance reviews for employees, you probably have heard of MBOs. While the basic ideas of MBOs were not original to Drucker, his influence helped popularize the concept.

In 1986 another management guru, Tom Peters, was credited with saying, "What gets measured gets done." Ever since Peters' rallying cry, companies have amped up their efforts to get smarter about how they measure what matters.

Let's look at a few principles that help shape how partners measure success.

Getting S.M.A.R.T. with Metrics

The concept of using "SMART" metrics was first introduced by George T. Doran in a 1981 article in the *Management Review* journal titled "There's a S.M.A.R.T. Way to Write Management's Goals and Objectives." Doran used the acronym S.M.A.R.T. as a framework for helping companies set better metrics. The acronym stands for:

S	Specific
M	Measurable
A	Achievable
R	Relevant
T	Time-bound

The thinking behind S.M.A.R.T. objectives is sound: that objectives need to be quantifiable in order to be tracked and followed. If objectives are too vague it's impossible to know if they're truly being fulfilled. It's possible, using S.M.A.R.T. objectives, to measure what matters and agree to clearly defined and measurable outcomes. But far too often that isn't the case, and employees are left tracking and following metrics that don't help them and the company to achieve their goals. Or they are pursuing achievable goals that are within reach instead of attempting transformative goals.

It's why management consultant and author Dick Grote listed S.M.A.R.T. goals among his three popular goal-setting techniques to avoid. As Grote wrote, "While the SMART test may be a useful minor mechanism for making sure that a goal statement has been phrased properly (in the same way that a spell-checker is a useful mechanism for flagging any misspelled words in a document), it provides no help in determining whether the goal itself is a good idea. In other words, a goal can easily be SMART without being wise."

Finding Your Balance

Dr. David Norton (a lifelong consultant) and Dr. Robert Kaplan (a Harvard Business School professor) began to collaborate to find a better way to measure success in business in the 1990s when they worked together on a KPMG-sponsored project. In the 1990s, most organizations tended to focus on financial measures—which really only measured past performance.

In 1992 the duo introduced the idea of using a Balanced Scorecard in a *Harvard Business Review* article. The premise was easy to grasp: companies should focus on metrics that went beyond financial metrics. The article suggested companies add three categories of metrics: customer metrics, internal process metrics and innovation and learning metrics.

The duo went on to found the Balanced Scorecard Institute, which even sold software to companies to help them create and manage corporate dashboards.

Measuring What Matters

By 2018, former Intel employee turned investor John Doerr popularized a third approach with his book *Measure What Matters: How Google, Bono, and the Gates Foundation Rock the World with OKRs*. The book became an instant hit.

OKRs stand for Objectives and Key Results and are made up of two parts: **objectives** (what you wish to achieve) and **key results** (measurable metrics that track progress). As with S.M.A.R.T. objectives, OKRs focus on measuring and tracking success. The thinking behind using metrics to define and track success was spot on and over the years has contributed to the success of many companies.

One of the notable examples in the book is how Google used OKRs to focus on search quality and user growth. The structure followed the typical OKR format:

Objective: Improve search quality and user experience
Key Results: (paraphrased examples)

1. Increase search result relevance scores by X%
2. Reduce page load time to under Y seconds
3. Grow daily active users by Z%

Doerr emphasizes throughout the book that successful OKRs should be cross functional in nature. In the Google example the OKR creates alignment across teams: engineers knew they needed to focus on both technical performance and user metrics, not just one or the other. Unfortunately, what is not spot on for many organizations is the execution. Many organizations have used OKRs too narrowly, creating OKR Overload (more on this later).

MONEYBALL: VIEWING METRICS FROM A DIFFERENT LENS

Billy Beane had a crazy idea.

Beane—a former major league baseball player and scout—was promoted to the general manager of the small-market Oakland Athletics (A's) baseball team in 1998. Beane's challenge? The Oakland A's were consistent losers. They came in last in the American League West division the previous season and were the worst team in major league baseball in winning percentage.

Some might have thought Beane was doomed for failure. The A's couldn't afford an A+ roster of players. In fact, when Beane took over the job, the A's player payroll budget was among the lowest among all major league teams at under $20 million, a fraction of the payroll of winning teams such as the New York Yankees, which topped $60 million.

Beane aimed to find a way to compete with baseball's best teams while maintaining a shoestring budget. Given his unique perspective of the game, Beane felt there might be a better way to track player productivity and uncover hidden talent that was being overlooked.

Traditionally, baseball teams relied on a handful of statistics to measure player performance. For example, a player's batting average, which is a player's likelihood of getting a hit. The best hitters in the league have a batting average of .300 or above, meaning they achieve a base hit 30% of the time; the other 70% of the time they record an out. Beane believed focusing on traditional stats like batting average was limiting. While batting average was easy to measure (simply divide the number of hits by the number of at-bats), Beane knew batting average alone didn't account for all the ways that a batter could reach base, such as by getting walked by the pitcher.

What Beane wanted was a different kind of scorecard. A scorecard that was more predictive in nature and helped scout and sign players who would give the A's the best chance at getting overall team success without having the budget to get the players with the best individual performance record. He wanted a scorecard that challenged the status quo of how players were tracked and how the team roster was developed.

It was a gutsy idea—one that challenged the status quo of scouting and player development.

Beane's sherpa? Paul DePodesta, a Harvard grad with an economics degree.

Together Beane and DePodesta embraced a newly emerging technique known as sabermetrics that eschewed the old-guard stats like batting average and instead focused on on-base percentage (the likelihood of a player reaching base) and slugging percentage (which measures batting productivity, or the total number of bases a player records per at-bat).

Beane's bold challenger mindset—paired with DePodesta's number-crunching savvy—focused more heavily on predictive measures that would gauge the potential success of the team, not just on typical player performance stats. In essence, they wanted to find metrics that could help them determine the best chance at helping the A's get to the future desired state: winning despite the fact they had a paltry player payroll budget.

The A's new scorecard refocused their efforts and scouting around a new set of metrics. The result? In 1998 after Beane and DePodesta's first season using the new metrics the A's leapt to 22nd out of 30 teams.

By 1999, they had the 10th-most wins, and by 2000, they were in 6th place—winning the American League West division and making the playoffs.

Beane and DePodesta's climb to their Mt. Everest was profiled in the popular book by Michael Lewis, *Moneyball: The Art of Winning an Unfair Game*, which was later adapted into a movie starring Brad Pitt as Beane. In the ensuing decades, other MLB teams embraced many of the A's measurement strategies for scouting and player development.

GETTING IT WRONG: PERVERSE INCENTIVES IN PRACTICE

Unfortunately, metrics misalignment is far too common. People and companies either follow the wrong metrics or create metrics that compete against each other. And they are not using the data they do have to help define the root causes behind missing their goals.

Let's look at some of the most common perverse incentives that undermine Vested Rule #3.

Driving Blind Disease

You might suffer from Driving Blind Disease if you are not actively using metrics that monitor your progress. I learned this the hard way by being on both the buy and sell-sides of large outsourcing deals. In the rush to strike a deal, companies often don't take the time to outline how they will measure success. This was especially true in the early days of outsourcing.

The good news is that most business relationships address this head-on with scorecards or dashboards. However, many have gone overboard falling into the trap of measurement minutiae trying to measure everything that moves rather than what matters. For example, I have seen one outsourced facilities management contract that had over 550 "service level agreements" metrics making it both hard and costly for the supplier to track and report on all of the metrics.

While some businesses avert Driving Blind Disease, it is especially common in personal relationships. Case in point: how often do couples get married and and lack a dashboard for what success looks like? They may say they want to retire early, but they don't actively track their retirement savings to make sure they can retire when they want. Friendships can drift without consistent check-ins. Or roommates can get on each other's nerves if they don't establish shared expectations about chores, cleanliness or bills.

OKR Overload

I've worked with dozens of companies that tied themselves in knots over OKRs—a perverse incentive I call OKR Overload. OKR Overload has two root causes. The first is measurement minutiae. While both the Balanced Scorecard and OKR approach promote the use of a few "key" metrics, it's common for teams and functional silos to get lost in the weeds and have too many metrics. The second root cause stems from conflicting goals. When this happens it creates a culture that does more harm than good because team members are working at odds with each other.

OKR Overload is real. Think back to the cheese company profiled in Chapter 2 which fell into a trap of OKR Overload. Having recently read John Doerr's book *Measure What Matters*, the CEO mandated that every department come up with five ORKs for their department. The problem? Success for one function often meant inadvertently harming a different department upstream or downstream. OKR Overload was rampant. Everyone was working feverishly to reach their own department goals at the expense of the success of the overall company. By embracing OKRs, departments wound up fighting against each other without realizing it.

The larger the company, the easier it is to fall victim to OKR Overload. One of my favorite examples is from a procurement department in a large oil and gas company. The Chief Procurement Officer had a department-level OKR to reduce supplier prices. To achieve the goal he mandated that purchasing managers use more competitive bidding to ensure the company was getting the best pricing. A purchasing team in one division took the mandate a bit too seriously and literally began to issue competitive bids on *everything*. The team went from 10-12 bids a month to nearly 500 bids per month, placing bids for frivolous items like $10 buckets when the company already had a strategic MRO (maintenance, repair and operations) contract that covered items like buckets. Even sadder? The team—determined to meet the new "requirement" to do more competitive bidding—hired seven additional people to keep up with the new added workload.

Definition Disconnect

Definition Disconnect is caused when partners are not defining success in the same way, a problem that led to the fateful demise of NASA's Mars Climate Orbiter in 1999.

The orbiter was meant to study Mars' climate and serve as a communications relay for the Mars Polar Lander, which was set to launch less than a month after the Orbiter. The Orbiter blasted into the sky on Dec. 11, 1998. The mission plan? An orbital insertion burn followed by a two-week "aerobraking" process to reduce velocity and move into a circular orbit. But that's not what happened.

On Sept. 23, 1999, as the Mars Climate Orbiter approached the red planet, NASA lost communication.

A NASA review board investigation found the Orbiter entered the Martian atmosphere at an altitude of approximately 57 kilometers instead of the planned 140-150 kilometers. This mistake led to a miscalculation of the spacecraft's trajectory where it encountered a much greater atmospheric drag than anticipated, leading to the destruction of the Orbiter.

A closer look revealed a definition disconnect. The ground software used English units while the onboard software worked in metric units. The miscalculation—roughly the driving distance between Baltimore and Philadelphia—was a critical gap. The definition disconnect led to a total destruction of the spacecraft, which had a total project cost of $327.6 million.

Watermelon Scorecard

My colleagues and I coined the term the Watermelon Scorecard to explain how it is possible to have a green scorecard but still be unhappy about your success. A Watermelon Scorecard gets its name because on the surface things look green (a watermelon is green on the outside). However, below the surface, things are not going so well (a watermelon is red on the inside).

The root cause is not that you lack metrics. Rather, it is that you are likely measuring only one aspect of your performance. For example a company might have great operations performance but lack innovation and "not be easy to do business with."

The watermelon scorecard is rampant in business relationships because they are often transactional and only measure operational performance metrics. Having a balanced scorecard approach does help but it still falls short for business partnerships because it fails to monitor the partners' relationship health (think Island Health and Newfoundland and Labrador Health Services).

TROUBLE ON THE HOME FRONT

Every month, Martin makes the same promise to his wife Maria: he's going to chip in more money so they can buy the house they'd always talked about. And every month, Martin comes up with another excuse. He had some unexpected expenses. Or he planned another golf outing with his buddies. He loves his golf outings, but they can become pricey. Martin justifies his golf outings considering how hard he works.

Maria falls into the same trap. Her closet often features new shoes and purses. "If Martin wants to have fun golfing, I'm going to spruce up my accessories," she tells herself, justifying the expenditures.

Martin and Maria are both putting themselves first. And that me-first thinking is keeping them from accomplishing their goal of buying a house. Both husband and wife think their actions are justified, increasing the likelihood of frustrations bubbling over.

Whenever Martin talks about going golfing, Maria rolls her eyes. And whenever Martin sees Maria with a new pair of shoes, he shakes his head. The partners are feeling shortchanged. Instead of addressing their concerns, they are providing less-than-consummate performance, something Nobel Laureate Oliver Hart calls "shading."

While Hart never studied Martin and Maria, he did study shading in real companies like Island Health and the Hospitalists. In the case of the acrimonious business partners, the relationship had soured in part because the Hospitalists felt Island South administrators were ignoring their need for a more manageable work-load; As the hospitalists grew more fatigued, some workers refused to accept the responsibility for admitting patients from the emergency room, leading the administration to temporarily suspend medical privileges for some hospitalists. Once shading starts, the relationship's downward spiral can accelerate quickly. Which is why getting and staying aligned on goals and metrics is so important.

THE VESTED WAY

How do you quantify greatness?

How do you track progress toward your future success?

Vested Rule 3 is designed to help partners map out how they will measure success against their desired outcomes. Think about it as carefully picking the right metrics you will use to monitor your success on the way up your own Mt. Everest. When the focus remains on the key indicators—and everyone is working together to achieve them—the incredible can happen. The alignment helps people show up in the partnership with a clear sense what they are contributing to the larger goal. What can you do to improve safety today? Or what little thing can you do today to reduce cost?

Getting Rule 3 (the metrics) right starts with Rule 1 (the desired outcomes). Recall from Rule 1 that a Desired Outcome is a future-focused statement about what you want to get out of the partnership. The statements are short and direct and few in number (typically five or less) which helps the parties stay focused.

Armed with your Desired Outcomes, you are ready to use a simple tool called a Requirements Roadmap to help put Rule 3 into practice.

Your Toolkit: *The Requirements Roadmap*

The Requirements Roadmap translates your high-level Desired Outcomes into a measurable performance roadmap. Think of it as the climbing plan for your Mt. Everest. When partners build a Requirements Roadmap together, they move from measuring activity to measuring progress toward their shared future state.

Download the Requirements Roadmap toolkit (see the next page for an example) to begin thinking about how to align metrics to your Desired Outcomes. While the Requirements Roadmap toolkit was originally designed to help business-to-business trading partners align on performance metrics, it can also be adapted to other types of partnerships. For example, at the end of the chapter, we share an example of how Maria and Martin adapted the Requirements Roadmap to help them align on a roadmap for saving for their dream home.

The tips below provide general guidance for completing a Requirements Roadmap.

Aligning Metrics to Desired Outcomes

The first columns (on the left-hand side) is where the partners identify what they want to get out of the partnership—the "Performance." This includes:

- **Desired Outcomes**—the high-level outcomes the parties want to achieve as a result of the partnership as defined in Rule 1

- **Objectives**—are more tangible and sometimes shorter-term objectives.

- **Metric/Standard**—the performance standard the parties want to strive for—the goal or target. There may be one (or more) metrics for an objective as illustrated in objective A-3 which has two metrics.

Desired Outcomes:

A
B
C

Desired Outcome	Performance			Incentive		Inspection			
	Objective	Metric/ Standard	Range/AQL*	Type*	Who	Data Source	Calculation	How Often Collected	
A…	A-1								
	A-2								
	A-3	A-3a							
		A-3b							
B…	B-1								
	B-2								

Alignment

*Optional information

- **Range/AQL**—the acceptable performance range. In a business setting this is often referred to as an AQL (acceptable quality level). This is an optional attribute if the partners want to have a range for their goal. For example, in some cases there might be a minimum target and a stretch target.

Incentives

The Requirements Roadmap also includes an optional column where the partner can note any incentives. Incentives can be used effectively in business relationships, especially buyer-supplier partnerships where the supplier may receive an incentive such as a performance bonus or contract extension for achieving goals.

Incentives can be monetary or non-monetary. For example, a contract extension is a wonderful way to reward a supplier for good performance.

Inspection

The last part of the Requirements Roadmap is the Inspection, which includes four columns. This part of the Requirements Roadmap is where the partners get more granular and define who will be in charge of capturing the data, where the data will come from, and how often it is reported. A good Requirements Roadmap also includes how the partners will calculate each metric, an essential step for preventing a Definition Disconnect such as what happened with the Mars Climate Orbiter.

Choosing the Right Metrics/Standards

The beauty of the Requirement Roadmap is that the goals you pick (the standard) for each metric can be as hard (or easy) as you would like. Think of the standard as the distance from your starting point and where you are going. Your targets will be much harder if you are climbing Mt. Everest versus if you are trying to conquer the bunny hill at your local ski resort. Or if you are a young couple saving to buy your house, the standard (your savings target) can be flexible. You'd have a smaller target if you were trying to save for a small condo and a larger target if you wanted to buy a starter home.

The rule of thumb for a good Requirements Roadmap is five or less desired outcomes supported by 15 or fewer objectives with metrics.

It seems simple enough, which is exactly the point. By focusing on the end game—the desired outcomes—you can in essence build a roadmap that will give you the best chance of conquering your Mt. Everest (or the bunny hill). The Requirements Roadmap can also be modified as needed. For example, in a personal relationship you may not have an incentive or AQL.

Failing to complete a Requirements Roadmap is like driving a car without directions or gauges and sensors to monitor key success factors like making sure you don't run out of gas. While you may arrive at your destination, you might find yourself suffering from one or more of the common perverse incentives resulting from metric misalignment shared previously.

> **Pro Tip:** When a partnership first kicks off you may not be collecting the data you need to measure your success. That is OK. Put in a placeholder and work to collect the data you need versus taking the easy route to just not measure something.

> **Pro Tip:** Best practice in business relationships is to automate your Requirements Roadmap into a dashboard and use it as part of your regular business reviews.

FROM THEORY TO PRACTICE

In practice, partners use a Requirements Roadmap to map their metrics to their desired outcomes. Taking time to properly complete a Requirements Roadmap helps you avoid the common perverse incentives associated with misaligned metrics. For example, you can abate OKR Overload because you are selecting metrics that are **we**-focused rather than metrics that promote a **me**-focused functional silo. And it helps avoid having too many metrics if you stay to the rule of thumb of having 15 or fewer metrics. In addition, you can sidestep a potential definition disconnect because you are clearly defining how you will calculate success.

Let's look at how EY is applying the Requirements Roadmap to a strategic relationship with Denmark-based ISS to achieve epic results in transforming their workplace experience. We'll also revisit how Island Health and the Hospitalists used the Requirements Roadmap to get on the same page for their relationship.

EY and ISS: An EPIC Success

EY, a leader in professional services, wanted to take its workplace services to a higher level. The company decided to make its Nordic region the focus of a pilot to make the shift to Vested. Claus Christensen, head of workplace experience for EY's Nordic countries, shared EY's purpose: "At EY, we believe a better working world is one where economic and people growth go hand-in-hand with environmental sustainability and people who thrive. We have the ambition to be a world leader and showcase the 'next-possible' by transforming the overall workplace experience, including the workplace services to support our people in the best way."

In order to achieve its Workplace of the Future transformation, EY would need to collaborate and move beyond a transactional approach with its suppliers. EY decided to make the bold shift to have one workplace service provider across all of the Nordic countries.

EY found a partner—their sherpa—in ISS, a global workplace services support company headquartered in Denmark. ISS had been one of two major suppliers in the Nordics region and was excited to have the chance to take their relationship with EY to the next level.

Out of the gate, a cross-organizational/cross-functional Deal Architect Team set out to create a name for their partnership. The name that stuck was "EPIC"; a phrase that would mark the cultural change they would be rolling down to the hundreds of team members working in the field after contract signing. EPIC stands for

E	EY
P	Plus
I	ISS
C	Collaboration

In Rule 1 the EPIC team developed their shared vision and five desired outcomes. In Rule 3 they began to blow this out into more tangible details that could be measured. Here they used the Requirements Roadmap and came up with eight objectives as shown on the following page.

With agreed objectives, the team then tackled completing the Requirements Roadmap by identifying what the best metrics would be and how each of the metrics would be measured. EY's Fredrik Nikolaev explains how the team did this. "It is common in outsourcing deals to fall into the trap of coming up with dozens (or even well over a hundred) service-level agreement metrics that measure the supplier's performance on how they perform tasks. But this is very transactional thinking. The Vested methodology forced us to think about how to measure where we were going."

REQUIREMENTS ROADMAP OBJECTIVES

Shared Vision: "Together we are building the greatest workplace experience, enabling our teams to deliver exceptional client service."

DESIRED OUTCOMES:

OBJECTIVES:

#1 Build the best workplace experience that attracts, retains and engages the right people for EY & ISS

- ☐ Achieve a highly attractive and satisfying workplace that creates well being for our employees
- ☐ Develop highly engaged ISS employees

#2 Create a seamless workplace experience that enhances the performance of our teams

- ☐ Improve productivity and workplace convenience

#3 Develop a sustainable workplace that reduces EY's environmental impact

- ☐ Reduce environmental footprint

#4 Optimize the total cost for the workplace service delivery

- ☐ Achieve a sustainable baseline-saving

#5 Live and grow the EY & ISS Collaboration (EPIC) successfully

- ☐ Continuously improving the relationship
- ☐ Onboard all relevant stakeholders
- ☐ Ensure seamless transitions (temporary objective)

ISS's Henrik Møhl agrees. "Prior to Vested, we used all kinds of random metrics, which, to be honest, didn't add value to the end user. What Rule 3 did was to help us rethink how we measure success aligned with our Desired Outcomes and where we want to be in the future."

In the graphic on the following page, notice that one of the desired outcomes was "Build the best workplace experience that attracts, retains and engages the right people for EY and ISS" and objective 1.2 was to develop highly engaged ISS employees. The team selected this objective because typically there is low worker engagement for those who work in workplace services jobs such as cleaning and dining services. As such, the EPIC team decided to measure ISS employee retention. Their goal was to increase retention by 10%.

Henrik Møhl, ISS Nordic Key Account Manager, explains the logic. "A common metric in an outsourcing agreement that has a heavy labor element is to measure employee turnover." So by improving turnover the EPIC team would reduce costs associated with recruiting and training new team members.

The Requirement Roadmap served EPIC well and by the end of year 1, EY's Magnus Kuchler reported "the EPIC team achieved epic results against the metrics defined in their Requirements Roadmap. This meant a great transition as well as lower costs and higher service for EY. As a result, ISS earned incentives meaning more profit and contract extensions—both wins for ISS."

But recall one of the attributes of a great Vested partnership is to have a Challenger Mindset and to challenge the status quo. With performance at peak levels, the EPIC team went back to the drawing board and challenged the original Requirements Roadmap in a Vested 2.0 initiative. Were targets too low? Had business conditions changed such that they needed new metrics?

Møhl reflects on how revisiting the Requirements Roadmap once the targets were met challenged the EPIC partnership to think even bigger. For example, the team challenged the conventional thinking about employee turnover. "If you think about it, it is much more effective if you are measuring how engaged employees are. When team members are engaged and giving their best, word gets around that the EPIC account is the best place to work and we attract the most talented people."

The EPIC team changed metrics to use a combination of a Net Promoter Score (NPS) measuring employee engagement and the Compatibility and Trust assessment to look at the overall the relationship health of the partnership.

EPIC REQUIREMENTS ROADMAP

Desired Outcome: Build the best workplace experience that attracts, retains and engages the right people for EY & ISS

DESIRED OUTCOMES:

 Build the best workplace experience that attracts, retains and engages the right people for EY & ISS

OBJECTIVES:

 Develop highly engaged ISS employees

Performance				How To Measure			
Objective	**Performance Metric**	**Standard/ Target**	**Tolerance**	**Who**	**Data Source**	**Caluclation**	**How Often Collected**
Develop highly engaged ISS employees	ISS retention rate	Increasing retention by 10%	Increasing retent on by 5%	ISS	Retention rate reports	Average result per country and aggregated to a Nordic Index, adjusted based on the weight used in the pricing model used to calculate the Nordic performance	Annually reported May/June

NPS is a satisfaction measurement asking, "How likely would you recommend working for ISS on the EPIC team." The NPS metric has a scale of -100 (would never recommend) to +100 (would always recommend). When EPIC first adopted the metric their score was just over +20, which is considered typical for a company in the services industry. For comparison, the average score across Scandinavian countries ranges between +10 and +30 based on industry with world-class scores falling over +70. Today EPIC tops in at +58, the highest level across all of ISS's accounts.

In addition to measuring NPS, EPIC uses an annual CaT assessment to monitor the relationship health between EY and ISS. Today the EPIC CaT ranks in the top 5% of all contracts the University of Tennessee has benchmarked.

For Isabella Liljeström, the ISS Contract Owner for the EPIC partnership, the success is not in the NPS or CaT scores themselves, but rather in the results stemming from a healthy workplace culture. Team members use adjectives such as "Trust," "Collaborative," "Innovative," "Transparent" and "Loyal" to describe the partnership (see the word cloud from the CaT assessment).

CAT ASSESSMENT WORD CLOUD

"This is truly amazing when you think about the nature of the work, which revolves around manual labor such as cleaning and dining services, which many people would think of as unrewarding."

Island Health: From Driving Blind to Aligned

Island Health and the Hospitalists—who'd clashed for years over contract negotiations—had started taking steps to repair their fraught relationship in their three-day alignment workshop. But they still had a ways to go. Any false move could undermine their progress.

To avoid backsliding into distrust, it was crucial for the parties to build on the high-level Desired Outcomes they'd developed during their initial three-day Alignment workshop. To jog your memory, these were:

1. A sustainable and resilient hospitalist service
2. Excellence in patient care
3. Relationship health excellence
4. A best value hospitalist service

As part of Vested Rule 3 the partners set out to refine their desired outcomes by co-creating their Requirements Roadmap. The Requirement Roadmap, as depicted on the following page, clearly linked seven objectives to their four desired outcomes.

In the case of Island Health and the Hospitalists, the partners were measuring lots of things—but these metrics did not always align to where they were going. They were suffering from a Watermelon Scorecard and even worse, they were Driving Blind in some cases. The partners knew they would need to work together to begin to capture the right data and they would need to do some work to determine what the right metrics should be. But that was not going to stop them. They adapted the Requirements Roadmap to create action items that would guide sub-teams into closing their gaps.

Let's take a closer look at one of the desired outcomes on page 141– *Excellence in Patient Care* (Desired Outcome #3). In this case, the partners wanted to improve how they measured quality of care. One of the things they wanted to challenge was how to improve how they measured quality of care. Their Requirements Roadmap drills down on one of their goals to "Develop a formal and robust quality structure." Rather than use the Requirements Roadmap to define how they would measure success, the partners adapted it to agree on the actions and responsibilities for how they would create a formal and robust quality structure which ultimately would include selecting metrics and developing a dashboard.

ISLAND HEALTH-HOSPITALISTS
DESIRED OUTCOMES/OBJECTIVES

Shared Vision:
- Together, we are a team that celebrates and advances excellence in care for our patients and ourselves through shared responsibility, collaborative innovation, mutual understanding, and the courage to act, in a safe and supportive environment
- We will be recognized leaders in health care
- We will achieve this vision by building relationships grounded in trust and respect, and anchored in the Guiding Principles and Intended Behaviors

DESIRED OUTCOMES:

OBJECTIVES:

#1 A Sustainable and Resilient Hospitalist Service

- Strengthen Hospitalist recruitment, mentorship, and retention processes
- Ensure the Hospitalist scheduling model is efficient and flexible
- Clearly define and articulate Hospitalist services and workload and develop stronger interdepartmental working relationships
- Support the development of current and future Hospitalist leaders

#2 Excellence in Patient Care

- Develop a formal and robust quality structure

#3 Relationship Health Excellence

- Continue to build and maintain a healthy relationship between Island Health and South Island Hospitalists, Inc (SIHI)

#4 A Best Value Hospitalist Service

- Proactively manage the budget, optimize recoveries, regularly review Workload, and optimize operational efficiencies

DRILL DOWN ON ISLAND HEALTH-HOSPITALIST

DESIRED OUTCOMES:

#2 Excellence in Patient Care

OBJECTIVES:

☑ Develop a formal and robust quality structure

Actions	Responsible for Work
Select two system program quality metrics for improvement annually. For year one, the focus will be on 1) improving care for COPD patients (reducing LOS and readmissions, and improving adherence to clinical guidelines), and 2) improving SIHI Member attendance at ward-based Structured Team Reports (with the goal that attendance will be 80% or better).	Excellence Team
Develop a dashboard of quality indicators for the Hospitalist program that includes anonymized physician-specific data within one year. The dashboard will be for the collection, reporting, monitoring, and analysis of Hospitalist program data and physician performance. The data will inform future QI projects.	Excellence Team
Develop two physician-specific quality metrics to be monitored annually by SIHI. The anonymized results will be shared with Island Health For the first year, Time to Consult will be measured and monitored. The second indicator is to be determined.	SIHI with oversight from Excellence Team
Implement Hospitalist Morbidity & Mortality rounds within six months.	SIHI with oversight from Excellence Team
Develop and administer within one year a patient and team (including specialist colleagues, allied health, etc.) satisfaction survey. Once data is collected, it will be reviewed for opportunities for improvement.	Excellence Team
Appoint a patient representative to the Excellence Team to ensure that the patient perspective informs quality discussions and decisions.	Excellence Team

*SIHI stands for South Island Health Inc., the legal entity in which the Hospitalists worked

After the contract signing, Courtney Peereboom (Island Health's Director of Special Projects) developed a simple yet highly effective dashboard to track progress against the Requirements Roadmap. Dr. Smith, a Hospitalist, loves the dashboard. "On the right-hand side each action is given a color (either green, yellow or red) and that means either you're on schedule, behind schedule, or completely behind schedule and that area needs a lot of work. It helps the sub-committees when they're steering to look at the current roadmap and find out where they're falling behind or where and what they need to put more effort in, to make sure that we're getting things done that we had on the roadmap."

Dr. Jean Maskey echoes this sentiment: "The Requirements Roadmap keeps us all on the same page and on track. There is a lot to accomplish on the Requirements Roadmap and it can feel very overwhelming. But it is broken down into small pieces and helps us stay focused, knowing where we need to help each other."

SUCCESS ON THE HOME FRONT

Maria and Martin's plan of buying their dream house was stuck, with both of them making empty promises and wishes without any action behind it. All of that changed when Maria went out to lunch with her friend Pam.

Pam mentioned how she was able to close on a new house. Maria had lots of questions.

"How did you make it work financially?" she asked.

"We budgeted and had a plan every single month, and we stuck with it," Pam said. "We had a goal to meet or exceed each month, and until we did so, we really held back on any discretionary spending. For each month, we mapped out our goals and the actions that would help us achieve them. If we hit our savings goal for that month and had leftover money, we took turns deciding if we wanted to do something with it or if we wanted to add it to our house fund. We even reached our savings goal early!"

Whatever it was—FOMO, or "Keeping up with the Joneses," or just a desire to make a change—Maria wanted to give Pam's suggestion a try. Maybe it could work for her and Martin, too.

Of course, such an approach would mean sacrifices. She wouldn't be able to splurge on new shoes and purses like she was used to. And she knew Martin wouldn't necessarily like cutting back on his golf trips. But those little actions could help them potentially move out of their cramped apartment.

Maria brought it up over dinner that night.

"I had a nice talk with Pam today … they just closed on a new house," she told Martin.

"How were they able to swing that?" he asked.

"Little by little," Maria said. "She said they set a monthly savings target for themselves and stuck to it. The key was every month they tracked their progress. You know … I think we could do the same thing."

They talked about it and mapped out a plan. Martin was on board, even if it meant cutting back on the golfing. With all of their savings and assets, they figured they would need to come up with an additional $40,000-$50,000 in savings within two years in order to be able to make a down payment. This came out to about $2,000 each month for two years.

Maria got out a pen and paper and made a list and began to put together a roadmap that could help them achieve their goal.

MARTIN AND MARIA'S ACTION PLAN

GOAL:

Save $2,000 each month toward down payment on a house for 24 months

- Set $500 aside each week, with $250 from each of their paychecks every week: *Martin and Maria*
- No golf trips until monthly goals are met and bills are paid: *Martin*
- No retail therapy shopping trips until monthly goals are met and bills are paid: *Maria*
- Track overall progress toward goal: *Maria*

GOAL:

Better communication and transparency on spending

- Make a list of all anticipated bills and expenses each month: *Martin*
- Discuss and get agreement on how to handle any expenditures costing $200 or more: *Martin and Maria*

A week after they started the plan, Martin came home with pep in his step. "Maria, I have a fun idea to motivate us with our savings goal. At work, they send out a weekly update on the United Way giving campaign. I noticed they use a thermometer to track the progress against the company's giving campaign goal. It's kind of hokey, but it might be fun to do something similar for our savings goal as a way to visually motivate us."

Maria loved the idea.

After dinner Maria took out the kids art supplies and asked the girls to help her draw a picture of a thermometer with lines representing their collective weekly savings target of $1000. On another piece of paper the girls drew a picture of a house representing the goal. When it was done, the girls used magnets to put the thermometer and picture of their house on the refrigerator.

Each week, Martin and Maria would sit down and track their progress. And each week the girls would color in more lines on the thermometer illustrating their progress.

For the months where Martin was a little bit short of his savings goal, Maria chipped in a little bit extra, and where Maria came up short, Martin made sure to set aside more money. For the first time in a long time, they both felt like they were truly aligned and collaborating to achieve success. By shouldering the burden together and putting their goals and actions in writing, they both felt empowered to follow through instead of their typical mode of talk without action or feeling slighted when the other didn't do what they had anticipated.

And before long, they had saved the money for the down payment and closing costs on a house.

TOOLKIT QUICK REFERENCE GUIDE

Requirememts Roadmap

- **Purpose:** To translate Desired Outcomes into clearly defined and measurable performance standards
- **When to Use:** After defining Shared Vision and Desired Outcomes and whenever performance expectations need refinement or reset
- **Components:** Desired Outcomes → Objectives → Metrics or Standards → Range or Tolerance if needed → Incentives if appropriate → Inspection including data source, calculation and reporting cadence
- **Guideline:** Five or fewer Desired Outcomes supported by fifteen or fewer objectives and metrics
- **Output:** A simply table providing a clear line of sight from strategy to measurement.
- **Perverse Incentives it Prevents:** Driving Blind Disease; OKR Overload; Definition Disconnect; Watermelon Scorecard

8

Rule 4: Focus on Gains, Not Games

"You can have everything in life you want, if you will just help other people get what they want." - Zig Ziglar

We all bring our own skills, talents and goals to group tasks, whether facing the harsh terrain of Everest or navigating workplace interactions. The power of a *WIIFWe* mindset is consciously seeking to optimize the success of the partnership by contributing what we do best. By the same token, we have our own weaknesses and the group could potentially help us forward.

With mountain climbing or other extreme weather challenges, it could mean helping a team member who is struggling on a task by assisting in ways that leverage your strengths. During an Antarctic expedition across icy terrain, Alison Levine experienced just such a scenario. Two of her teammates, George and Eric, recognized Alison was struggling with the weight of her sled. Alison—at 5'4" and just over 100 pounds—was much smaller than the others and it made it difficult for her to keep up.

George and Eric suggested offloading some of Alison's sled weight even though that would increase their load. As Alison wrote in her book *On the Edge*, "I'd convinced myself that my teammates wanted to get rid of me because I was the weakest person on the team. But instead, these two men were secretly strategizing on how to help me."

Alison wanted to return the favor and found the perfect solution: shoveling snow and ice to make ice blocks to protect them from the elements. The others, because of their heights, had a tough time shoveling. But since Alison was shorter and closer to the ground, she could shovel more easily. "I would never overcome the fact that I could not pull the same amount of weight as my larger teammates, but I felt I could—and should—contribute in other ways," she recounts in her book.

Probably no other topic creates as much apprehension as trying to determine what is fair: whether that involves money, bartering, a trade-off of services or trying to find ways for everyone to pull their own weight on an Antarctic expedition. Collaborators often find themselves on opposite sides of the table using classic negotiation tactics to get the best possible deal. Or they find themselves silently suffering like Alison because no one is transparently talking through fair ways to allocate work and resources.

Think of the grievances that emerge when you feel that you aren't being adequately compensated. Gallup estimates employee disengagement and attrition are costing companies massive amounts of money, time and effort—nearly $10 trillion in lost productivity. Or think about the frustrations you feel when you're hit with an out-of-nowhere surcharge. Customers, feeling taken advantage of by add-ons and surcharges, are increasingly seeking out alternatives because they are disappointed by their service. The value proposition is no longer there for them.

Parties often fight over taking bigger slices of the pie instead of combining their talents to make a bigger pie. But focusing on gains, not games, speaks to the importance of setting fair terms that bring out the best in everyone.

FOUNDATIONAL THEORIES

Vested Rule 4 is focused on gains, not games. At its heart, Rule 4 helps partners create value for the partnership while consciously avoiding gamesmanship where one partner could have a short-term win at the expense of the other partner.

Let's look at Rule 4 in terms of going on an interview for your dream job. It's the perfect role in a great office near where you live—the ideal growth opportunity. You meet with the CEO of the innovative startup you've been following.

"You're an awesome candidate, and I have so many plans for the future," the CEO tells you. "I want you to come work for us. However, we are a small startup company, and we only have a limited amount of money to spend on salaries while we are ramping up. I can't meet your anticipated salary. But we're growing, and as the company flourishes, I hope to be able to reward you in the future with stock options and a higher salary."

You take stock of your goals. You don't feel great that the money isn't close to your anticipated range, but the upsides are so high, especially if you can earn stock options based on your performance. You swallow your pride. Yes, I accept.

Fast-forward a year. You're crushing it at work. Your clients love what you do. You're a revenue driver for the company. At review time, you anticipate a raise and stock options. You've proven yourself and paid your dues.

Now it is time for your performance review.

First, the CEO is nowhere in sight when it comes to review time to reflect on the promises made. Rather, your direct boss does the review. It starts off well. "Everyone loves your effort," your boss tells you. "Keep up the great work!"

Then the bomb drops. "I wish the financial news was better, but we're still scraping by as a startup, and as a result, we're not raising salaries for the time being." You do get some stock options, but far fewer than what you had thought was fair.

With the cost of living increasing and your salary flat, your paycheck is worth less now than it was when you first got hired. And there is no sign of when (or if) the stock options will generate any value.

The same happens in business partnerships. Far too often, companies fight over prices with one party winning at the expense of the other. When the buyer wins with a price decrease, it is a loss for the supplier—and vice versa. Shifting to a WIIFWe pricing model with incentives can align the partners' interests on the same goals rather than pit them against each other. One way is to shift to a transparent pricing model where the supplier is rewarded with an incentive when they drive down the cost structure. The lower the cost structure, the more incentives (profits) for the supplier. From win-lose to win-win.

Through flexibility and creativity, partners can accomplish amazing things. But getting to a true win-win means thinking about what game you are playing when it comes to crafting the economics of your partnerships.

What Game Do You Play?

What game you play depends a great deal on how you see the world. Much like the optimist and the pessimist who view a half-filled glass differently, economists have shown that people view the world by the type of games they play. Some economists and mathematicians study the games people play and put them into two categories: zero-sum games and non-zero-sum games.

Think about a pie. Do you remember those sibling or childhood feuds over the last piece of pie or the scoop of ice cream that was far too little to share? In many cases your parents intervened and made everyone play nice.

Yet, in a way, didn't you and the other person both feel as if you had lost? After all, you had to share the pie or ice cream; you didn't get it all. Sharing has come to mean you get less than what is optimal; you lost something you could have, or should have, had.

In a zero-sum game, there is always a winner and a loser. In order for winners to gain, they must take something from the losers.

Many people view the world through this lens of scarcity. There is only so much ______________ (fill in the blank: money, opportunity, innovations, etc.). If someone has a lot, it must be because they took it from someone else. There's only so much pie in the world.

How Much Pie Is There?

When faced with that last piece of pie, why not simply look at the world through a lens of abundance? Instead of walking away thinking you have to sneak the last piece of pie or face Mom cutting it in half, why not respond with "Let's bake another pie."

Seeing the world through a lens where opportunities are not limited and everyone can win opens up an entirely new world to explore.

Economists call this approach a non-zero-sum game. In this case, parties work together to expand the pie. Losers can be winners, as there is enough for everyone.

In this game, you might say that 1 plus 1 equals 11. No, this isn't fuzzy math; rather, it's a different way of viewing the world. Is it possible? Absolutely. And a smarter approach.

Partners work together bringing their unique skills and resources to the relationship. Together, they can achieve more than by going alone or against each other in a conventional transaction-based approach. They can figure out how to dominate market share, radically reduce cost structures, dazzle customers, or build a bridge and clean up a nuclear waste site exponentially faster than anyone thought possible.

How to Divide an Orange

Roger Fisher and William Ury rocked the business world with their concept of interest-based negotiation. In their bestselling book *Getting to Yes*, the authors tell the tale of how to divide an orange. Their story illustrates the conventional philosophy regarding mutual gain. In the orange story, two sisters negotiate to divide one orange. Positional bargaining would split the orange in some fashion—in half or perhaps with the party with the most power getting two-thirds and the weaker party getting one-third.

But what if the negotiators weren't actually interested in getting half of the orange, but instead one wanted the fruit to eat and the other wanted the peel for baking? Each side often wants different things. Fisher and Ury's interest-based bargaining approach allows the parties to seek creativity in their negotiations to achieve their interests.

In Fisher and Ury's analogy, the parties' self-interests are maximized, with each person getting exactly what is wanted, creating a win-win solution.

The problem? Fisher and Ury's approach falls short of achieving real mutual gain where the parties create value, not just find a creative way to share the value of one orange.

The Vested way? Rather than fight over one orange (or even creatively dividing a single orange), collaborate to find solutions for planting an orange tree and allowing both parties to prosper. Think about the power of collaborating by looking through the problem with a value creation lens. If both parties are patient and take a long-term approach to focus on potential gains from leveraging each other's skills, the partners stand to create far more value than simply finding a way to negotiate over *one* orange.

Prospect Theory

Nobel Laureate Daniel Kahneman, an expert in psychology of judgment and decision-making and behavioral economics, posited the concept of prospect theory with his longtime collaborator Amos Tversky.

As the duo wrote in a 1979 research paper, *Prospect Theory: An Analysis of Decision Under Risk*, people underweight probable outcomes in relation to certain outcomes—people are risk-averse with choices involving sure gains and risk-seeking when choices involve sure losses.

More simply put, people hate to lose more than they like to win. This, in turn, triggers behaviors where people focus on ways to mitigate their short-term loss in spite of the fact that they could have a much larger potential gain by working collaboratively with their partner. In the context of how to divide the orange, it means the sisters will most likely opt for fighting over the orange or, at best, seek a strategy where they find a creative way to split the orange rather than seek longer-term opportunities such as collaborating to plant an orange tree.

The concept of loss aversion explains so much of our attitudes toward risk—and it reinforces the way that slights, real or perceived, stick with us. Losses are painful and feel more intense than the pleasure from gain. You might not always recall the gains of a relationship, but you definitely remember the games. Think about this in terms of something that happens in your life. You probably don't remember all the times someone paid you for something they owed you. But you definitely remember the times someone didn't and you had to chase them for payment or eat the costs. The frustration and losses are acute. They are front of mind.

Prospect theory and entrepreneurship, as a result, go hand in hand. Entrepreneurs thrive on risk. They embrace it. Risk is part of the allure. However, most larger established companies and governments operate differently; they often fear change and embrace the status quo.

The Carrot Principle

Managers often try to lead with either carrots (rewards) or sticks (penalties). While sticks can potentially drive people in the short-term, carrots are much more effective in the long-term. The same carrot-and-stick principle applies in personal relationships—especially in parent-child relationships.

Adrian Gostick and Chester Elton studied the effectiveness of using carrots and sticks in a 200,000-person study. They popularized their findings in their bestselling book *The Carrot Principle*. The study's key findings? Recognition can lead to better results and lower turnover, and leaders who exhibit recognition are viewed as stronger in goal-setting, communication, trust and accountability.

Multiple studies, in fact, have shown that carrots (incentives) are more effective than sticks.

We often think of incentives and recognition in terms of money. And yes, money is nice. But as Gostick and Elton argue, there are many forms of carrots and one of the best is simple recognition. "Just ask yourself, did you save the bank deposit slip from the last time someone gave you a $200 cash bonus? Is it tucked away in a scrapbook of memories? Of course not. But what about something useful and tangible that was given to you as a reward? Not a baseball cap, T-shirt or canvas tote bag, but something usable and valuable. Chances are that even years later, you still own it and can picture the award in your mind."

People want to feel wanted and appreciated. And the littlest bit of recognition, even when money isn't involved, can make a massive difference. Unfortunately, we are often slow to offer recognition, rewards or incentives. Gostick and Elton found that three-quarters (74%) of managers don't practice recognition. Additional studies reveal similar results. Studies have shown that more than half of workers feel only somewhat valued or not valued at all by their organization, with communication a main cause of the problem. Younger workers have increasingly felt undervalued, and nearly half of them (45%) feel lonely and feel like others do not see the value in their ideas.

When workers feel undervalued, they often check out and disconnect. But what about when workers are engaged and empowered?

ROCKY FLATS: CREATING VALUE AND SHARING VALUE

Let's revisit the story of Rocky Flats cleanup project, which required an unprecedented collaboration to close and clean up the former nuclear weapons site. Chapter 2 illustrated how the Department of Energy (DoE) and Kaiser-Hill (the contractor) applied Vested's Rule 2 what-not-how mantra to open the door to innovation. Let's now look at how the partners rethought how to create win-win economics where the Department of Energy, Kaiser-Hill and the union employees all came out winners by collaborating to create (and share!) value because of the innovations.

Prior to the Kaiser-Hill contract, the Department of Energy (DoE) had worked with other contractors without getting traction to close and cleaning up Rocky Flats. Cost estimates developed for Rocky Flats Closure Project included a 1995 Baseline Environmental Management Report that estimated the project would take between 65 and 75 years and $37 billion.

The partners devised what was at the time a "first-of-its-kind" contract for the closure of Rocky Flats. It was here the partners devised a win-win approach that focused on the gains (creating value and sharing value) with a transparent pricing model with incentives for the safe, clean and cost-effective clean-up and ultimate closure of Rocky Flats.

One important design principle was that Kaiser-Hill's profit was connected to the final cost; namely, it would generate more profit for keeping the DOE's costs down. Kaiser-Hill had a vested interest in beating the baseline budget estimates, which aligned Kaiser-Hill's interests with the DOE's interest. In practice, it meant Kaiser-Hill put up to 85% of their profit at risk. But it also meant there was a significant reward where Kaiser-Hill could earn a substantial amount of additional profit the more efficient they were. Kaiser-Hill ultimately earned yielding a profit margin of 11.6%—nearly three times the 4.1% average profit margin for other DOE projects.

A key point is that the pricing model was structured such that when Kaiser-Hill "won" with more profit, the DOE "won" with lowered costs. The contract also had incentives aligned to the other desired outcomes—safe, clean and fast closure.

Another important feature was the DOE also had skin in the game. Kaiser-Hill could request adjustments to cover the actual cost of DOE delays to the project. This brought DOE performance into the light and assured accountability because now both DOE and Kaiser-Hill had visibility to the end-to-end effect of not working together. This also greatly helped to eliminate the finger-pointing often seen in outsourcing agreements where the buying company does not provide the inputs needed for the supplier to achieve the proper outcomes. Now the DOE and Kaiser-Hill were in the cleanup together.

With so much at stake, Kaiser-Hill developed strategies to recognize and manage risk, even using simulation techniques to gauge the schedule duration and cost estimates.

Notably, the rewards—the carrots—trickled down to the workers. Kaiser-Hill offered performance-incentive contracts for all subcontracting work and passed 20% of their incentives to workers. This created a three-way win where there were incentives for everyone (even union employees) to pull on the rope in the same direction. Creating value. Sharing value. Together. The results were nothing short of spectacular.

The DOE was a winner with Rocky Flats being closed 65 years ahead of schedule and $30 billion under independent baseline costs estimates.

Colorado citizens were a winner, with the measure of radioactive soil contamination (known as picocurie per gram or pCi/gm) reducing from a high of over 1000 pCi/gm in some areas of the plant to final cleanup of below 50 pCi/gm.

Kaiser-Hill was a winner, earning $576 million in incentives, giving them a profit margin almost three times higher than the average DOE contract. Employee safety also improved by 800% and union grievances went down from over 900 to a mere handful.

Employees were winners, getting 20% of the incentive money.

GETTING IT WRONG: PERVERSE INCENTIVES IN PRACTICE

Money can make people do stupid things. In fact, Professor Kathleen Vohs' research into the psychology of money shows how money makes us egoistic. In one experiment, individuals were exposed to words and thoughts about money and some were not. The individuals were then tested for their willingness to help others. Those individuals exposed to money before being asked to help others showed a lower willingness to help than individuals not exposed to money.

Perverse incentives are often fueled by money, with people playing games to earn a short-term dollar rather than collaborating to focus on potential gains. Moving past gamesmanship requires partners to view their partnership through a longer-term lens of value creation instead of short-term transactional value exchange or worse—value extraction where one partner is winning at the other partner's expense.

Let's look at common perverse incentives that occur when partners play games instead collaborating with a WIIFWe mindset to create mutual gains.

The Activity Trap

If money can make you do stupid things, thinking about money through a transactional lens can make people do really stupid things. A transactional mindset charges for work completed (per unit, per hour, per mile, per shipment). While transactional pricing is easy, it can easily create a perverse incentive because one party can take advantage of the other. Think of the writer who gets paid by the word, without a limit, and decides to write and write and write—even at the expense of the story. Or the taxi driver who gets paid per mile for driving a passenger to their destination.

Let's take a deeper look at the perverse incentives for taxicab drivers and how they game the system. One study researched Uber trips versus traditional taxis on metered airport routes between New York City's Midtown Manhattan and LaGuardia Airport. The study revealed the cabbies' routes were 8% longer, and even worse with nonlocal passengers. Why? Since the Uber drivers' fares are fixed ahead of time, there is little incentive for them to take the "scenic route" and take a longer time driving passengers to their destination. Simply put, they can't run up the passenger's fare with a longer trip.

The researchers provide further insight: the detour incentive is greater on metered airport trips, which reward delays and longer distances traveled. Not surprisingly, the taxi drivers on metered airport trips tended to take longer routes and longer travel times with nonlocal passengers, which... you guess it... led to higher fares.

The Activity Trap Redux

Uber has also suffered from drivers who try to game the system through the lens of "surge pricing," which kicks in when there are a rush of riders or deficit of drivers in a specific area.

You need a ride in the worst way. The concert is over, the weather is fierce, the hour is getting late.

The Uber model makes sense in practice, but it also showcases how the perception of trying to one-up a collaborator or take advantage of a situation—playing games—can create ill will. To add insult to injury, reports have suggested some Uber drivers are triggering fake surge pricing periods by coordinating their log-off times—creating a deficit of nearby drivers and pushing added costs onto customers similarly to taxi cab drivers running the meter for additional driving time. And it can be shocking for users to open the app to find a "surge pricing" notice where their typical ride now costs two, three, or four times the usual amount.

As Uber explains on its website, "Because rates are updated based on the demand in real time, surge can change quickly. Surge pricing is also specific to different areas in a city, so some neighborhoods may have surge pricing at the same time that other neighborhoods do not."

Surge pricing reflects what users view as an unfair game, not gains. As professor Utpal M. Dholakia wrote in an essay about Uber's surge pricing, "Uber's surge pricing offers a good example of how technology and economics have combined to create a sophisticated pricing approach without adequately bringing customers into the equation. After all, it is riders who choose Uber over a taxicab or a bus, experience the service, and pay the asking price. So it is vital that their assessment of the approach be considered carefully."

Playing games with pricing is not something unique to Uber. Research shows the gamesmanship has inflicted the economics of concert tickets, airline flights, and even Wendy's fast food.

Zero-Sum Game

Let's return to the concept of game theory. Recall a win-win game is when all the partners are winners. Unfortunately there is often an urge to game the system and win at the expense of your partner when the pie is truly limited. This is especially true when there is not a relationship and the nature of the interaction is transactional.

We often think of Zero-Sum Games in business relationships (if I use my power and negotiation savvy, I will get a lower price, which in turn lowers your profit). But often in business there is a way to turn a zero-sum game into a non-zero-sum game (collaborate to create efficiencies which lower the cost structure and the savings can be shared) as shown in the Rocky Flats closure project.

But sometimes there truly are situations where a Zero-Sum Game applies. Consider what is at stake for siblings when an elderly parent needs to make their will and is trying to determine the best way to split their inheritance among their children. There is a limited pie (inheritance) to split, creating a zero-sum game among the siblings. This can create an opportunity for perverse incentives for the siblings. For example, would one of the siblings provide care not out of love, but to position themselves as the "deserving" heir? Or perhaps go so far as to isolate the parent from other siblings to gain more influence over the estate decisions?

Or consider the flip side: one sibling feels like they have shouldered the burden of being caretaker, but feels slighted when their freeriding sibling gets the same amount of inheritance they did.

In cases like this, it is even more important for the siblings to work through the Vested methodology and create a Statement of Intent (Rule 1) and workload allocation (Rule 2) for what is most fair to optimize their upside (potential inheritance) and minimize their downside (exhaustion and stress from taking on the added responsibility for care).

Penny-Wise and Pound-Foolish

When's the last time you bought an inexpensive belt or pair of shoes? They probably fell apart on you pretty quickly, leaving you to buy a replacement again a few months later. Or maybe you opted to skip the additional insurance coverage on an inexpensive electrical device, only to have it come back and bite you. Or you chose the lowest-bid contractor on your bathroom repair work only to have it redone a few years later because shoddy plumbing caused a leak.

One study of the construction industry linked selecting the lowest price contractor to higher claims and disputes. For example, when organizations selected a contractor with a bid price of 10 percent below average, they were over 40 percent more likely to have a claim. The results are even more dramatic when the contractor bid price was 20 percent lower than the average bid price—resulting in a 70 percent increase in the likelihood of having a claim.

Companies also suffer from being penny-wise and pound-foolish, often believing it is better to continuously search for lower-price suppliers. This can lead to a vicious cycle of bidding and transitioning, bidding and transitioning, bidding and transitioning.

The danger in focusing on the cheapest offer is that trade-offs are made in quality and service. This approach can quickly derail relationships by driving away good partners who tire of being squeezed on price, only to have their efforts rewarded by losing the work to a lower bidder the next time. In one extreme example, a company rebid its transportation services every three months. This company had churned through nearly all of the top 20 suppliers until it was forced to work with suppliers of lesser quality. The consequence was that the company had several truckloads of its product drive off, never to be seen again.

Even if you are not constantly switching suppliers, companies that are too Penny-Wise and Pound-Foolish easily find themselves with suppliers that are forced to cut corners. Being penny-wise and pound-foolish doesn't engender trust—and it often costs you more in the end to fix the problems created as a result.

Sandbagging

As noted early, using incentives (the Carrot Principle) is a powerful way to drive behavior. But using incentives can backfire if not used properly. One such example is Sandbagging. The case of Ukrainian pole vaulter Sergey Bubka provides a classic example of Sandbagging.

Bubka was one of the world's best pole vaulters during the 1980s and 1990s. His sponsors rewarded him every time he set a world record—netting him $40,000 each time. Bubka found the perfect way to game the system; the Olympic gold medalist kept breaking the world record, 35 times in all. He would set new world records by a centimeter, all so he could recoup the bonus. Soon he would set another record, and another, and another. The bonus payments kept coming.

As one reporter noted, "Bubka is no fool. He doesn't smash his own records, but nibbles at them, replacing them a fraction at a time." Bubka's nibbles were mighty valuable to him.

TROUBLE ON THE HOME FRONT

Martin and Maria were beaming. After visiting dozens of open houses, they finally found their dream home. A true gem with a lot of space, an open vestibule, and a finished basement that could be turned into a play area.

The girls' rooms were especially bright and happy. They were going to love living there.

It was perfect. And at the right price, too. "It's the lowest price on the block," Martin smiled when he did the financial research.

They made an offer and waited for the home inspection to come in.

But there was a problem.

The reason the house was priced so low was because the previous owner had basically kicked the can down the road, leaving several issues for the next homeowners, Martin and Maria, to get the house up to code.

Before they could move in, they would need to do a few repairs.

Martin did some quick research and got some estimates for the repairs and worked with the mortgage broker.

"Good news!" he exclaimed after getting the estimates and working the finances. "We can use the money we saved on the house to cover the cost of the repairs."

There was one small issue. "The contractor says it may take a month or two to get the repairs done because the town is especially finicky and slow about getting permits."

Maria tried to stay optimistic but was nervous. "But Martin, that means we'll need to pay rent on our apartment and the new mortgage. We don't have enough money to do that."

Martin and Maria began thinking how they could make it work. After all they were so close. And the house—once it got repaired—would be perfect.

They'd struck a fair deal that would allow them to cover the short-term gap so they could finally move into their dream home. Maria would log extra client work a few days a week, while Martin would increase his share of family duties—picking up the children from school, helping them with their homework and cooking dinner. They'd both cut out any extras with Martin skipping golf and Maria taking a break from her Pilates classes.

It was not going to be fun, but they both agreed they could stick it out for a couple of months.

Things were going swimmingly. Martin enjoyed having more Daddy time. And as long as Maria didn't complain about his cooking he didn't mind taking on the added work.

But two months turned into three. And then four.

They were both growing frustrated.

While he enjoyed spending more time with the kids, he felt disregarded. He committed to a few days a week of expanded home and family duties, not being an all-hours taxi driver, ushering the girls here and there.

Then one day, Maria flew off the handle after a particularly taxing day.

Martin was taken aback. Yes, Maria was working more. But he was also doing double duty on the home front. How could she feel so entitled to complain?

THE VESTED WAY

Following Vested Rule 4 means a partnership should be fair and motivating—for all partners. In a business relationship, the focus may be on the value of what is bought/sold, or on optimizing how business partners create value for each other. In a personal relationship, it may be about the effort the parties put into the relationship (how to divide chores or take care of an aging parent). Regardless of the context, partners need to feel good about what they are putting into the relationship and their return on time and investment.

Because money can make people do stupid things, Rule 4 leverages four design principles to help partners focus on the potential gains from their relationship rather than being tempted to play short-term games to win at the expense of their partner.

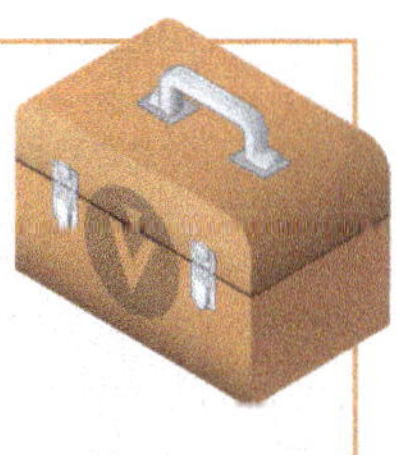

Your Toolkit: *Economic Model Framework*

A co-created transparent economic model that aligns the partnerships interests to partners Desired Outcomes to encourage win-win (versus win-lose) behaviors.

Let's do a deeper dive into each of the four design principles used to create an economic model for your partnership.

A Flexible and Fair Economic Framework

A properly structured Vested partnership reflects a fair and balanced framework where the partners win together and lose together. In a business relationship this means moving away from a *price* to a *pricing model*.

Think of the differences this way. A price is the $5.67 you pay for your grande two-pump vanilla latte at Starbucks. It's transactional in nature, which makes it easy. The seller sets the price and the buyer pays. While you don't negotiate with your local barista, companies are often expected to negotiate prices with their trading partners. This pits the buyer and supplier against each other, where there is usually a winner and a loser. If the buyer gets a lower price, the seller loses. This in turn often triggers shading behavior where the supplier tries to get even after the contract is signed by cutting back on service, replacing the A team with the C team, or charging extra claiming "scope creep."

Making the shift to a transparent pricing model (vs. a price) helps trading partners look at the cost structure and create a flexible framework where the partners win and lose together. For example, when Vested partners collaborate to drive efficiencies that lower the cost structure, the savings can be shared between the buyer and supplier.

Making the shift to a pricing model also has a secondary benefit because a model (vs. a fixed price) enables flexibility which helps sustain a healthy business relationship over the life of an agreement when situations change and the cost structure goes up or down.

In a personal relationship, a pricing model would consider how to fairly compensate the parties for the effort they put into the relationship. For example, siblings would transparently work through Rules 1-3 to determine the best solution for caring for their aging parent. Then in Rule 4, the siblings would come up with a fair way to compensate each sibling for their costs and effort either directly through the estate or after the fact through the sale of any assets from the estate. A key point: the siblings create the flexible framework proactively, thinking through a fair approach versus after the fact.

Link Incentives to Desired Outcomes

Recall the Carrot Principle? A Vested partnership leverages the Carrot Principle by using incentives when value is created.

Think of a time when you got a bonus or recognition for a job well done. It likely made you feel good to get the positive reinforcement. Incentives don't have to be monetary; they can be anything that is valued by the party receiving the incentive. This can be time off, stock options or even a contract extension for a supplier.

A well-structured Vested partnership links incentives to the partners' Desired Outcomes and not simply to an activity of one party. Linking incentives to Desired Outcomes aligns the interests of the partners as they both have a vested interest in generating added value; when one partner wins, the other partner wins. It also avoids sandbagging (e.g., Sergey Bubka) because it helps prevent gaming where one party wins at the other's expense.

I used incentives with my son Austin when he was little by using a simple ladder system. My husband built a small, three-foot ladder with Velcro on each step. We inserted Austin's picture in a plastic name badge holder and put Velcro on the back of the badge. The goal of the ladder system is to reward kids for climbing the ladder when they demonstrate good behavior. Austin's reward for good behavior? Toy cars.

Austin was obsessed with the movie *Cars*, and each week we'd go to the store where he could pick out a miniature toy car from the movie to add to his collection. But instead of getting the toy car immediately he had to earn it by following our family rules. We had five simple rules in our house: safe, happy, respectful, responsible and try hard. When Austin demonstrated one of the behaviors (e.g., being responsible by cleaning up his toys before going to bed) he would get to move his plastic badge holder with his picture up the ladder one notch. And if he misbehaved? Oh the torture as he would have to move the picture of himself down the ladder.

The simple system was a game-changer in our house because it aligned Austin's and our interests. As parents, we wanted good behavior and he wanted a new toy car. While my husband and I were out of pocket $5 each week for the cost of a new car, the added cost was well worth it in terms of having a safe, happy, respectful and responsible child.

Share Risks/Shared Reward for Risks

Recall prospect theory and that people want to avoid losses. The conventional approach for transaction-based relationships is to shift risk to the other party whenever possible. After all, if the other party will take the risk, why not let them? But this creates a negative reaction because our natural instinct is to optimize for ourselves and not necessarily for the partnership.

Think of building a bridge or even a new home. There are often many unknowns that can impact the costs. Will there be issues with the soil after breaking ground? When risk is shifted to the contractor (either in the form of operational risk, legal terms and conditions, or unknown risk) the contractor is forced to factor the risk into its pricing. This is known as a risk premium. Savvy contractors factor in the risk and add a risk premium to their costs in order to mitigate their losses. And when forced to estimate the cost of the risk, it is in their best interest to estimate high, which ultimately leads to a higher price than needed. And if the risk does not happen? The contractor wins at the expense of their customer.

A Vested partnership is different because it sees risk as something that should be mitigated and managed with a high degree of transparency and collaboration—not simply transferred.

Use Guardrails and Triggers to Ensure Continual Alignment

A properly designed Vested partnership means partners always win—or lose—together. But sometimes business (or life) happens, and what was once fair may no longer be fair under the new circumstances. And when a partner finds themselves in what they perceive as an unfair situation, it can lead to *shading*.

Recall shading happens when a party isn't getting the outcome expected and feels the other party is to blame or has not acted reasonably to mitigate their losses. The aggrieved party often retaliates by stopping cooperation or using countermoves to get even (e.g., cutting back on performance in subtle ways, such as justifying buying a new pair of shoes versus putting money into savings as a reaction to a spouse's lavish golf expenditures.)

To prevent shading, a Vested partnership uses Guardrails and pre-planned triggers that signal that one or both partners are not comfortable because they are close to their pre-defined Guardrails (their risk zone).

So how does this work? Partners pre-establish Guardrails based on what they think is fair at the outset of their partnership. Guardrails in Vested partnerships act just like they do on a road; they are put in place to keep people safe. And when the situation changes and one (or both) of the partners is nearing a Guardrail, it is a trigger to do a formal review and realign as needed—or perhaps even decide if it no longer makes sense to continue the relationship because it is too risky (violates one or both of the partners' risk tolerance levels).

In a business relationship, the triggers often take the form of margin matching and are associated with the profit margin or ROI targets the partners have pre-agreed as fair targets. For example, in a complex construction project, the partners will face many unknowns. The partners agree that the contractor should have a minimum profit margin (the lower margin trigger), ensuring the contractor does not lose money on the project. Likewise the partners agree to an upper profit margin that factors in the highest-end profit margin the contractor will make if they achieve all of the incentives.

As a general rule of thumb for a strategic buyer-supplier Vested partnership, the supplier's lower margin should be 50% of market margin for the type of good/service they are delivering and an upper margin of three times market margin in the form of incentives (meaning if market margin is 10% the guardrails are a low profit margin of 5% and a high profit margin of 30%).

In a personal relationship, the triggers are often related to the effort the partners put into the relationship (e.g., finding an equitable way that creates the most value for the partnership). Let's consider the situation Maren and Mikhail faced when they found themselves needing to care for their aging mother. They proactively sat down and worked through an approach they both felt was fair.

Maren had a high-profile job and two school age children at home. As such, she could not take on her fair share of the days to take care of their mother. Mikhail, on the other hand, was a freelance graphic artist, but his income was far smaller than Maren's and he could not afford to pay for his half of the cost of the daily home health service their mother needed.

The solution? Mikhail would play the role of primary caretaker Monday through Friday, and Maren would cover the full costs for the home health service on the weekends, which would give Mikhail much-needed time off (his trigger). Maren would also take the cost savings from only paying for the home health service for weekend days (8 days a month vs 15 days a month) and allocate the savings to Mikhail to compensate him for his time.

Both felt the solution was fair and importantly Mikhail felt his time and effort was being valued.

From Games to Gains

Following the four design principles will help you stay focused on the potential gains of your partnership and avoid the pitfall of playing games. As part of our research, my colleagues and I developed a toolkit in the form of a simple table for buyer-supplier strategic relationships (see following page).

As you work through Rule 4, use the toolkit, the design principles shared previously, and the associated examples as a source of inspiration to help you think through creative ways to help you focus on unlocking the potential gains of your partnerships. Below are some pointers on how to get started. While these tips are more suited for business relationships, you can check out how Maria and Martin were successfully able to apply the concept of gains not games on a personal level at the end of this chapter.

- Start by reviewing your transparency commitments and your Statement of Intent. You will want to lean on these as the foundation for developing the economics associated with your partnership.
- Use the example generic economic model framework toolkit – as well as examples shared later in the chapter – for inspiration. Agree on a framework that best represents the economics and effort associated with your partnership. Begin to populate your framework.
- Review your Requirements Roadmap for which objectives and metrics you indicated you wanted to incentivize. Map your incentives to your framework (e.g., which incentives are tied to each of the pricing model framework buckets in a buyer-supplier relationship).
- Jointly identify known and unknown risks that may prevent you from achieving your Desired Outcomes. Make sure the partner(s) bearing any risks are adequately rewarded if your partnership bears gains.

- Before finalizing your economic model, review any guardrails you have created for your partnership and establish triggers you will proactively watch out for to ensure you stay within the Guardrails. Commit to a regular review process and cadence to review the economics of your partnership.

ECONOMIC MODEL FRAMEWORK

	Service Delivery			Transformation
	Base Service	**Other Services**	**Governance Structure**	**Transformation Incentive Framework**
Logic				
Economics				

FROM THEORY TO PRACTICE

Staying aligned through Vested Rule 4 and focusing on gains not games isn't easy—but the four design principles are meant to guide partners along their journey to create a win-win partnership. The rest of this chapter revisits the EY-ISS EPIC partnership and how Martin and Maria put Rule 4 into practice.

EY-ISS: An EPIC Win-Win Deal

In conventional buyer-supplier relationships companies purchase services for a transactional fee (cost per hour, per unit, per shipment, per pallet storage, etc.). In a Vested partnership, a buyer and supplier jointly develop a pricing model with incentives that reward the service provider when mutually defined Desired Outcomes are achieved. In short, the service provider is vested in the buyer's success and vice versa: the better the supplier helps their client achieve the Desired Outcomes, the more incentives they earn.

For the EY-ISS team, putting win-win into practice started with a foundation of a "cost-is-the-cost" mantra.

Next, the team physically created the pricing model (not a price) by aligning the ISS's scope of work (from Rule 2) into four "buckets."

EPIC PRICING MODEL FRAMEWORK

	Service Delivery			Transformation
	Base Service	**Other Services**	**Governance Structure**	**Transformation Incentive Framework**
Logic	Ongoing workplace services (e.g., cleaning, dining and reception) with a stable volume and can be budgeted for	Work that is variable and not part of ongoing budgeted work. • User paid services • Client paid services • Projects delivered by ISS. • Subcontracted projects • Projects ISS is asked to support outside of scope.	Funding for the core governance team and specialists that are brought in as needed.	Transformation initiatives that create cost savings (both within budget and beyond budget looking at TCO) Transformation initiatives that deliver on non-cost-related Desired Outcomes.
Economics	Costs pass through with a below-market benchmark profit margin	Variable fee with a "fair" market margin based on industry benchmarks	Management Fee to secure the "A" governance team	High percentage of profits tied to innovation

The first step in developing the pricing model was to align the services in each of the cost driver buckets (e.g., ongoing work such as cleaning, dining and receptionist services was mapped as a "base" service while projects ISS is asked to support outside of base services is considered "other services"). The second step was to determine the fair "base" profit targets, with a baseline minimum profit target below market benchmarks. The rationale? ISS should not be highly compensated for simply showing up to do the work, but they should get rewarded heavily for delivering transformation initiatives that created value and made progress towards the Desired Outcomes.

With the pricing model framework developed, the team went to work aligning incentives to the framework using their Requirements Roadmap (from Rule 3). Each metric in the Requirements Requirement has a corresponding incentive—with some incentives being monetary and others being non-monetary. For example, ISS could earn contract extensions. They team then estimated the value associated improvements for each metric and developed incentive targets which ISS could unlock.

Andreas Horwitz was the Business Development lead for ISS and had a front row seat in developing the EPIC pricing model. "As the business development leader, I had seen firsthand how money moves the world around. Vested Rule 4 is where the rubber hits the road with Vested because you translate your intentions into an economic model. The Vested methodology helped us think outside of the box, where we could start to align the economics and incentives to our intentions and Desired Outcomes."

Aligning interests on the economics of their partnership has been game-changing in terms of helping EY achieve its vision of building a Better Working World.

The results? The EPIC team is putting up record results.

1. EY is winning with a lower cost structure—with year-on-year cost savings exceeding baseline targets by 50-100%.
2. ISS is winning with more revenue (51% more) and more profit (50%+ more) due to incentives and contract extensions.
3. EY employees are winning with a better working environment, including record high satisfaction levels and an improved environment (e.g. 70% reduction in CO2 emissions).

SUCCESS ON THE HOME FRONT

Maria and Martin found themselves at an impasse. Martin, struggling to take on extra responsibilities and Maria so busy with her client work she was working late in the evenings. Martin decided to initiate a conversation so they could work out a better solution.

"I recognize that we agreed to this arrangement, and I'm happy to go the extra mile, but this is going beyond the scope of what I anticipated," he told her. "Let's rebalance and find an approach that works well for both of us."

"I appreciate you saying that. We are so close to our dream of moving into our new house—but all of this extra work is…well…it's just a lot," Maria admitted. "My most demanding client is winding down soon, so things at work should be less stressful. But let's make sure, moving forward, that we have a better system in place."

Maria paused to reflect on the challenges Martin was having as well. "What are the biggest challenges you're facing?"

She took time to let Martin vent. He rubbed the back of his neck. "Time. I just don't have enough time to do everything and be everywhere, and cook dinner, and get the kids ready for bed, and juggle my work on top of it. To be honest, I never knew how much effort you put into keeping the kids so organized and the house running so smoothly."

Maria smiled. She felt appreciated, and that was something she needed after working with a demanding client for the last two months.

"I know it's a lot for one person," she said sympathetically.

Maria made a suggestion. "Would it help if we shifted our schedules a bit? I can get up early and get a jump start on my client work and then take a break to get the kids ready in the morning every other day. That way you can sleep in a bit later."

"Yep—that would help for sure."

Martin jumped in with an idea. "What if you invited your mom to pick up the girls from school and get them to their activities a couple of days a week? She's always talking about wanting to see the kids more."

"She would love that. And the kids would, too."

Martin was on a role and jumped in with another idea. "One thing that I think would really help is if we could prep for dinners for the entire week on Sunday. That would streamline the time for cooking dinners each night and free up some time."

"That's a great idea. We could get the girls to help as well."

Martin paused and asked Maria what could help her relieve some of the stress she was having with her added workload.

"Moving forward, I definitely need to set firmer boundaries with clients. I know when they call I fall into my people-pleasing trap and get taken advantage of. But I really need to be realistic and setting boundaries so I don't wind up feeling abused."

Martin was sympathetic. "I know that is tough for you."

Martin paused and offered some advice. "One thing that has really helped me at work is to be transparent with expectations upfront. One trick I got from my boss after getting promoted to manager is what he called an 'expectations sharing matrix.' Now when a new employee joins the team we collaborate to share expectations. To be honest, it was game-changing for me and it's been an easy way to be aligned on expectations."

"Wow Martin. That would be great if you could show me how the expectations sharing matrix works."

Maria and Martin were pleased with how easy it was to have what could have been a difficult conversation.

Martin had an idea. "Maria, we've made such incredible progress. Let's take a minute and jot down our go forward plan and then at the end of every week and sense check if what are are doing is working."

CURRENT	ADJUSTMENT	OUTCOME
Martin cooks dinner, gets kids, ready for bed, juggles work	Shifted schedules - Maria gets kids ready in morning every other day	Free up Martin to sleep in
	Maria's Mom picks up girls and gets them to activies twice a week	Free up time for Martin Grandma is happier
Plan dinner, day by day	Prep dinners on Sunday	More time for both Maria and Martin
Maria overcommits to clients	Expectations Sharing Matrix	Maria less stressed out by having clear expectations

After just one week, both Maria and Martin both had more energy and enthusiasm.

And, just three weeks later they got great news. The permits were approved and the contractor was ready to get started. They would be in their dream home before summer.

TOOLKIT QUICK REFERENCE GUIDE

Economic Model to Promote Gains, Not Games

- **Purpose:** To design an economic structure that motivates partners to collaborate to achieve the Desired Outcomes
- **When to Use:** When establishing or renegotiating the financial foundation of a strategic relationship
- **Components:**
- **Guideline:** Five or fewer Desired Outcomes supported by fifteen or fewer objectives and metrics
- **Output:** A framework document (e.g., a table with the logic and incentives aligned to the model), document risk allocation, guardrails and triggers used for monitoring the the economics of the relationship
- **Perverse Incentives it Prevents:** The Activity Trap; The Activity Trap Redux; Zero Sum Game; Penny Wise and Pound Foolish; Sandbagging

9

Rule 5: Stay Aligned

"Planning tries to optimize tomorrow the trends of today. Strategy aims to exploit the new and different opportunities of tomorrow."
- Peter Drucker

It helps to think of the journey up Everest not as a straight climb going higher day by day, but as a series of ascents and descents from one camp to another in order to acclimate to the altitude. The entire journey typically takes about 40 days to finish and involves sherpas—who do much of the hard work and carry heavy loads—along with support staff.

The journey to the summit is a weeks-long series of hikes to reach and retreat from various camps along the mountain in order to prepare one's body for higher altitudes. But even with that altitude training, the body can't acclimatize at the highest levels. Mountain climbers have an ominous name for altitudes above 26,000 feet, or 8,000 meters: the "death zone." At such heights, oxygen levels get critically low, meaning every single step is a struggle. Every breath feels, on your lungs, like a hard run on a hot day, and you just can't catch … your … breath …

Nausea and confusion are common at such high altitudes, and extended stays in the "death zone," as the name suggests, can result in physical harm or death.

As if the physical journey isn't difficult enough, there are uncontrollable external factors that can turn the perfect plan into pandemonium. Storms can emerge at a moment's notice, making an already harrowing climb all but impassable due to whiteout conditions where you can barely see inches in front of your face. Or there could be crowding on the climb route. Or perhaps you might have an unplanned equipment failure. Simply put, shit happens. Life happens. Business happens.

When shit happens on Mt. Everest, it can lead to a failed summit attempt—or worse—death.

The death rate of personal and business partnerships is far worse than for climbing Mt. Everest. Well over half of business partnerships—50-80%—fail in the first few years. And about 40% of marriages are destined to end in divorce.

With so many changes going on around us, the state of flux can lead to misalignment over time. And misalignment means that partners may no longer be operating on the same page. What worked well at the beginning of a partnership may not be as fruitful or as fit for purpose anymore. When this happens, frustration or even shading, which we explored earlier, can slip in where one party feels slighted and takes steps (consciously or unconsciously) to level the playing field so they are no longer on the bottom of the pile of shit raining down on them.

With such a dynamic world, how do you identify opportunities and challenges before they become harmful? How do you account for that flexibility and stay aligned with your most valued partners?

A good system for identifying potential issues and opportunities and making timely decisions is the answer. In a business context, this "good system" is known as governance. But governance sounds very bureaucratic, doesn't it? Maybe that is the reason so many business relationships don't invest the time to put in the necessary governance mechanisms to keep partners on the same path. In personal relationships, the concept is almost always overlooked.

Rather than getting bogged down in the bureaucracy of the concept of governance, let's instead focus on what that term really means: the ability to stay aligned and pivot when appropriate.

Like when it snows on Everest.

Or when there is an economic downturn and budgets are constrained.

Or when you unexpectedly lose your job.

Or when there is a product recall.

FOUNDATIONAL THEORIES

Let's put Rule 5 in context to the other four Rules. If Rules 1-4 help you get in alignment with your partner, Rule 5 keeps partners in alignment when business, life (or shit) happens. The importance of Rule 5 is to establish the mechanisms partners use to navigate the path forward when there is a snowstorm on their Mt. Everest. Good governance—staying aligned and pivoting when necessary—allows you to maneuver bumps, roadblocks, and even pandemics better. The following three pioneering theories, when applied, can keep partners aligned over the life of their partnership.

Insight vs. Oversight Approach

When thinking about governance it often comes with an oversight mindset. For example, companies put in "supplier relationship managers" for their most strategic supplier relationships. The concept seems smart and shows a commitment to maintaining a strong relationship. But instead it often fails because the role represents an *oversight* instead of an insight mindset. The thinking goes, "I am the supplier manager, I am here to manage you."

When thinking about how to implement Vested Rule 5, it's important to consider the definitions of insight and oversight. While *oversight* is the action of overseeing, *insight* represents a deep understanding of something. Good governance is not simply about managing (or worse, micromanaging) a business partner. And it's definitely not about watching over your husband as he loads the dishwasher to make sure he does it up to your standards. Rather, it's about ensuring you have the right mindset coupled with open and timely communication protocols and processes. The byproduct? Allowing for collaborative decisions that make the most optimal decision, not the decision for what is best for just one of the partners.

Carol Dweck, a professor at Stanford University on mindset theory, provides compelling support for why insight-based governance succeeds where oversight-based approaches fail. Her distinction between fixed and growth mindsets correlates with the oversight-versus-insight paradigm.

Let's look at how Dweck's theory applies to how an organization manages supplier relationships.

When a buying organization operates with a fixed (oversight) mindset, it assumes the supplier capabilities are static and require constant monitoring to prevent decline. This creates a defensive posture where the focus shifts to catching mistakes rather than fostering improvement. This in turn inhibits performance and innovation because it inadvertently creates what Dweck terms "performance goals" rather than "learning goals." Suppliers in these relationships focus on avoiding criticism and meeting minimum standards rather than pushing boundaries or proposing innovative solutions. The constant evaluation and judgment inherent in oversight models trigger defensive behaviors that shut down the very collaboration and creativity that strategic partnerships require. This defensive dynamic explains why many well-intentioned supplier management programs fail to generate the strategic value they promise.

In contrast, insight-based governance embodies what Dweck refers to as a "growth mindset." When a buying organization looks at a supplier relationship as a dynamic partnership with untapped potential, it changes its perspective. Rather than asking "Are you meeting our standards?" insight-based approaches ask, "What are we learning together, and how can we apply these insights to create greater value?" This reframing transforms governance from a compliance exercise into a strategic capability, where partners are incentivized to share challenges early, experiment with solutions, and view setbacks as learning opportunities rather than relationship threats. The result is not just better supplier performance, but true partnership innovation that neither party could achieve alone.

This same paradigm is equally relevant in personal relationships.

Grit and the Power of Pivoting

No matter how much you plan and how hard you try, you can't account for every single scenario that could occur. The COVID-19 pandemic made it strikingly clear that many companies lacked good relationship management and governance with their suppliers. Most companies scrambled to align supply and demand and found themselves facing a supply chain full of chaos.

It's no wonder that a post-pandemic survey by Bain & Company found that flexibility and resiliency are the leading priorities in supply chains in the coming years.[147]

A leading authority on getting flexibility and resiliency right is Angela Duckworth, a psychologist at the University of Pennsylvania and author of *Grit: The Power of Passion and Perseverance.*

Duckworth's groundbreaking research on "grit"—defined as the combination of passion and perseverance toward long-term goals—emerged from over a decade of research studying thousands of participants across diverse settings, from the West Point Military Academy to the National Spelling Bee.

Her findings? A simple but profound observation: talent and intelligence aren't the primary predictors of success. Instead, those who demonstrate unwavering commitment to their objectives, coupled with the resilience to persist through failures and setbacks, consistently outperformed their more naturally gifted peers. Central to Duckworth's framework is the concept of "deliberate practice." Her studies reveal that truly gritty individuals don't just work harder; they work smarter by continuously adapting their strategies while maintaining their overarching goals.

Let me repeat. *They continuously adapt their strategies while maintaining their overarching goals.* This requires a flexible mindset that can embrace failure as information rather than defeat, adjust approaches based on feedback, and maintain motivation despite temporary setbacks. Like when it snows on Mt. Everest.

DISCOVERY HEALTH'S PIVOT

Adrian Gore, an actuary, founded Discovery Health in South Africa in 1992 with the focus of enhancing people's lifestyles and helping them become healthier. It would become one of the South Africa's—and what some argue as the world's—most progressive insurance platforms.

An unforeseen shift happened six years after Gore founded Discovery Health. South Africa passed a law requiring insurance providers—called "medical schemes"—to become non-profit entities. Gore was left with the challenge of how to meet the new mandate. The decision? Discovery Health was split into two entities: The Discovery Health Medical Scheme (the Scheme) and Discovery Health (Pty) Limited, a medical scheme administrator.

Discovery Health was cleaved in half.

As a result of the legislation, the medical scheme faced the challenge of creating an outsourcing contract for work it had once performed in-house. The Scheme and Discovery Health Pty worked hard to carry forward the strong relationship they'd forged when they operated as one.

Getting on the same page wasn't a concern. The entities were already on the same page.

But staying on the same page was another matter. Recall the statistic that 50-80% of business partnerships fail. The new legislation brought forth many new changes that would test the parties, which now had seemingly different goals. The scheme operated as a non-profit entity and Discovery Health Pty operated as a for-profit entity.

A falling out and heaps of friction could have occurred, especially given that the partners faced evolving landscapes of new regulations and increasing competition. In addition, Discovery Health Pty began to offer administrative services to other clients.

But through thick and thin the partners have had an unwavering commitment to world-class governance, enabling them to stay aligned.

As a highly regulated non-profit medical scheme, the Scheme is not shy about auditing how well things are going. Discovery Health knows the importance of staying aligned and welcomes the periodic reviews. One such review occurred when the Scheme engaged Deloitte to conduct a formal Operating Model and Governance Review. The study, conducted in 2013, suggested the Scheme review and optimize their outsourcing contract which was coming up for renewal.

That's when then-CEO Milton Streak began to learn about the Vested way of working with strategic outsourcing partners. Initially Streak led the partners to create a Vested agreement to following the Vested Five Rules. Streak and a cross-collaboration, cross-functional team to create a Vested agreement following the Vested Five Rules. The new contract addressed governance front and center and included a robust governance structure and protocols, helping the parties navigate the dynamic nature of the health care industry. Howard Snoyman, the Scheme's Head of Legal and Ethics, had a front row seat in redesigning the partnership, including helping create a governance structure and protocols.

Most recently, PG Governance conducted a comprehensive audit of the partners' governance structure and processes. The findings? An "excellent" score at 100%.[148] That score was achieved across all six dimensions that were assessed.

The audit results are indicative of the partnership's success, which has been nothing short of spectacular. At a time when most medical schemes were shrinking and losing members, the Scheme grew significantly and rose to capture over 50% market share while simultaneously containing costs at a better pace than other medical schemes. Their tight alignment has helped them innovate at a speed far faster than the market, helping the partners become market leaders in customer satisfaction and efficiency. It also helped the partners pivot quickly during Covid-19 as well as enabling them to navigate the ever-changing and stringent regulatory requirements.

Unfortunately, when partners lack a sound governance system for navigating through changing dynamics, things can heat up and go sideways.

TASTE THE HEAT

Just seeing a bottle of Sriracha makes you taste the sweet, tangy heat. Huy Fong Foods, the maker of the famed "rooster sauce" brand of Sriracha sauce, owned the hot sauce market for decades until a lack of governance led to the demise of the company's pivotal pepper partnership.

Huy Fong's bottles feature a rooster logo, a green cap and fire engine red sauce. The ingredients are simple and include chili, sugar, garlic, salt and distilled vinegar. You can't confuse it with any other condiment—Sriracha stands apart. In fact, industry pundits have credited Huy Fong with creating the entire category. Documentaries and songs have been devoted to the beloved sauce. It's been the subject of countless brand collaborations and influenced items as random as board games and candy and lip balm and shoes.

Sriracha's main ingredient is pureed red chili peppers. Amazingly fresh and high-quality peppers sourced locally through a strategic partnership with Underwood Ranches.

For nearly three decades, Huy Fong's owner David Tran had a symbiotic relationship with Craig Underwood, the owner of Underwood Ranches. Underwood Ranches was Huy Fong's only chili supplier, and the Sriracha maker's manufacturing plant was located in close proximity to Underwood Ranches, creating a predictable supply of the beloved bright red bottles of the famed rooster sauce. Huy Fong needed peppers and Underwood Ranches grew the best juicy red jalapenos. For years the two men would jointly plan how to manage for projected demand and growth as Sriracha sauce went from being just another condiment to a staple in restaurants and people's homes.

The more successful Huy Fong was at selling Sriracha, the more successful Underwood Ranches was. The partnership came to a standstill ahead of the 2017 growing season when Tran argued over payment for the next season's crop. Tran believed Underwood had overcharged him for the 2016 crop, and his feelings were stewing. As a result, Tran refused to fund the customary pre-payment Underwood Ranches needed to plant the 2017 crop.

The situation left both partners in precarious positions. Underwood was locked into long-term leases and did not have a buyer, while Huy Fong lost its only supplier. The misalignment turned to mayhem when the companies sued each other.

Ultimately Tran was found in breach of contract and a jury awarded Underwood Ranches more than $24 million in compensatory and punitive damages, while Underwood was ordered to repay Huy Fong about $1.5 million in overpayment for the 2016 growing season.

But the impact for the Sriracha producer has been far more than the $23 million it was forced to pay. In leaving its key supplier, Huy Fong needed to find new sources of peppers. Unfortunately, Underwood Ranches was the only large-scale pepper grower in California, so Huy Fong had to turn to growers in Mexico. But those other peppers haven't always been as plentiful, as hot, as red or as fresh as needed, leading to shortages and production gaps.

Meanwhile, Underwood has gone on to produce its own popular hot sauce, Dragon Sauce, that rivals Sriracha.

Huy Fong and Underwood Ranches could have prevented the demise of their partnership by using a sound governance system where they could openly discuss issues and find a path forward to realign. And—if continued alignment was not possible—leverage a pre-agreed exit management plan outlining how the partners could pivot in a manner that would have saved millions of dollars in litigation costs.

GETTING IT WRONG:
PERVERSE INCENTIVES IN PRACTICE

Many partners use the word "partner" loosely, simply tossing the word around rather than putting in the hard work to create and maintain alignment. With that realization has come a hard lesson: not putting in place and rigorously following governance protocols is almost always the start of strategic drift, shading and the other ailments profiled below. Let's look at a few of the perverse incentives that happen when you don't follow Vested Rule 5.

Strategic Drift

Strategic drift occurs when partners don't put in the work needed to keep abreast and update their strategic priorities as business happens. Strategic Drift often occurs when one (or all) partners get complacent. Think of the concept of the seven-year itch in a marriage, which suggests marital happiness and satisfaction decline around seven years into a relationship. The same kind of itch can happen in successful business relationships too.

A case of strategic drift involves Cellino & Barnes, a personal injury law firm founded by Ross Cellino Jr. and Steve Barnes in 1998. Their TV jingles had a distinctive ring: *Cellino & Barnes, injury attorneys, 800-888-8888.* The partners appeared in numerous commercials together and were synonymous with one another.

But over the years, Cellino and Barnes' relationship started to drift.

For example, Barnes hired his brother and girlfriend into the firm. But when Cellino wanted to bring his daughter into the firm, Barnes balked. When a tit-for-tat cycle emerges it often results in partners losing sight of the potential of their partnership and one (or both) partners starting to drift.

Cellino began second-guessing the partnership. He eventually grew so frustrated he analyzed the firm's revenues and approached his partner with an idea to split their responsibilities: Buffalo and Rochester to himself, New York City for Barnes. Barnes rejected the plan and even confronted Cellino's wife about it. Their bickering led to shouting matches, and in 2017, Cellino filed to dissolve the firm.

The lawyers known for helping their clients in court now faced their own legal battle between each other. The partners ended up forming separate law firms that competed until Barnes was killed in a 2020 private airplane crash.

Shading

Recall the concept of shading as popularized by Nobel Laureate Oliver Hart. Shading is prevalent in trading partner relationships where unanticipated costs, budget overruns, schedule delays and reimbursement refusals occur. For example, an aggrieved supplier may try to recoup losses by replacing the expensive A-team it currently has on the project with its less costly C-team. Or an aggrieved buyer may hold back on payment or squeeze the supplier for a price reduction.

Let's revisit the Huy Fong and Underwood Ranch partnership through the lens of shading, which created a slippery slope of distrust in the relationship that eventually became a death spiral.

Recall, the partnership came to a standstill ahead of the 2017 growing season when Tran accused Underwood of over-charging for the next season's crop.

Court records reveal that the friction started well before that, with shady behaviors by David Tran, Huy Fong's owner. Tran started another company to buy and sell peppers—one that Underwood's leader, Craig Underwood Ranches', didn't want to work with. Then Tran tried to hire Underwood Ranch's COO. And when the COO insisted on staying at Underwood Ranches, Tran took drone footage of Underwood's harvesting and sorting operations that he later shared with other farmers to teach them how to harvest efficiently.

In the eyes of an appeals court, Huy Fong's shading behavior was a sign he made the decision to terminate its relationship long before the fateful disagreement.

It's just as easy to fall into a negative tit-for-tat trap of shading in personal relationships. For example, a spouse could feel resentful that their partner has more "free time" than them and start to schedule nights out with their friends. "It's your turn to watch the kids," they say, keeping score of each partner's hours and responsibilities.

New Sheriff in Town

You know the scenario. The new sheriff rides into town to make a name for himself... most often leaving dead bodies in his wake. In the movies, the new sheriff is usually the good guy, as in Gary Cooper's Oscar-winning performance in *High Noon*. The bad guys become the dead bodies and it's a happy ending. The good guys win, the bad guys lose.

Unfortunately in business relationships the reverse is often the case. All too often the New Sheriff in Town is a power-hungry new executive looking to enhance their name and image; along the way, they throw good-standing suppliers under the bus for the name of "lower costs" or "a new strategic direction." The New Sheriff seeks short-term gains to make them look good, and then they are often gone in a flash to the next company to repeat the situation.

For a real-life example of a New Sheriff in Town look no further than Randy Mott. Randy rode into GM as the newly-minted CIO after stops along the way at Wal-Mart, Dell and HP. Mott's shake-up plan? Move 90 percent of its outsourced IT services back in-house within three years.

The dead bodies in this case? GM's Information Technology service providers—namely HP, IBM, Capgemini and Wipro--who lost contracts valued at nearly $3 billion a year. An interesting twist is that one of these suppliers, HP, was named GM's Supplier of the Year twice (including just the year before) for its "dedication and loyalty" for supporting GM during its dark years of bankruptcy. GM insiders attribute HP for helping GM bounce back from its bankruptcy. However, HPers were left wondering whether the significant investments they made to help GM during their bankruptcy were worth the effort. Regardless of which side is right, "dedication and loyalty" went by the wayside when Mott rode in as the New Sheriff in Town.

TROUBLE ON THE HOME FRONT

Ava, 15, rummaged through the messy piles of clothes and soccer gear in her room in a frantic search for her cleats. They were somewhere. But where?

Meanwhile, Liv, 13, ignored her mother's calls to set the table, one of her chores. But it felt like every mealtime, Liv was nowhere to be found or failing to finish the task.

The years had flown by for Martin and Maria. They'd worked through so much—getting aligned on their shared goals, starting and raising a family, finding balance, and buying their dream home. The years had been great for the family.

But now that the girls were teenagers, things seemed to be spiraling out of control. It was all a lot. Ballet rehearsals. The science fair. Permission slips. After-school clubs. Adding more money to the girls' cafeteria accounts.

Meanwhile, Martin was stuck traveling for extended sales meetings. Maria had lots of work responsibilities of her own. She was a manager now, running a team of eager employees.

The biggest complication?

The girls weren't great at disclosing all of their obligations like forgotten assignments and shifting practice times. Maria spent a full weekend day helping—or completing, depending on your definition—Ava's big science project for school. It had been assigned two weeks earlier, but Ava "forgot" until the last minute. While Maria helped save the day for Ava it set the mother back from her own responsibilities.

When Maria asked Ava why she hadn't mentioned it earlier, the girl stated she had. "I told dad about it. I guess it slipped his mind," she said. Ugh.

The hectic nature of their schedules left Martin and Maria pitted against each other for rides and support and permissions. Both of the parents were carrying their own frustrations, along with different versions of the day's schedule.

It was pure chaos. And something needed to change.

THE VESTED WAY

Even the most promising relationships fall out of sync and struggle to get back on the same page when they have lost their way or distrust has set in. In some cases partners can hug it out like *Friends* characters Joey and Chandler did and move on to continue with a productive relationship. But other times the frustration grows and once-successful partnerships ended up in court in a nasty divorce or lawsuit fighting over who was right and who was wrong such as Huey Fong and Underwood Ranch.

When you enter into a relationship with the intent of it being long-term in nature, it's essential to invest in appropriate governance mechanisms to help you stay aligned and pivot when needed. The Tool in the Vested toolkit to help you apply Rule 5 is a Governance Framework checklist (see following page) and associated design principles. In addition, a sample governance structure has been provided.

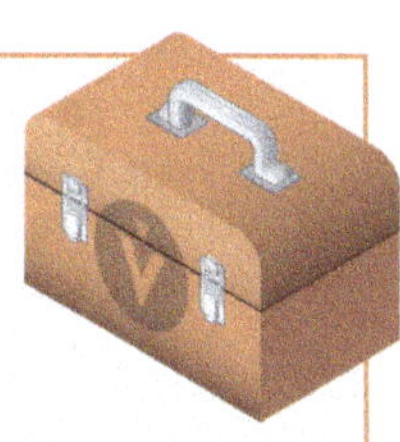

Your Toolkit: *Governance Framework*

A co-created governance system that establishes how partners manage their relationship, helping partners stay aligned when conditions change.

Collectively, Vested Rule 5 includes 22 design principles spanning four key elements partners should incorporate into their partnership: relationship management, transformation management, exit management and special concerns.

When partners embed a governance framework using proven mechanisms into their relationship, it helps partners stay in alignment when you find yourself facing an inevitable bump in the road. And when a turn in the road becomes so significant that it may be time to end a relationship, Vested Rule 5 ensures partners think through how to navigate a graceful exit to mitigate losses while allowing partners to go their own way.

Governance Checklist for a Buyer-Supplier Relationship

RELATIONSHIP MANAGEMENT

Key question: How will the relationship be structured, maintained and stabilized?

- ☐ Tiered Management Structure
- ☐ Separate Management Roles
- ☐ Peer-to-Peer Communications
- ☐ Communications Cadence
- ☐ Relationship Management
- ☐ Relationship Health Monitoring
- ☐ Issue Resolution Management
- ☐ Continuity of Resources

TRANSFORMATION MANAGEMENT

Key question: How will the partnership evolve and adapt over time?

- ☐ Transition Management
- ☐ Continuous Improvement
- ☐ Invention
- ☐ Structured Innovation Management Process
- ☐ Contractual Change Management

EXIT MANAGEMENT

Key question: How will separation be handled?

- ☐ Termination Notice Process
- ☐ High Level Exit Transition Plan
- ☐ Exit Team, Governance and Reporting
- ☐ Transfer of Resources

SPECIAL CONCERNS & EXTERNAL REQUIREMENTS

Key question: What external constraints shape the partnership?

- ☐ Understanding Concerns and Requirements
- ☐ Incorporation into the Agreement
- ☐ Responsibility to Update
- ☐ Links to Regulations

GOVERNANCE STRUCTURE

Buyer
Supplier
Standing Neutral

	Service Delivery - Base Services	Service Delivery - Projects	Innovation Managers	Commercial Managers
Executive Steering Group				
Strategic Level				
Tactical Level/ Country				
Processes	Reporting & Performance Measurement	Reporting & Performance Measurement	Transition	Pricing Model Governance
	Risk Management	Risk Management	Innovation & Continuous Improvements	Change Management
	Continuity regarding involved individuals			
	Escalation process			
	Measures on termination of the agreement			

Relationship Management

Relationship management refers to the processes and protocols partners use to manage the ongoing partnership and decisions they need to make during the course of their partnership. Whether you are in a business or personal relationship, trust and communication are at the center of relationship management. That is why good governance should be grounded in the partners' Statement of Intent—so if a difficult issue comes up, the partners can work through it in a healthy manner.

The types of relationship management mechanisms you adopt for your partnership will vary greatly based on the type and complexity of the partnership. But all partnerships can tap into common design principles to tailor how you manage the relationship with your partner. The following is a checklist of some of the most common principles partners should think about when designing the governance for their partnership with some being unique to business relationships.

Applicable to All Types of Partnerships	Primarily Applicable to Business Partnership
• Communication Cadence • Relationship Health Monitoring • Issue Resolution Process	• Tiered Structure with Peer-to-Peer Alignment • Key Role Definition • Continuity of Resources/ Onboarding

Each is described in more detail in the callout box. In addition, many academics and business professionals have written about governance best practices. (See the endnotes for some suggested resources).

High-Level Overview of Proven Relationship Management Mechanisms

Issue resolution management. Partners should co-create a process for how they identify and work through issues. In business relationships, a best practice is a formal process that includes a joint issue log and process for resolving issues while they are small. Likewise partners should have a joint risk register where they identify and actively manage risks.

In a personal relationship, it could be as simple having as having a sign or signal to help your partner recognize frustrations are building. For example, in my family we have a "pet peeve rule" where we vocally express our pet peeves and commit to not doing whatever it is that bugs the other person. This has been great in helping prevent irritations that get under each other's skin. Whatever processes you use, the key is to establish mechanisms that resolve issues while they are small.

Continuity of resources. In a marriage, partners—by design—stay in a relationship for life unless the partners agree to end the marriage or one of the partners dies. In business relationships it is common for key people to come and go. That's why it is imperative that partners identify key personnel and develop a process for getting new team members up to speed on the why, what and how of the Vested partnership.

Tiered Structure with Peer-to-Peer Alignment. With a tiered management structure, each tier has specific responsibilities for managing different aspects of the business. This structure creates vertical alignment among the upper management, middle management, and day-to-day workforce. Each layer is accountable for examining the relationship and business success from its own point of view and is accountable for ensuring that the relationship is focused on the strategic and transformational components as well as the tactical elements.

Key Roles. The people in an organization who are most familiar with their business partner—and thus, have the most insight into the relationship. Individuals in key roles are a great resource in uncovering challenges and opportunities in Vested relationships. The University of Tennessee's research on strategic trading partner relationships suggests partners include a minimum of three key roles:

- Relationship Management (manage the overall relationship)
- Operations Management (manage the day-t- day operational aspects of the partnership)
- Commercial Management (manage any commercial elements such as contract change management, managing the budgets, invoicing/ payments) and managing the overall governance (such as ensure proper reporting and quarterly business reviews are being scheduled).

Strategic partners that are new or are striving to collaborate on innovation initiatives should also include the role of Transformation Management (managing ramp up a new partnership and post stabilization manage any continuous improvement or transformation management initiatives).

Continuity of Resources/Onboarding. In business partnerships people come and go. That is why good governance of a business partnership includes processes for ensuring continuity of resources. High-level guidelines include:

- Mutually identify a limited number of personnel who are designated as key personnel for both parties.

- Establish a provision that prevents either party from unilaterally removing, replacing or reassigning key personnel for a specific timeframe. Two to three years is a reasonable duration that enables promotions.
- Develop a process for communicating key personnel changes. For example, establish communications protocols when key personnel become unavailable (e.g., sickness, jury duty, resignation, etc.).
- Establish a provision for replacement of key personnel. This might include having the service provider propose a replacement resource three months prior to the replacement or enabling the company to interview a limited number of potential replacements and approve the new person.
- Use a formal escalation process for personnel mismatch concerns. For example, we have seen employees of one party (typically the company outsourcing) denigrate or verbally abuse the service provider's personnel. This is intolerable. The agreement should have provisions that address escalating improper behavior between the parties or between employees.

Transformation Management

One of the reasons Vested relationships are so successful is that they leverage each partner's expertise to enable each to do more together. Transformation management governance mechanisms support the parties' transition from the current state to the new state—the desired outcomes.

Transformation management differs from relationship management. Think of relationship management as managing the relationship for today, while transformation management helps the partners manage for tomorrow. In a business scenario, this may be about how to collaborate on new products or services or how to implement a new strategy. In a personal relationship, this may be about how to collaborate to save for your first home or transition in managing the evolving needs of growing children.

Exit Management

Face it. Business relationships—and marriages—often fail.

One reason is because the future is unknown: no matter how promising the start or how successful the partnership has been, sometimes partners go in different directions. Conditions can change, people move on, projections fall short, and companies get acquired. For example, a supplier may decide to no longer operate in a certain country. Or a company that works with a stra-tegic supplier is acquired and part of the acquisition plan is for the company to streamline suppliers. The same is true for personal relationships. Longtime friends might drift in different directions because they move to different cities or their interests shift. Or romantic partners could find themselves misaligned due to distrust.

An exit management plan is a commitment to unwind a relationship in a fair and respectful way when circumstances change.

In personal relationships, a pre-nuptial agreement is a form of an exit management plan. The parties think about what will happen in the event of a divorce. Unfortunately, pre-nuptial agreements often have a negative connotation because they are created when one party in a marriage-to-be has more power and wealth that the other. As such, the weaker party is often asked to sign the pre-nup as a way to protect the more powerful party.

That doesn't mean that a husband and wife must sign a prenup before getting married, only that having a plan can provide agreed-upon guidance to make the separation as straightforward and respectful as possible if a breakup happens.

A better way to think of an exit management plan for a personal relationship is for a couple to collaboratively develop an approach they will follow in the event that circumstances change and they grow apart. How will they work together to ensure the kids grow up in separate but harmonious households? How will assets be split based on the contribution to the relationship?

Business relationships should develop a formal exit management plan that is akin to a pre-nuptial agreement in a marriage. In most cases, businesses are already thinking about an exit when they enter a business relationship. For example lawyers almost always include contract clauses such as a termination-for-convenience clause. While these contract clauses are a good start at putting down the termination rights for the parties, the simplistic nature of the clauses fall far short of having a well-thought-out exit management plan designed to mitigate risk when parties do find themselves needing to exit a relationship.

Organizations without a well-thought-out exit management plan can find themselves disappointed with their breakup—or worse, in a lawsuit such as Huy Fong and Underwood Ranches.

It may sound like a silly idea to create an exit management plan, especially if you are in a healthy relationship. But having a good exit management plan with pre-approved processes the parties agree to follow "just in case" can significantly reduce headaches and heartaches by helping partners exit their relationship smoothly. For example, children exposed to bitter conflict after their parents' divorce "are more depressed and show more psychological symptoms than children whose parents have only minor conflict," according to a study published in the *Journal of Child and Family Studies*. And my research following 150+ Vested partnerships has not seen any Vested deal have an acrimonious exit. Simply put, having an exit plan can help you avoid having an overly difficult and taxing exit.

Special Concerns

Today's businesses face an increasing demand to comply with complex, unique needs and business regulations. For example, an outsourcing relationship may call for the service provider to have unique IT data specifications, which may hinder operations if not followed. Or a manufacturing contract may address how the partners will stay on top of the ever-changing regulatory landscape around environmental compliance—especially for organizations that operate in Europe, where the European Union is imposing strict environmental regulations.

When entering into personal relationships, there may be hidden special concerns the partners should put on the table. Does one partner have significant debt from school loans that may prevent the couple from saving enough money for a down payment on a house? Or working through the fact that your family has an unspoken requirement to attend Sunday dinners at Grandma's house.

When special concerns do exist, partners collaborate to identify the best way to manage compliance requirements. In the words of one executive, "When you get it right, you can be in control without being controlling over your partner".

> **Pro Tip:** The University of Tennessee's has published a comprehensive guidebook for designing a governance framework for trading partner relationships. Download at www.vestedway.com.

FROM THEORY TO PRACTICE

In practice, partners create an appropriately scaled governance structure for their unique relationships by building on the four elements of governance outlined on the previous pages. In a personal relationship this might be a simple weekly review of the family schedule or a monthly review of the checkbook. In business relationships, the best practice for large and complex business relationships is to have a formal governance schedule as part of your actual contract. The key is to include all of the elements and co-create how you want to manage the relationship.

When done right, the parties not only agree on—but they also use—the governance mechanisms that help them stay aligned in their relationships.

Let's look at how business relationships apply governance elements in practice. We'll end the chapter seeing how Martin and Maria and their girls created an appropriately tailored governance system to reduce the chaos in their household.

The Insight Behind Rebuilding the I-35 Bridge

Most large construction projects are fraught with changes. Why? It's inevitably hard to imagine all of the what ifs that might occur along the way. For a benchmark, consider that 98% of megaprojects face cost overruns, with the average cost and time overruns relative to a project's original budget and schedule being 70% and 61%, respectively.

The big hairy audacious desired outcomes of the bridge rebuild meant both MnDOT and Flatiron-Manson would need to collaborate well beyond the day-to-day project management team. For example, stakeholders included federal, state and community elected officials, subcontractors, local labor unions and even concerned citizens. To prevent misalignment, mishaps and contractual maladaptation, MnDOT and Flatiron put a heavy emphasis on how they governed their partnership.

This started with the partners devoting several full-time dedicated roles to the partnership's success to provide core governance work to keep the project safe, on time and under budget and with the highest quality standards. MnDOT's Jon Chiglo and Flatiron-Manson's Peter Sanderson represented quintessential two-in-a-box leaders for jointly managing the partnership. Chiglo was MnDOT's project manager while Sanderson was Chiglo's counterpart for Flatiron-Manson.

"Jointly" managing is the key attribute. While there was a formal governance structure the partners knew conventional hierarchical approaches would have created a bottleneck and slowed the process. To achieve success, each man relied on collaborative working protocols to ensure everything was going according to the aggressive project schedule and manage any issues that arose on in a timely manner.

One of the first things the partners did to improve the fast and efficient communication flow was incorporate personal proximity through co-location. A joint co-location space was set up and included the key personnel from MnDOT, Flatiron-Manson, Federal Highway Administration, and OSHA (Occupational Safety and Health Administration). It became easier for them to develop further "2 in a Box" relationships when they were all positioned in the same literal box.

As Chiglo recalled, "Phone conversations and emails aren't sufficient. Communication works better when you're face-to-face. You can read body language, see facial expressions, and just know the other person better. Direct interaction minimizes misunderstandings and saves time."

As the site was small, other key players were located in offices within walking distance of the construction site. The objective was clear: ensure the free flow of information, non-stop collaboration, and timely response to any situations that may arise. As such, the partners cascaded down governance protocols to subcontractors and employees so everyone was on board. For example, the partners routinely infused daily quality checks and progress reports in a collaborative manner with two FIGG team members (the architect) supporting the field inspection efforts and incorporating independent testing located on or near the project site to accomplish lab tests.

On the surface the rigorous quality controls—including duplicative quality checks and over 20 signatures for concrete pouring—could have significantly delayed progress. But the partners knew doing things wrong would likely create even longer delay. So instead of resisting rigorous quality controls, the partners embraced ways to collaboratively and expeditiously integrate quality into their daily ways of working.

A similar philosophy applied to safety. The partners were commitment to a desired outcome of NO lost time and a #1 safety site—which was achieved.

The success of the I-35 bridge rebuild–completed in just 13 months, under budget, and winning almost two dozen quality and industry awards with no significant safety issues—could only be delivered together. It meant challenging the status quo of the way work was done. It also meant embracing (not fighting) the dynamic nature of the project when the unexpected happened. For example, artesian water was discovered in the bottom of a 100-foot test shaft. Or creating a solution for the rock that appeared close to the surface in an area where piles would be driven.

EY and ISS: Innovating to Win

Let's return to the EY-ISS EPIC partnership. Recall from Chapter 3 the partners had some fairly lofty Desired Outcomes to take workplace services to new heights in the pursuit of creating the Workplace of the Future.

While the partners carefully followed Rules 1-4 in order to get to a Vested agreement, applying great governance under Rule 5 would ensure they were on track to deliver the needed transformation to achieve their Desired Outcomes. Collectively the partners had more words in the contract on how they would collaboratively govern the partnership than in the deal points (Rules 2, 3 and 4). The EPIC deal architect team formally embedded governance into the contract using four governance schedules applying proven governance design principles spanning four contractual elements.

Schedule	Core Contents	Governance Design Principles
Schedule 4: Relationship Management	Outlines the partners commitments to how they will manage the relationship.	• Tiered governance structure with defined cadence • Defined management roles with peer-to-peer "2-in-a-Box" communications • Relationship management protocols including monitoring relationship health • Issue resolution management • Continuity of resource and onboarding protocols
Schedule 5: Transformation Management	Outlines the partners commitments to how they will evolving the partnership to meet ongoing businesses need.	• Transition Management Plan for initial ramp-up • Continuous improvement process • Innovation management process • Contractual change management process
Schedule 6: Exit Management Plan	Outlines the partners commitments to how they will collaborate in the event one or both partners need to end the partnership	• Termination notice process • Exit Transition commitments • Exit team, reporting and governance commitments • Commitments and process for transfer or resources if needed
Schedule 9: Special Concerns	Provided guidance and commitments to how the partners will address special concerns associated with the partnership.	• Internal concerns/special requirements (for example, audit rights and requirements for EY's global security policy that is required at every EY location). • External regulatory requirements, including links/references to actual compliance guidelines and regulations (e.g., OSHA, GDPR, etc.) • Responsibility and process for who will monitor/communicate requirement changes

Let's dig deeper into how the EPIC team incorporated four of the governance design principles.

Tiered Structure with Integrated Peer-to-Peer Roles

The EPIC partners adopted a three-tier governance structure (see graphic illustration on following page) that included an Executive Steering Group (highest level), Strategic Level (mid-tier), and Tactical Level/Country Level (lowest

EPIC GOVERNANCE STRUCTURE

GOVERNANCE STRUCTURE

	Service Delivery - Base Services	Service Delivery - Projects	Innovation Managers	Commercial Managers
Executive Steering Group	• Representatives from each party • Standing Neutral			
Strategic Level	• Contract Owner • Contract Manager		• Contract Owner • Contract Manager • Innovation Manager • Transformation and Development Manager	• Procurement • Commercial
Tactical Level/ Country	• Country Facilities Management Coordinators • Country Key Account Manager		• Innovation Manager • Transformation and Development Manager	
Processes	Reporting & Performance Measurement	Reporting & Performance Measurement	Transition	Pricing Model Governance
	Risk Management	Risk Management	Innovation & Continuous Improvements	Change Management
	Continuity regarding involved individuals			
	Escalation process			
	Measures on termination of the agreement			

tier). Each tier has defined members with clearly defined roles, agenda and cadence.

Within the structure, the partners agreed on 12 full-time key governance personnel that were mapped as six peer-to-peer "2-in-a-Box" relationships, meaning that for each key governance role, there was a counterpart within the other organization. The 2-in-a-Box partners are expected to collaborate with their peers to create the optimal way to accomplish the work associated with their role, including resolving any issues at the *lowest possible level*. By design this empowers 2-in-a-Box partners to solve problems at the lowest level with a "no-blame" culture. The approach that keeps the partners from being tempted to escalating issues to internal managers without putting in the proper time to do a root cause analysis at the lowest level.

Escalation Management

The partners formalized an escalation management process as part of their contractual commitments to each other. The process is supplemented by a five page appendix to the governance schedule which "sets out the process for addressing issues arising for either Party."

EPIC ESCALATION MANAGEMENT

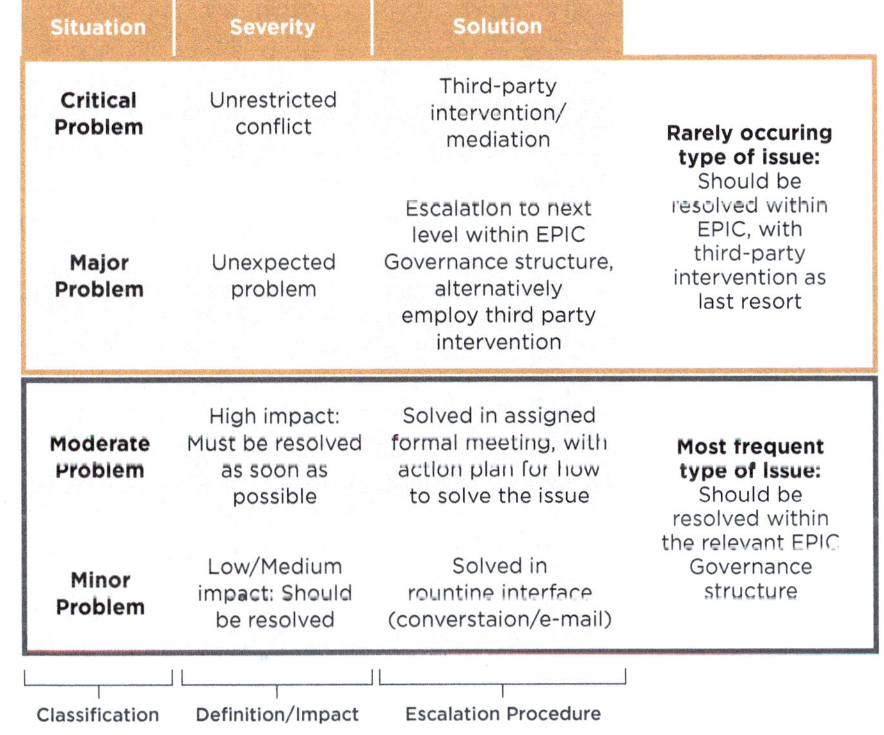

Per the appendix the "Parties acknowledge that it is critical to the success of the Parties' relationship that the Escalation Procedure is complied with to the extent possible in order to mitigate any misalignment of interests that may arise during the Term." A key function of the process is to help team members facilitate healthy issue resolution at the lowest level and promoting a no-blame culture using root cause analysis. The process also provides guidelines for how team members should escalate unresolved issues in a timely manner to the appropriate "2-in-a-Box" governance team leaders who are best able to resolve the issue.

Innovation Management

Achieving EPIC's Desired Outcomes would require innovation. For this reason the partners devoted an entire schedule to how they would find potential Ponies through the collaborative efforts that would create value for the partners.

One of Ponies that delivered both cost savings and employee satisfaction for EY and more profit for ISS came from reimagining how EY delivered IT support services.

The EY IT department had a high volume of tech-related end-user questions such as handing out chargers, setting up laptops and phones, and solving a wide range of Tier 1 IT issues that are relatively easy to solve. Many of these requests were something a less expensive ISS team member could do with a little training. The idea was for ISS to create a highly visible and service-minded Tech Lobby to support the "First Line of IT." EY employees now receive assistance by simply stopping by the Tech lobby rather than submitting a ticket and waiting online. Since launching, the Tech Lobby services have expanded and now include almost 90% of end-user IT-related tasks.

The solution has helped EY by freeing up its high-end IT workers to focus on other, more complex IT-related work. End users also get quicker, more efficient service. ISS also wins with higher revenue and expanded service. It's a win-win-win.

The Bottom-Line Benefits

The bottom line for EY and ISS? Bottom-line improvements for both partners. In the first three years after making the shift to Vested the partnership delivered year-on-year annual savings exceeding baseline targets by 50-100% for EY, with EY needing only six team members managing $20 million in end-to-end workplace services spend. ISS is also a winner with a long-term win-win contract that has led to 51% increase in revenue and 50%+ increase in profit margin growth due to incentives.

The partnership also led to happier employees and lower turnover. EPIC adopted a global standard called "Net Promoter Score," which is a satisfaction measurement asking, "How likely would you recommend working for ISS on the EPIC team?" The NPS metric has a scale of -100 (would never recommend) to +100 (would always recommend). When EPIC first adopted the metric, their score was just over +20, which is considered typical for a company in the services industry. Under the Vested partnership NPS performance has increased to +58—considered world-class in a services industry such as outsourced facilities operations.

McDonald's Rapid Response

McDonald is a behemoth in the quick-service restaurant category. With over 40,000 locations around the world, McDonald's serves upwards to 60 million people a day. Food safety has been a top priority for McDonald's for many decades, starting with its founder Ray Kroc's unwavering demand for food safety. After an E. coli outbreak in 1982 McDonald's and its system of supply chain partners made a commitment to create bulletproof food safety processes and protocols.

In short, they went back to the drawing board to see how they could govern their supply chain—with their supply chain partners—to create the world's safest supply chain.

Key meat processing suppliers such as Lopez Foods and Keystone Meats openly share their rigorous quality processes. Ed Sanchez, CEO of Lopez Foods, posted a video highlighting his company's hourly 100-point quality inspection process on McDonald's website. Similarly, Keystone Meats opened up its doors for a USA Today tour, which revealed McDonald's food is "safer than school kids' lunch" because McDonald's tests their beef up to 10 times more than companies selling beef to school programs.

If you do that math, it's statistically amazing the level of food safety McDonald's has achieved. Hundreds of millions of people have been served without food safety issues between the 1980s and 2024.

When people started getting sick after eating McDonald's Quarter Pounder burgers in 2024, McDonald's took it very seriously and stopped selling the popular burgers in states where there were reported issues. The culprit? E. coli

E. coli is spread through fecal-oral transmission. For McDonald's, shit literally happened. The fast-food giant was ready, responding quickly in collaboration with the Food and Drug Administration, something not easy to do when you don't know where to start. Was it the beef burgers? Or an ingredient that went into the Quarter Pounder? And was the issue in the McDonald's restaurants or somewhere along the many stops in the supply chain?

McDonald's robust governance "system" operates with a Systems First mindset where supply chain partners operate with a spirit of collaboration and transparency. The swift response uncovered the culprit: Slivered onions from a supplier, Taylor Farms, tested positive for E. Coli. The onions, also sold at other restaurant chains, were ultimately blamed for 104 illnesses, 34 hospitalizations and one death.

Joe Erlinger, President of McDonald's USA, took responsibility in a video statement. "I know that our relationship is built on trust. You trust us to serve you safe food every time. On behalf of the McDonald's system, I want you to hear from me: we are sorry. For those customers affected, you have my commitment that, led by our values: we will make this right."

Note the word choice Erlinger used—the McDonald's "system." That world-class governance *system* enabled McDonald's to respond quickly when business happened.

How quickly? An investigation into the outbreak by the Centers for Disease Control and Prevention and Food and Drug Administration was closed after five weeks. Because McDonald's has been a pioneer in food traceability far superseding current standards, it was well positioned to address the problem quickly, and it did.

Compare how McDonald's handled their E. coli outbreak to how Boar's Head managed its own outbreak. Boar's Head, an iconic deli meat brand that dates to 1905, was faced with a similar situation when a listeria outbreak caused 10 deaths and dozens of hospitalizations. The culprit? A Virginia Boar's Head plant which violated numerous federal regulations "including instances of mold, insects, liquid dripping from ceilings, and meat and fat residue on walls, floors and equipment."

In the wake of the damning US Department of Agriculture report, Boar's Head closed the plant and established a Food Safety Advisory Council. Additional inspection reports released in 2025 revealed further unsanitary conditions at several other Boar's Head plants, including one inspector who noted "general filth" at an Indiana plant.

Where the investigation into the McDonald's outbreak was over in five weeks, the Boar's Head investigation started in July and dragged on for more than four months. And, unlike McDonalds leadership, no Boar's Head top-tier leaders from the company personally came forward to take accountability. Rather messages from the company were simply signed "Boar's Head."

Following the outbreak, many longtime customers stopped buying Boar's Head products. And thousands of restaurants, grocery stores and delis that used or sold their products lost trust in the brand.

SUCCESS ON THE HOME FRONT

After one more missed practice and another last-minute take-out dinner, Martin and Maria called a family meeting.

"Girls, come down. Let's have a talk. And no phones."

OK...

Maria started the conversation. "This has been a really hectic couple months, and it just feels like we're all running in different directions. It's been tough to keep track of everyone's schedules. And because of that, there's been a lot of scrambling."

"We gotta get on the same page here," Martin added. "It's been really tough to understand what everyone's up to in a given week, or even in a given day."

"I know my soccer schedule has been really demanding," Ava said. "It's been a big commitment with practices picking up as we entered the playoffs and end-of-season tournaments."

"And I've had more ballet lessons than usual as we get ready for our recital," Liv added.

The parents paused. "This isn't about one specific thing. We want you to participate in the things you love to do. What we are talking about is the need for us to all stay on the same page so there are no surprises and missed commitments. That's why we wanted to try something new," Maria said.

With that, she pulled out a whiteboard she borrowed from the office and a bunch of markers. "We have an idea we want to run by you. What if every Sunday we have a family planning session and map out the week? Each person can add their school schedule, practice and events, homework deadlines, work responsibilities and anything else we need to remember. From there, we could even map out a dinner schedule for the week. What does everyone think?"

Ava had a question. "What about things like invitations to go to a friend's house? Sometimes those pop up on that day."

"I guess we'd have to check the calendar to see if we can make it work," Maria said. One thing that Maria was adamant about: both parents have to agree before saying yes to an invitation. No pitting one parent against the other. Maria was used to getting caught in the middle of functional silos at work and didn't want it happening at home.

Liv had a question. "What if we have a schedule conflict between me and Ava? How do we figure out whose event gets priority?"

"Good question," Martin said. "You girls should try to solve it between the two of you. If you can't figure it out, that's when you should ask me and Mom."

Martin took the lead next. "You girls have great questions. But they seem to be all about the fun stuff you are doing. There's more to it than just keeping track of your soccer, ballet and friend events. We want to make sure we are also keeping track of your homework and chores, too."

The girls' excitement waned.

Maria jumped in. "We've been thinking we don't want to make keeping track of everything just another chore. So we have an idea we want your help with."

The parents shared an incentive system they learned about from a mutual friend where the children had gotten points for chores completed, and after accumulating enough points from chores, the children were rewarded with a toy of their choice.

"We know you're too big for toys but we want to try to find something that will be rewarding for you. Can you think of something that would be an incentive you would like to earn if you do a good job of keeping the calendar updated, your homework done and your chores complete?"

The ever-enthusiastic Liv didn't hesitate. "I'd love to earn crochet kits of some of my favorite characters!"

Ava was a bit slower to jump in. "I think I would like movie tickets and gift cards I can use for when I go shopping with my friends."

Liv chimed in. "Can we start now? And can we pick our own marker colors? If so, I choose green!"

"Of course you can pick your own marker color, but before we start I have one more thing for us to think about," said Martin. "Your Mom and I have been thinking it would be good to spend more family time together. What do you think if one weekend day a month, we plan something fun together as a family? We could spend the day at the beach in the summer or go ice-skating in the winter."

"Can we go to the Nutcracker ballet for Christmas?" squealed Liv. "It would be so amazing to see professional ballerinas!"

"Let's start by making a wish list of good ideas and then we can come up with a fair way to decide," said Maria.

With that, the family got to work creating their color-coded calendar with their commitments.

They had a communication cadence in the form of weekly meetings, as well as issue resolution management through the girls' system for handling issues before raising them to their parents. They also created a fair decision process for deciding how to pick their monthly Sunday Funday family day.

On top of that, the girls ranked every week with a happy face scale—either a smiley face, a frown face, or a neutral face.

WEEKLY PLAN

	Sun	Mon	Tue	Wed	Thu	Fri	Sat
Martin	Sunday Funday: Bike around lake 3-6 Prep for weekly dinners	Work from Home Take Liv to ballet	Office 7-4:30 Take Liv to ballet	Office 8-5	Office 8-5 Work Dinner	Work from Home	Ava's soccer game
Maria	Sunday Funday: Bike around lake 3-6 Prep for weekly dinners	Office 8-5	Office 8-5	Office 7:30-3:30 Pick up Ava at school/ take to soccer	Office 7:30-4:30 Take Liv to ballet	Work from Home Drop off Liv on way to dinner	Ava's soccer game
Ava School		Study for Math test Science project	Math test Science project	Science project due	Study for History test	History test	
Sports		Soccer 4-5:30 (get ride from friend)		Soccer 4-5:30			10-11 soccer game
Fun	Sunday Funday: Bike around lake					Movie with friends (ride with friends)	Karaoke night with friends at house
Chores	3-6 Prep for weekly dinners	Dishes	Garbage Night	Dishes			Clean Room
Liv School		Daily Homework	Daily Homework	Permission Slips Due	Daily Homework		
Sports		Ballet 5-6	Ballet 5-6		Ballet 5-6		
Fun	Sunday Funday: Bike around lake					Sleep over at Sally's	2pm - Back from Sally's (Sally's mom to bring home)
Chores	3-6 Prep for weekly dinners	Set Table	Set Table Dishes	Set Table	Set Table Dishes		Clean Room
Dinner Plans	6:30pm	6:30pm	6:30pm	6:30pm	Martin/ Liv Get get take out dinner on way back from ballet	Marie/ Martin Date Night	Pizza

Every month, Martin and Maria reviewed the month's progress and provided a "happy home" score, a chance to provide a relationship health check. The family stuck to the plan—and the positive change soon became completely obvious. The system turned chaos into a constructive process for managing the family's commitments. The usual scramble had become more orderly and calm. Ava and Liv got into the swing of things to check with each other before requesting to add unscheduled outings with their friends. And they loved earning their incentives.

Maria and Martin were proud parents. The kids stopped pitting their parents against each other.

And the whole family enjoyed their planned Sunday Funday outing to their town's annual carnival.

Together the family had a real plan. They could tackle anything that emerged.

TOOLKIT QUICK REFERENCE GUIDE

Governance Processes, Protocols and Mechanisms that provide insight versus oversight

- **Purpose:** To design governance Processes, Protocols and Mechanisms that provide insight versus oversight
- **When to Use:** Ideally done at the onset on a relationship to set expectations on how you will manage the relationship. However, it's never too late for rethink your governance if there is friction in the relationship
- **Components:** Relationship management, transformation management, exit management, and special concerns/compliance management
- **Guideline:** There is no one size fits all governance. Work through the checklist and discuss which areas apply to relationship and co-create the processes, protocols and mechanisms you will use to stay aligned in yrou relationship
- **Output:** The output will vary based on the formality of your relationship. Partners in contractual relationship should create a governance schedule for their partnership that is part of their contract.
- **Perverse Incentives it Prevents:** Strategic Drift; Shading; New Sheriff in Town

10

Don't Cherry-pick the Rules

Following the Vested Five Rules can help ordinary people achieve extraordinary results.

Like rebuilding the I-35 bridge under budget with award-winning quality levels in less than a year. Or helping Island Health Authority and their Hospitalists get past a bitter contract dispute and turn an adversarial and toxic culture into a collaborative and trusting relationship where the partners are focused on maximizing patient care given Island Health's limited budget.

But getting the full potential of Vested requires partners to fully adhere to all five rules. Not one rule. Not three rules. All five rules.

Why? Because the rules work together to form a high-performing system.

SYSTEMS THINKING

Systems thinking represents a way to make sense of how the parts of a system work together for the greater whole.

There are all sorts of systems, including economic systems, biological systems, social systems and political systems. Your own body is a good example of a complex system. While each organ has a function, the individual parts are interconnected and interdependent on the other parts. The heart pumps blood, but it relies on the lungs for oxygen, the brain for regulation, and the muscles for demand signals. No single part can thrive—or even survive—on its own; each must work in concert with the others. When one element is out of balance, such as when the liver fails or the immune system overreacts, the entire body feels the consequences. True vitality comes not from the strength of any one organ, but from the seamless coordination and alignment of all parts working together toward a common purpose—life itself.

Dr. Russell Ackoff, an early pioneer of systems thinking, explains, "A system is never the sum of its parts; it's the product of their interaction," meaning that the performance of a system depends not on how individual parts perform separately, but on how they work together.

Later, Peter Senge popularized systems thinking in his best-selling business book *The Fifth Discipline*. Donella Meadows, a pioneering environmental scientist and educator, further propelled the concepts to a much broader audience in her book *Thinking in Systems*. Today, Meadows' book is considered one of the most influential works on systems thinking. As she wrote, "A system is an interconnected set of elements that is coherently organized in a way that achieves something. If you look at that definition closely for a minute, you can see that a system must consist of three kinds of things: *elements, interconnections,* and a *function or purpose.*"

A fundamental point of systems thinking is that a carefully crafted system can unlock latent powers when intentionally structured to do so. But the system must be designed properly. To illustrate the power of systems thinking Meadows used the example of a Slinky toy. The toy appears to magically walk downstairs by itself. All that is needed is to take it out of the box, put it in the right place, and let it go with a gentle push. That gentle push releases the energy that is latent in the toy's structure, keeping it moving. The careful design of the Slinky's system makes it possible for the slinky to "walk" down stairs by itself.

Vested, similarly, works best as a system—it has elements (five rules), interconnections (the rules working in tandem), and a function (to help partners win together).

I'll be the first to admit relationships aren't the same as a metal coiled toy. They do, however, in essence form their own systems and therefore need mechanisms in place to keep their unique system running at peak performance. When applied to collaborative partnerships, systems-first thinking promotes partners to work together to solve problems that yield the maximum benefit for the group, rather than making decisions that prioritize short-term interests. Ray Kroc intuitively got the concept of systems-first thinking.

BUILT TO LAST: MCDONALD'S SYSTEM

Many businesses enter into strategic partnerships with intent they will last. McDonald's is credited with having one of the most successful supply chains in the world in large part because they have a conscious strategy to create strong relationships with their most important suppliers that are built to last. Many of McDonald's most strategic supply chain relationships are decades long. Take for example McDonald's and Coke. They have been together for over 70 years in a symbiotic relationship that has helped both be better.

A key reason McDonald's has such a successful supply chain relationship is that they have built a system that promotes staying tightly aligned with strategic suppliers. Ray Kroc, the driving force behind the global growth of McDonald's, formed partnerships with owner/operators and suppliers so solid and so dependable that they became known as the "System." The System's promise? When McDonald's succeeds, the partners also succeed. In the System, everyone succeeds.

And when business happens? At the heart of their success is a "System First" philosophy to solve problems that help them create a competitive advantage through their supply chain partnerships. System First thinking leads to some behaviors that are hard to imagine in the "real world," such as competing suppliers collaborating on how to improve the products they sell to McDonald's. Or a company creating a new product and then teaching competitors how to make it—all because it's good for the System.

It's no wonder that Gartner consistently ranks McDonald's as one of the best supply chains in the world.

McDonald's System First mentality has been in place since Ray Kroc founded the company. In the case of the McDonald's and Coke relationship, it started when Kroc called Claude "Waddy" Pratt, Coca-Cola's district manager for fountain sales, with a business proposition. Pratt traveled to Des Plaines, Ill., northwest of Chicago, to meet Kroc at his yet-to-open restaurant location.

"I'm opening a restaurant and I want to sell Coke because it's the best goddamn product there is."

But Kroc had a plan much grander than the one yet-to-be-opened restaurant; open up restaurant locations all over the world and serve Coca-Cola in each of them.

"We'll put Coke in every store that you open," Pratt said.

That was it. McDonald's and Coke began their relationship with a handshake and a promise during an impromptu meeting in a parking lot.

That was in 1955. To this day, the companies still don't have a formal contract.

Even without a contract, the partners made—and keep—a commitment to giving the best to each other. As McDonald's grew and opened in new locations, Coca-Cola often helped with offices and logistics. And McDonald's has its own division devoted to Coke.

McDonald's and Coke work together to make sure Coke is extra refreshing at your local McDonald's. No, your taste buds aren't deceiving you: Coca-Cola just tastes better at McDonald's. That sip of Coca-Cola at McDonald's doesn't taste better *just because*, it tastes better because the brands have made a decades-long commitment, through science and data and marketing, to uphold their collaboration and win together at every turn.

For starters, the way Coke syrup is delivered—not in plastic bags, but in stainless steel tanks—makes a big difference in ensuring freshness. But the list goes on all the way down to the straw, which is slightly wider than a typical straw *"so all that Coke taste can hit your taste buds."*

I spent several weeks studying the McDonald's System and "Systems First" thinking as part of my research and profiled how their Systems First governance mechanisms has allowed their strategic relationships to grow and respond to challenges and opportunities together in the book *Vested: How P&G, McDonald's and Microsoft are Redefining Winning in Business Relationships.*

UNDERSTANDING A SYSTEM'S POTENTIAL

One of the ways I teach organizations to consider the power of systems thinking is through the interconnectedness of the steps in an assembly line. Let's say a company has four steps in the manufacturing of a widget and each step has a goal to have a 95% quality level for their step. That sounds like a high standard!

But if each step has a 95% quality level the total system performance is actually only 81%.

Why? Because 5% waste occurs *at each step* in the manufacturing process and the end result is an *accumulation* of waste far greater that 5%. In fact—total waste is almost 20%, which is quite poor. Let's look at the math on how this works, considering the first step in the process starts with 1000 raw material widgets that will go through each step in the manufacturing process.

- Step 1—starts with 1,000 units. At a 95% quality rate only 950 units will pass to the next step.
- Step 2 —starts with 950 units. At a 95% quality rate only 902 units pass to the next step.
- Step 3—starts with 902 units. At a 95% quality rate only 857 units pass to the next step.
- Step 4—starts with 857 units. At a 95% quality rate only 814 units pass to the next step.

Thus—the total system performance is just over 81% and can be predicted by multiplying the quality level at each step (95% x 95% x 95% x 95% = 81.4%).

Let's use that same analogy to look at the potential system performance from following all five of the Vested rules. For fun let's say that you can score a partnership on how well they follow each Vested rule using a five-point scale. When you are fully following a rule you get a score of 5 and when you are not following that rule at all there is a score of 1. So if you implement all five rules at optimal levels the total system potential would be 3,125.

$$5 \times 5 \times 5 \times 5 \times 5 = 3{,}125$$

Consider if one of those values isn't five. Maybe Rule 4 isn't fully activated. Let's give that rule a score of three. Now the system performance is 1,875.

$$5 \times 5 \times 5 \times 3 \times 5 = 1{,}875$$

Now let's see the impact when Rule 2 is only activated to a score of 2 on the 5-point scale. In this case the total system performance goes down to 750.

$$5 \times 2 \times 5 \times 3 \times 5 = 750$$

When I say that leveraging the Vested five rules provides the power to unite where 1+1=11, this is what I mean. When we focus on total systems performance instead of individual elements, true transformation can happen. But on the flip side, it's easy to be tempted to cherry-pick the rules that resonate for you. But where will that leave your collaboration? How might things go sideways or lose steam?

Can you get benefits from doing only one or two of the rules? Absolutely. But if you don't follow *all* of the rules, don't expect a preferable outcome. And definitely don't expect to achieve your impossible. The magic of Vested comes through partners working in harmony following the same set of rules—the Vested five rules. Not one rule. Or three rules. Or even four rules. Both (or all!) partners following all five rules.

BEWARE OF CHEATING ON THE RULES

At the beginning of Part 2, I shared the importance of having rules in games. In practice, I find many partners are tempted to cheat on the rules. Why? Psychologists would say because it is people's nature to cheat.

Dan Ariely, professor of psychology and behavioral economics at Duke University, explains that people talk themselves into believing it is OK to cheat or steal—at least sometimes. He has run experiments with about 30,000 people on the psychology of cheating and found that while very few people lie or cheat a lot, almost everyone does those things a little bit. It's basically a bug in our moral code that affects our personal lives and business relationships, and we're pretty adept at it. Ariely describes those experiments and the results in his book *The (Honest) Truth about Dishonesty: How We Lie to Everyone—Especially Ourselves.*

People cheat in lots of ways, both small and big. They tell "white lies" to spare another person's feelings. They move an extra space in a board game when no one's looking. They lie about not skipping ahead on a popular streaming show they promised they'd wait and watch together. They get the test answers from another student's sheet.

And yes, businesses aren't always faithful in relationships. You've likely been a victim of late payments or missed shipments. Perhaps they were honest mistakes. Or perhaps it was the results of shading behavior in an effort to get even when one party felt slighted.

Ariely makes an interesting point when observing cheating; it's often contagious. Ariely's research shows that group dynamics and behavior have a powerful effect on each individual. To make the point Ariely points to the downfall of Enron. A person that consulted for Enron while the company was in a state of rapid demise said he "hadn't seen anything sinister going on." In Ariely's interview he found people like the consultant in fact had fully bought into the worldview that Enron was an innovative leader of the new economy right up until the moment the story was all over the headlines.

Even more surprising, Ariely relates that once the story of Enron's corruption broke, there was a sense of shock that people had "failed to see the signs all along."

Ariely calls this phenomenon "wishful blindness" and the result is that groups can easily create a culture that tolerates cheating. Case in point is when one party in a business deal proceeds in a conversation with the phrase "nothing personal, it's business."

This temptation to take advantage (or even screw over the other person!) often leads to the partner who feels slighted turning to more adversarial behaviors themselves.

The tendency to get even is so common it is researched by psychologists and game theorists around the world. Their finding? Cheating is met with cheating, leading to a downward spiral of negative tit-for-tat behaviors. Ariely and other leading academics points to the need to find ways to prevent the negative cycle that so often leads to us-versus-them behaviors.

So how can you prevent the cycle? By recognizing early warning signs.

Tools of the Trade

Are you in business-to-business relationship? Visit www.vestedway.com to take the 10 Elements self-assessment to determine how well your existing agreements stacks up against the Vested Five Rules and 10 contractual elements.

COMMON AILMENTS

Recall in Part 2 I shared common perverse incentives from not following each rule. I think of these perverse incentives as "ailments" that can inflict relationships. The ailments are often an early warning sign there is cheating on the Vested rules.

Let's review the most common ailments that occur when you cheat on the Vested Five Rules.

Rule 1 Ailments

- **The Activity Trap.** One of the biggest perverse incentives stemming from traditional transactional agreements is the Activity Trap. Under a transactional approach, trading partners are paid for every transaction (per hour, per unit, per shipment, per mile, etc.) The more transactions performed, the more revenue for the trading partner. There is no incentive to reduce the number of non-value-added transactions because such a reduction would result in lower revenue.
- **The Honeymoon Effect.** At the beginning of any relationship, the parties go through a honeymoon stage: your partner can do no wrong. But that stage often makes way for frustration and disappointment. Partners initially jump through hoops to make their partner feel happy, but over time the extra effort wanes and the relationship cools. Things happen that make you question yourself or your partner … and in some cases, to wonder if someone else might be a better partner instead. When the Honeymoon Effect kicks in, it is frustrating because you want to get the magic back.

Rule 2 Ailments

- **The Outsourcing Paradox.** The Outsourcing Paradox happens when you recruit an expert to help you and then tell them how to do the work. This is especially common in outsourcing relationships where the company outsourcing work develops a "perfect" set of tasks, frequencies, and measures, but paradoxically gets no input from the supplier it has hired as the expert. Thus, the "perfect" statement of work (SOW) or specification then contractually obligates the supplier to perform the work as told— effectively locking the buying organization into a status quo way of working.
- **The Junkyard Dog Factor.** The Junkyard Dog Factor occurs when one of the partners hunkers down and draws a line in the sand, claiming that certain processes simply "must" be done the way they have always

been done. Junkyard Dogs are often known for being "anal retentive" or "micromanagers," which almost always leads to duplication of effort and frustration.

Rule 3 Ailments

- **Driving Blind Disease.** You might suffer from the "Driving Blind Disease" if you are not actively using metrics that monitor your progress. In the rush to strike a deal, companies often don't take the time to outline how they will measure success. While most business relationships address this head-on with scorecards or dashboards, driving blind disease is fairly common in personal relationships.
- **OKR Overload.** It's common to for teams and functional silos to get lost in the weeds and have too many metrics. Additionally, different teams or workers often have conflicting goals (recall the cheese company!). When this happens it creates a culture that does more harm than good because team members are working at odds with each other.

Rule 4 Ailments

- **The Activity Trap.** If you let the Activity Trap slip in from not following Vested Rule 1, you will likely see it rear its ugly head in Rule 4. Why? If money can make you do stupid things, thinking about money through a transactional lens can make people do really stupid things. A transactional mindset is to charge for work completed (per unit, per hour). While transactional pricing is easy, it can easily create a perverse incentive because one party can easily take advantage of the other.
- **Zero-Sum Game.** There is often an urge to game the system and win at the expense of your partner when the pie is truly limited. This is especially true when there is not a relationship and the nature of the interaction is transactional. We often think of zero-sum games in business relationships (if I use my power and negotiation savvy, I will get a lower price, which in turn lowers your profit). But often in business there is a way to turn a zero-sum game into a non-zero-sum game (e.g., collaborate to create efficiencies which lower the cost structure and the savings can be shared).
- **Penny-Wise and Pound-Foolish.** This is one of the easiest ailments to identify. It happens when a company or individual chooses business partners based purely on costs. When we make decisions based only on the price tag, we can find ourselves continually searching for lower-price options—leading to lost trust, weakened commitments, and long-term trouble for the sake of short-term gain.

- **Sandbagging.** Using incentives is a powerful way to drive behavior. But incentives can backfire if not used properly. With sandbagging, a partner attempts to achieve just the amount of improvement needed to get the incentive. The wrong incentives, in essence, can cause parties to chase the wrong goals instead of achieving its best.

Rule 5 Ailments

- **Strategic Drift.** Strategic drift occurs when partners don't work to maintain their relationship or put in the work needed to keep abreast and update their strategic priorities as business happens. Strategic Drift often occurs when one (or all) partners get complacent. Strategic drift is akin to the seven-year itch in a marriage which suggests marital happiness and satisfaction decline around seven years into a relationship. The same kind of itch can happen in successful business relationships too.
- **Shading.** Recall the concept of shading as popularized by Nobel Laureate Oliver Hart. Shading is prevalent in relationships where unanticipated costs, budget overruns, schedule delays and reimbursement refusals occur; an aggrieved supplier may try to recoup losses by, for example, replacing the expensive A-team with its less costly C-team. Or an aggrieved buyer may hold back on payments or squeeze the supplier for a price reduction.
- **New Sheriff in Town.** New sheriffs often ride into town with the goal to shake things up. In some cases, this can be a good thing. In many cases the new sheriff does not take time to understand how the existing system works and what is a good change versus a negative change. And when this happens, one or both of the partners find themselves in chaos in the name of change for the sake of change itself.

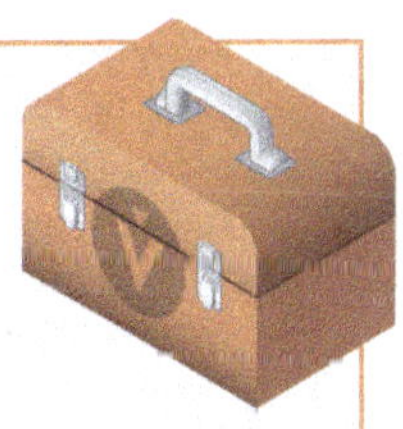

Tools of the Trade

Are you in a business-to-business relationship? Visit www.vestedway.com to take the 12 Ailments self-assessment to determine to what extent your relationship may be suffering from the most common ailments.

STOP CHEATING; START CO-CREATING

The easiest way to stop what is ailing you in your partnership is to stop cheating on the rules that are causing your ailments and double down on co-creating how you will follow the rules with your partner.

Start by taking stock of your partnership. Which rules are you cheating on? Which ailments are you suffering from?

For EY, the Vested journey started when Magnus Kuchler started to challenge the value the company was getting from their outsourcing efforts in the Nordics. Kuchler—an expert in outsourcing—wanted EY to think bigger and achieve more value from our outsourcing efforts.

At Kuchler's nudging, EY started by doing soul searching on their existing ways of working with their two primary facilities management suppliers. A deep dive review of EY's contracts showed the contracts fell into the classic WIIFMe trap, with contract terms that were more one-sided and in favor of EY. One contract referenced "Supplier shall" 92 times, whereas "EY shall" was cited only 16 times. The contracts also had a one-sided termination for convenience that created a perverse incentive for suppliers to not be willing to invest in innovation and continuous improvement.

A key part of EY's soul searching was critically reviewing the ailments that were inflicted them and digging below the surface to understanding where and how they were cheating on each of the Vested Five Rules. The following graphic is the team's self-assessment against how well their existing contract followed the Vested Five Rules and associated 10 contractual elements.

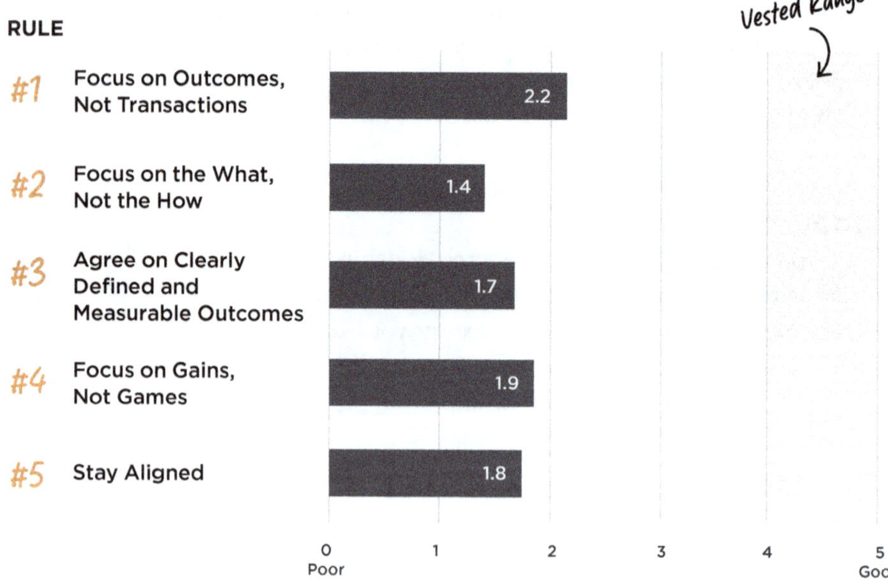

The review helped EY see they had far more potential to create value than the traditional ways of working. The result? The launch of a Request for Partner to determine which of their current partners would be the best fit for helping EY transform their workplace services operations.

After a 12-week process to pick the best fit partner, EY picked their sherpa: ISS. The partners formed a cross-organizational/cross-functional team commitment to resetting their relationship by going through each of the Vested Five Rules and rethinking how they worked. Consider the before and after results with regards to closing the gaps against each rule.

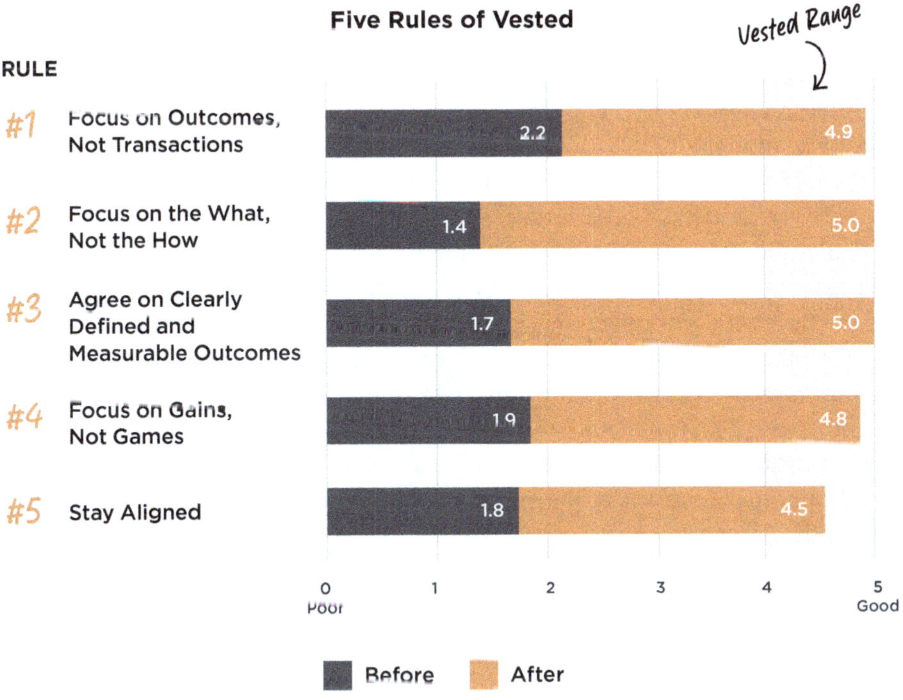

It's easy to see from the chart how far the team came in terms of following the rules.

Let's put their efforts through the "systems performance" math test.

Prior to going through the Vested process, their system performance was 16.5.

$$2.17 \times 1.4 \times 1.67 \times 1.86 \times 1.75 = 16.5$$

After going through the Vested process, the system performance rose to 2,673.

$$4.92 \times 5 \times 5 \times 4.83 \times 4.5 = 2{,}673$$

That boost in system performance is paying off. Today their collaboration is helping them revolutionize workplace services and build a working world. Rather than a transactional fee-for-service contract, they now operate under a formal relational contract with a shared risk/shared reward outcome-based economic model.

As highlighted in chapter 5, a win for EY is a win for ISS—and vice versa; they are *vested* in each other's success.

The results have been transformational. EY has realized year-over-year cost savings exceeding baseline targets by 50-100% while also increasing end-user satisfaction with workplace services to record high levels. ISS is also winning with a long-term contract where they have increased their revenue by 51% and a 50%+ increase in profit margin from earning incentives. And employees are winning too. EY employees have a world-class workplace and ISS employees enjoy working with a client that brings out their best—achieving the highest Net Promoter Score for employee engagement across all of ISS's thousand+ accounts.

Now that is a powerful system!

Conclusion

Us vs. Them?
This side vs. that side?
With us or against us?

We began this book by considering the tensions and divisions holding us back. Let's close, instead, with possibility.

I hope this book has not only inspired you with stories of the art of possible, but it also motivates you to take the needed next steps to transform your own relationships to achieve your "impossible," whether you are rebuilding bridges or trying to strengthen a valued personal relationship. And I hope the book—and tips and tools—become the starting point on your own Vested journey.

SHIFTING FROM ME TO WE

As you take the steps to get and stay Vested with your most important partners, here is some final guidance.

First, getting and staying Vested starts with being humble enough to recognize that "We" is more powerful than "Me." It is a recognition that together you can achieve more than by going it alone. Sometimes you need a Sherpa to reach your highest potential.

If you are seeking out a new partner, consider how you can lay a strong foundation by purposefully choosing to lean into trust and transparency to give your relationship the much-needed fuel to get out of the gate on good footing. Actively seek out others with a good cultural fit: not a partner who is exactly like you in terms of race, religion or political views. But a partner with the skills and insights to help you achieve your impossible. Someone who will help you find a Pony where others simply see a pile of manure.

And if you are in an existing relationship and feel stuck? Recall the powerful story of how Island Health and the Hospitalists turned around their relationship by putting the trust elephant in the room and openly discussing how negative behaviors created a slippery slope, leading to an adversarial, opaque and even toxic relationship.

If you're not sure where to start, consider using resources such as the Compatibility and Trust assessment and a neutral facilitator to create a safe environment for having difficult discussions. I'd be happy to recommend one of the neutrals trained in the Vested methodology.

Regardless of your starting point, your journey requires a true commitment to play by the rules. A commitment to play the long game versus being tempted to cheat on the rules for a short-term win at your partner's expense. Consider reflecting on the list of common perverse incentives that creep into relationships that don't follow the rules. Openly discuss how cheating on the rules is holding you back and use the tools I have shared to help you co-create a better way—a Vested way—of working.

MY INVITATION TO YOU

I realize you are constantly being bombarded with information from emails, apps, newsfeeds and Netflix—and yet, you had time to finish reading this book. That tells me that you truly care about collaboration and you want more out of the relationships in your lives.

For those who want to dig in deeper and drive real change in your most precious relationships, I encourage you to go beyond this book and join the Vested movement. I encourage you to share your notes with suppliers and teammates. Consider hosting a lunch and learn at work and brainstorm how Vested could improve cross-functional collaboration. Or starting a book club to discuss how the rules can improve how you collaborate on community initiatives. Better yet, pass on your highlighted book to a local politician and encourage them to choose a better way to work that builds a better community.

For those who want a deep dive, enroll in one of my Executive Education courses at the University of Tennessee—ideally bringing your partner with you (learn more at www.vestedway.com).

If you find yourself feeling friction in a personal relationship, consider sharing your learnings with your family members to create a healthier home life. Start by reflecting on how Maria and Martin adapted the Vested Five Rules to help them get on the same page when it came to chores and saving for their dream home. Set aside time like Martin and Maria over a date night or Sunday morning coffee to discuss how some of the tools shared in the book can reduce the friction you might be having. Or host a brainstorming session with your kids to create a new system to help you get control of the chaos in your house.

Whatever your journey, I urge you not to fall into the trap of doing nothing. I am 100% confident that you will be successful if you apply the concepts I have shared. Use your notes and the tools to develop your own playbook, preferably with your partner. And when (not if!) you are successful, please share on your social media sites (using #VesstedWay) so both myself and others can learn from and be inspired by your success.

Here's to achieving your impossible!

Afterword
The Vested Story: From Research to Relevance

The Vested movement represents two decades of studying the art, science and practice of how to get collaboration right in relationships. I often get asked how a research project sparked a movement.

The truth? It started with a philosophical discussion over a beer.

In 2009, Dr. Alex Miller and I sat down over a beer to discuss the findings of a recent research project I led to study complex outsourcing relationships. As part of my research, I spent six years exploring why some relationships were highly successful while others floundered or even failed.

The key finding was the parties involved created symbiotic relationships where collaboration and "win-win" was not a glib marketing term or wishful thinking. Rather, win-win thinking was deeply embedded in all aspects the partners' relationship. The partners' mindset and management mechanisms influenced how they worked together enabling them to achieving unprecedented collaboration and often remarkable results.

I took the learnings from the research and had an early framework of the five rules that would later become the Vested methodology. As part of the research our small research team has also developed several simple tools, such as the Requirements Roadmap (shared in Rule 3) to help organizations get aligned on key operational issues like performance metrics.

Alex and I had a hunch. The research and early work on how to operationalize collaboration into a true win-win co-creation process could have the transformative impact such as Lean or Six Sigma. But there was a sticking point. First, the business world does not typically adopt or embrace academic research. And to make matters worse, great research often remains trapped inside university walls and bureaucracy.

Our casual conversation turned into philosophic banter. "Just how could we unlock the potential of our research and inspire individuals and organizations to adopt rules that often fly in the face of how traditional businesses work with their trading partners?"

We had an epiphany. The answer was right in front of us; take the emerging Vested business model and apply the rules and principles to create collaborative Vested relationships with thought leaders and experts from the academic and business world. These experts could then take the Vested methodology and help institutionalize it across all types of organizations, in all industries, all across the world.

That meeting was in 2009. That prophetic discussion gave a glimpse into the potential of what might be possible if we took the lessons from the research and put it into practice to solve our own problem. *Our own Mt. Everest.*

That night I have never been more motivated than ever to start a climb to the top of a Mt. Everest sized problem I was passionate about. I didn't know how I was going to get there. I didn't know who the various sherpas I would need to find. But I was equipped with the five rules that I knew had the power to drive radical collaboration.

For the next year our tiny research team set out to build out tools and courses that have become the foundation of what is now Vested. Simultaneously, I set out to find a small group of sherpas that could help us operationalize the Vested methodology from research into a relevant and repeatable business model. These experts could test the tools and provide field-based educational support and coaching to organizations who wanted support in putting Vested into practice

With this as the context, I'll share how Vested evolved from a research project to being named by Thinkers50 as the *Breakthrough Idea of 2025.*

BEGINNINGS

The seeds of the Vested movement were planted in 2003 when Alex recruited me to lead the initial research project for UT. I still remember his phone call. I was sitting in my car about to head into a meeting at Microsoft where I was doing some supply chain consulting. Alex had some seed money to study complex performance-based outsourcing deals and he needed someone to lead the project.

"It pays like crap, but it will be fun as hell," he shared.

As Alex shared the problem the research project was trying to solve for I still to this day recall telling him; "Alex, if we can spend some solid time studying this problem and potential solutions I am confident we can crack the code on how to get strategic and complex deals to work exponentially better than they do today."

My gut feeling was more than a hunch. I had seen the problem Alex was describing first hand. Recall, I had been in the trenches operating from all angles in business relationships. I'd worked on the development/buy-side (Microsoft), the supplier/sell side (Stream International) and the manufacturing/marketing side (P&G) of business. I'd also spent time as a consultant (Accenture), so I had seen how easy it is to create fancy reports and pretty presentations that gets stuck on someone's shelf or lost on their hard drive.

That day I found my calling.

Leading the University of Tennessee's research initiative allowed me to transcend being in the trenches and instead spend significant time trying to find better ways to collaborate.

RESEARCH PHASE

The early phase of my research set out to study complex performance-based contracts. The research got lift when the Air Force provided substantial funding allowing me to expand the research to deep dive behind the scenes into some of the world's most successful buyer-supplier relationships.

For example, what made the Procter & Gamble strategic partnership with Jones Lang LaSalle so successful that JLL won Supplier of the Year twice in less than five years? Or why was Microsoft and Accenture's "OneFinance" partnership winning so many industry awards? And how was the US Department of Energy's "unique" partnership with Kaiser-Hill so successful that the Rocky Flat's Closure project was closed and cleaned up 65 years ahead of schedule and $30 billion under budget?

Many of the partnerships we studied described their partnerships in terms of almost being a unicorn—something that just seemed to work because of the deep-seated trust that "just happened naturally". In some cases, the trust and transparency breakthrough was only unlocked after a critical inflection point in the partners' relationship.

My colleagues and I began to unpack what these companies were doing and had developed several tools and resources for the Air Force as part of our funded research. But we knew there was so much more potential. This is what sparked the philosophical discussion with Alex over a beer and motivated me to take the lessons from our research and codify them into a methodology with the secret sauce for developing successful partnerships.

CODIFICATION OF THE METHODOLOGY

The codification phase was a key part of our work. The goal was simple: set out to codify a methodology that could be not only be taught, but could be repeated.

We purposeful narrowed the focus to strategic outsourcing relationships because that was both a core focus of our original research and there was a significant need to teach organizations how to get outsourcing right. The Vested methodology was formally introduced in the book *Vested Outsourcing: Five Rules That Will Transform Outsourcing* published in 2010.

We launched our first course on Vested as part of the University of Tennessee's Executive Education program. Interest grew—especially from European countries such as the Nordics and the Netherlands, where collaboration and transparency come more naturally in the way people work. We went on to expand our courses launching the University's first online course in 2011.

It was also during this time that I set out to find individuals and organizations who had a similar passion for helping organizations make the leap from transactional relationships to trusting and transformational relationships. These partners helped sense check the original courses, which today are the foundation for our field-based Vested Centers of Excellence. Many of these partners have gone on to collaborate on additional research, provide field-based testing of tools and resources and even co-author books me with. One partner – Elizabeth Kanna – provided much needed branding savvy including helping us name the methodology to Vested.

Together we shared a common passion, and a light-hearted mantra emerged – to change the world one relationship at a time. As a group, we went on to create a network we refer to as the Vested community and adopted our own Statement of Intent and Requirements Roadmap to track our success.

The Vested Community's Shared Vision:
To create a movement where Vested's *What's in it for We* mindset is the methodology and business model that will create value to enable sustainable, measurable results never thought possible.

PROOF OF CONCEPT PHASE

The next phase was much harder and longer; proving the Vested methodology would work in practice. In the early days there were skeptics. Lots of skeptics. I recall doing a presentation at a conference and someone came up to me after my talk and patted me on the back. "Nice theory. It will never work in practice."

I went on a mission with those early advocates to help put our theory into practice, proving that the lessons from the "unicorns" we studied could be consciously created.

Dell and Intel were the first two organizations to give the Vested methodology a try. In both cases, they had supplier relationships they were deeply frustrated with, but did not want to throw in the towel with their partner yet. As these and other organizations had success, we spent the time to document their stories. The more successes, the more our program grew and the more organizations started to pilot their own Vested partnerships.

Along the way we also spent the time to learn from the organizations on what was working and where we needed go deeper with our research and toolkits. For example, Vancouver Coastal Health's head of strategic partnerships wanted to know if it was possible to get to a Vested relationship when the Canadian government needed to do a bid process. This led to our development of the Request for Partner process. And there was the constant question, "But how do I know if there is enough trust to make the leap to Vested with my partner?" which inspired my collaboration with Dr. Karl Manrodt and Dr. Jerry Ledlow to develop the Compatibility and Trust Assessment.

One of my favorite deep dives was a collaboration with David Frydlinger (one of the early advocates for Vested who leads a Vested Center of Excellence in the Nordics) and Oliver Hart (2016 Nobel Prize winner and Harvard economic theorist) around deeper work into formal relational contracts which led to a Harvard Business Review article—*A New Approach to Contracts: How to Build Better Long-Term Strategic Partnerships* and later the book *Contracting in the New Economy*.

Most recently, I collaborated with the International Institute for Conflict Prevention and Resolution which led to the book *Preventing the Dispute Before It Begins: Proven Mechanisms for Fostering Better Business Relationships*, showcasing how many of the Vested tools reduce friction and prevent contractual disputes.

By 2025 my research and collaborations had led to eight books and 10 courses as part of our Certified Deal Architect program. I am proud to say that almost all of those early partners are still a key part of the Vested community.

BUILDING A MOVEMENT

Today, public and private sector organizations around the world are deploying the concepts taught as part of UT's Vested program, with over 150 Vested initiatives to date spanning five continents. I am honored 46 leading organizations such as Intel, bp, JLL, Discovery Health, Compass, Telenet, EY, ISS and the Canadian government have allowed me to profile their success stories—some of the stories which I share in this book. In addition, over three dozen more organizations have been public about their shift and success to Vested such as IBM, Securitas, Leidos and AstraZeneca.

What is even more remarkable is the active engagement from people being genuinely curious about how Vested can be deployed. Almost 100 individuals have collaborated on various aspects of our research leading to 27 white papers which are also all open source and shared in the Creative Commons. Equally amazing is the fact that over 50 universities and trade associations are actively incorporating some (or a lot) of our research and work into their curriculum helping sow the seed to inspire the next generation of leaders how a collaborative WIIFWe approach can help individuals and organizations get past us versus them dogmas that so often prevail in today's workplaces and society.

What is truly inspiring is how people are being creative in applying the Vested way to solve tough problems *outside the business realm.* I am constantly impressed by the stories of how Vested tools are being put into practice to solve both personal and community issues. This book is my first attempt to share how the Vested Five Rules go beyond business relationships and can even help individuals collaborate in healthier ways in their home and communities.

I hope you too will join the Vested movement!

If this book sparked new ideas for your personal relationships, team, organization or community, or if you have questions, I would love to hear from you. DM me on LinkedIn.

Subscribe to my newsletter for insights, research, and real-world examples on how leaders and organizations use Vested to achieve what once seemed impossible. Visit **www.vestedway.com/newsletter** to subscribe.

Acknowledgements

In writing *The Vested Way* I stand on the shoulders of many talented collaborators.

First and foremost, I'd like to thank **Alex Miller** for bringing me into the UT family and giving me the opportunity to study the big, hairy, audacious problem of why complex business relationships which led to Vested. A shoutout to **Karl Manrodt**, **Steve Rutner**, **Steve Brady**, and **Mike Winchell**, who were part of the original research team when the research started out by looking at performance-based contracts and why some were successful while many failed.

It's also important to highlight how good research needs good funding and sponsors, so for this I'd like to recognize the following folks from the U.S. Air Force and Defense Acquisition University who championed my original research on outsourcing: **Blaise Durante**, **General Wendy Masiello**, **Col. Mark Hobson**, **Col. Dave Searle**, **Marie McManus**, **Edie Ryan**, **Lt. Col. Chris Moore**, **Sandy Schwartzwalder** and **Lyle Eesley**. I am also grateful for the amazing support from the University of Tennessee, and I'd like to give a shoutout to UT's **Global Supply Chain Institute** as well as **Ted Stank** and **Amy Cathey** for being longtime champions of my work. I want to thank Rohan Satija, a Texas teenager I profiled in a *Forbes* article, who inspired me to change my phrasing of 1+1=3, 4 or 5 to 1+1+11.

Next, I want to recognize two of the smartest people I know: **Elizabeth Kanna**, you offered the vision for what could be, and the tools and guidance necessary to make that vision a reality; and **Laurie Harting**, you were quick to understand the power of Vested and provided valuable strategic direction on not only my first book—but most of the books that followed. I still remember you saying "Kate, you don't have one book, you have five! Vested will be as big as Lean or Six Sigma."

This book, my ninth, is near and dear to heart because it is my first book that is specifically being written for a broader audience outside of the "professional" book market. I am deeply grateful for **Dan Good**, who is a masterful strategic and technical editor, and **Tricia Principe** for the beautiful cover and graphics inside the book. I'd also like to thank the following individuals who took the time to review the book and provide feedback and endorsements.

Because Vested is so much more than this book, I'd be remiss if I did not call out the various academics and practitioners I have collaborated with that have put in the hard work into various research initiatives that have led to the previous eight books, white papers and case studies.

Authors & Contributors

Sanjiv Aggarwal	David Frydlinger	Donna Massari
Jim Bergman	Jean H. Gagnon	Peter D. Moore
Marisa Brown	Adrian Gonzalez	Hank Mullen
Daniel Bumblauskas	James P Groton	Steve Murray
Mike Burnette	Lynnette Guess	Fredrik Nikolaev
Emmanuel Cambresy	John Hayes	Jeanette Nyden
Howard Carsman	Mary Holcomb, Ph.D	Todd Snelgrove
Michèle Coquis	Sarah Holliman	Wendy Tate
Phil Coughlin	Julia Jakus	Joe Tillman
Jacqui Crawford	Katherine Kawamoto	Dawn Tiura
Tim Cummins	Bonnie Keith	Astrid Uka
Ruud de Groot	Jeanne Kling	Alan Van Boven
Bill DiBenedetto	Srinivas Krishna	Jeroen van de Rijt
Sibrecht Diender	Magnus Kuchler	Ellen Waldman
J. Paul Dittmann, Ph.D	Jerry Ledlow, Ph.D	Allen Waxman
Andrew Downard, Ph.D	Mike Ledyard	Richard Wilding, Ph.D
Michele Flynn	Karl Manrodt, Ph.D	Wiebe Witteveen

I'd also like to thank the following consulting firms/law firms that have helped test and deploy the concepts in the field with real companies:

C&I Consultants	Covecroft	Neller Davies
Cirio	Incendium Consulting	Seiersen Enterprises Inc.
EY (Ernst & Young)	Prowez - Yellow Everest	Y- Africa
PerformWorks	The Forefront Group	
Ci-advisory	CIOC	

A special thanks to the professional associations that have been cheerleaders of our work. Thank you for the time you spent reviewing early versions of our work and providing endorsements.

- American Bar Association
- CORE (Center for Outsource Research and Education)
- Council of Supply Chain Management Professionals
- International Association for Outsource Professionals
- International Institute for Conflict Prevention and Resolution
- NEVI (Dutch Association for Purchasing Management)

- NIGP (The Institute for Public Procurement)
- Procurement Leaders
- SILF (Swedish National Association of Purchasing & Logistics
- Sourcing Industry Group (SIG)

I also want to extend my gratitude to the very special and talented team members behind the scenes: Mike Watts, Mike Ledyard, Janet Foldenhauer, Gui Andrade de Paula, Jennifer Werner, Chelsea Johansen, Izabela van Deest, Kelle Knight and Rhonda Watts.

And last, but certainly not least, I am fortunate to have the support of my family, Greg and Austin Picinich.

Keep Learning

"An investment in knowledge pays the best interest."
- Benjamin Franklin

Want to learn more? I encourage you check out the amazing resources I leaned on to write this book.

Chapter 1

1. Thomas R. Eisenmann, "Why Start-Ups Fail," Harvard Business School, https://www.hbs.edu/faculty/Pages/item.aspx?num=60200.
2. Wendy Wang, "Divorce in Decline: About 40% of Today's Marriages Will End in Divorce," Institute for Family Studies, December 15, 2015, https://ifstudies.org/blog/divorce-in-decline-about-40-of-todays-marriages-will-end-in-divorce.
3. Arthur C. Brooks, "The Friendship Recession: The Lost Art of Connecting," Harvard Kennedy School—Happiness Studies, February 2025, https://www.happiness.hks.harvard.edu/february-2025-issue/the-friendship-recession-the-lost-art-of-connecting.
4. Jessica Winter, "Why So Many People Are Going No Contact with Their Parents," The New Yorker, October 30, 2023, https://www.newyorker.com/culture/annals-of-inquiry/why-so-many-people-are-going-no-contact-with-their-parents.
5. Society for Human Resource Management (SHRM), "Civility in the Workplace," SHRM, https://www.shrm.org/topics-tools/topics/civility.
6. Association of Corporate Counsel, 2022 State of Corporate Litigation Report (Washington, DC: ACC, 2022), https://www.acc.com/sites/default/files/2022-10/ACC_State_Corp_Litigaton_Report.pdf.
7. Vanderbilt University, "Latest Vanderbilt Unity Index Shows the U.S. Continuing Its Trend Toward Increased Political Polarization," February 14, 2024, https://news.vanderbilt.edu/2024/02/14/latest-vanderbilt-unity-index-shows-the-u-s-continuing-its-trend-toward-increased-political-polarization/.
8. When I first started referencing the analogy of climbing Mount Everest, my collaborator Karl Manrdodt researched the history behind it, and a

version of the story of the first team to reach the summit appeared in an ebook, *The Vested Way*, that Karl and I wrote together.

9. Burt A. Folkart, "Tenzing Norgay : Sherpa Who Led Hillary to Top Dies," Los Angeles Times, May 10, 1986, https://www.latimes.com/archives/la-xpm-1986-05-10-mn-4940-story.html.

10. "Controversy Rages On Who Was First at Top," The Daily Mercury, June 23, 1953, Newspapers.com, https://www.newspapers.com/image/1001457680/.

11. Tenzing Norgay, Tiger of the Snows: The Autobiography of Tenzing of Everest (New York: Bantam, 1955).

12. Logan Kane, "U.S. Net Worth and Wealth Data: Married vs. Single," TheStreet, 2025, https://www.thestreet.com/personal-finance/us-net-worth-wealth-data-married-vs-single.

13. Alicia Adamczyk, "Inflation Makes Married Couples Between 24 and 35 Nine Times Richer Than Singles," Fortune, August 17, 2022, https://fortune.com/2022/08/17/inflation-makes-married-couples-between-24-35-nine-times-richer-than-singles/.

14. Diego De Leo et al., "Marital Status and Risk of Suicide," Journal of Affective Disorders 201 (2016), https://www.sciencedirect.com/science/article/abs/pii/S0165032716315828.

15. David A. Sbarra et al., "Divorce and Health," Perspectives on Psychological Science 6, no. 3 (2008), https://pmc.ncbi.nlm.nih.gov/articles/PMC2566023/.

16. National Center for Health Statistics, "Mortality by Marital Status in the United States, 2010–2017," Centers for Disease Control and Prevention, https://www.cdc.gov/nchs/data/hestat/mortality/mortality_marital_status_10_17.htm.

17. H. West, "A Chain of Innovation: The Creation of Swiffer," Research-Technology Management 57, no. 3 (2014), https://doi.org/10.5437/08956308X5703008.

18. West, "A Chain of Innovation: The Creation of Swiffer."

19. A. G. Lafley and Ram Charan, The Game Changer (New York: Crown Business, 2008), 134–135.

20. Procter & Gamble, Annual Report 2024, Procter & Gamble, https://us.pg.com/annualreport2024/.

21. Peter Robinson, How Ronald Reagan Changed My Life (New York: HarperCollins, 2003), 15–16.

22. Kate Vitasek et al., How P&G and JLL Transformed Corporate Real Estate (University of Tennessee Vested Case Study, 2022), https://www.vested-way.com/wp-content/uploads/2022/06/PG-Case-Study-final-TEACH-

ING-case-OK-for-Distribution-v2.pdf.

23. Susan Helper and Rebecca Henderson, "Management Practices, Relational Contracts, and the Decline of General Motors," Harvard Business Review, February 12, 2014; Oliver E. Williamson, "Outsourcing: Transaction Cost Economics and Supply Chain Management," Journal of Supply Chain Management 44, no. 2 (2008): 5–16; and Robert Axelrod, The Evolution of Cooperation (New York: Basic Books, 1984).

Chapter 2

24. Gayle King and Oprah Winfrey, "Gayle King and Oprah Uncensored," O, The Oprah Magazine, https://www.oprah.com/omagazine/gayle-king-and-oprah-uncensored-the-o-magazine-interview/all.

25. Warren Littlefield with T. R. Pearson, Top of the Rock: Inside the Rise and Fall of Must See TV (New York: Doubleday, 2012).

26. Friends: The Reunion, directed by Ben Winston, HBO Max, 2021.

27. Pew Research Center, "What Does Friendship Look Like in America?" October 12, 2023, https://www.pewresearch.org/short-reads/2023/10/12/what-does-friendship-look-like-in-america/.

28. Andrew Hutchinson, "Facebook Statistics That Matter to Marketers in 2017," WordStream, November 7, 2017, https://www.wordstream.com/blog/ws/2017/11/07/facebook-statistics.

29. Kate Vitasek, Karl Manrodt, and Jeanne Kling, Vested: How P&G, McDonald's, and Microsoft Are Redefining Winning in Business Relationships (New York: Palgrave Macmillan, 2012).

30. Key P&G Suppliers Honored with 2024 Partner of the Year Awards | P&G. https://us.pg.com/blogs/partner-of-the-year/.

31. Armstrong & Associates, "Trends in 3PL/Customer Relationships—2017" (Milwaukee, WI: Armstrong & Associates, 2017).

32. McKinsey & Company, "Six Emerging Trends in Facilities Management Sourcing," McKinsey & Company, https://www.mckinsey.com/~/media/McKinsey/Business%20Functions/Operations/Our%20Insights/Six%20emerging%20trends%20in%20facilities%20management%20sourcing/Six-emerging-trends-in-facilities-management-sourcing.pdf.

33. Kogod School of Business, 2024 Kogod Index: Closing the Gender Leadership Gap, American University, 2024, https://kogod.american.edu/autoindex/2024.

34. Grand View Research, U.S. Business Process Outsourcing Market Size, Share & Trends Analysis Report, 2023 2030, Report ID GVR-4-68040-067-1, https://www.grandviewresearch.com/industry-analysis/us-business-process-outsourcing-market-report.

35. Newspapers.com, "The 150th Anniversary of the Transcontinental Railroad," https://blog.newspapers.com/the-150th-anniversary-of-the-transcontinental-railroad/.

36. University of Washington Magazine, "At the 1936 Olympic Games, UW Crew Pulled Together to Make History," https://magazine.washington.edu/feature/at-1936-olympic-games-uw-crew-pulled-together-to-make-history/.

37. University of Washington, "UW Rowing Team Legacy," Boundless, https://www.washington.edu/boundless/uw-rowing-team-legacy/.

38. "Friends Cast Reunion Interview," YouTube video, 1:54, posted by [channel name], https://www.youtube.com/watch?v=KCxCG_lUsSE&t=114s.

Chapter 3

39. Douglas M. Lambert and A. Michael Knemeyer, "We're in This Together," Harvard Business Review, December 2004, 114; Geert Hofstede, Culture's Consequences: International Differences in Work-Related Values (Beverly Hills, CA: Sage, 1980); Vijay Pothukuchi et al., "National and Organizational Culture Differences and International Joint Venture Performance," Journal of International Business Studies 33 (2002): 243–265; Kate Vitasek et al., Unpacking Trading Partner Trust (Knoxville: University of Tennessee, October 2022).

40. Warren Littlefield with T. R. Pearson, Top of the Rock: Inside the Rise and Fall of Must See TV (New York: Doubleday, 2012).

41. "Ben Affleck and Jennifer Lopez Split: What Went Wrong," People, https://people.com/ben-affleck-jennifer-lopez-split-what-went-wrong-exclusive-8701617.

42. Kate Lloyd, "The Fantasy of Bennifer," Vogue, August 22, 2024, https://www.vogue.com/article/the-fantasy-of-bennifer.

43. Ibid.

44. Society for Human Resource Management Foundation, Retaining Talent: A Benchmarking Study, archived March 4, 2016, https://web.archive.org/web/20160304185746/https://www.shrm.org/about/foundation/research/documents/retaining%20talent-%20final.pdf.

45. Beth Kowitt, "Patagonia's Radical Approach to Hiring for Culture," Business Insider, October 2019, https://www.businessinsider.com/patagonia-hiring-company-culture-add-vs-fit-dean-carter-2019-10.

46. Lorraine Grubbs-West, "How Southwest Airlines Hires Such Dedicated People," Harvard Business Review, December 2015, https://hbr.org/2015/12/how-southwest-airlines-hires-such-dedicated-people.

47. Southwest Airlines, "Our People," Southwest Airlines Citizenship, https://www.southwest.com/citizenship/people/.

48. After Hours, podcast, Harvard Business Review, October 2018, https://hbr.org/2018/10/podcast-after-hours.

49. Susan Cartwright and Cary L. Cooper, "The Role of Culture Compatibility in Successful Organizational Marriage," Academy of Management Executive 7 (1993): 57–70.

50. McKinsey & Company, "Organizational Culture and Performance," https://www.mckinsey.com/~/media/mckinsey/dotcom/client_service/Organization/PDFs/775084%20MM%20culture%202%2010.ashx.

51. Kate Vitasek et al., Unpacking Trading Partner Trust (Knoxville: University of Tennessee, October 2022).

52. McKinsey & Company, "Organizational Culture and Performance," https://www.mckinsey.com/~/media/mckinsey/dotcom/client_service/Organization/PDFs/775084%20MM%20culture%202%2010.ashx.

53. Newspapers.com, "David Crane and the Casting of Friends," https://www.newspapers.com/image/1028563481/.

54. Warren Littlefield with T. R. Pearson, Top of the Rock: Inside the Rise and Fall of Must See TV (New York: Doubleday, 2012).

55. "Friends: Documentary Footage," television documentary.

56. Procter & Gamble, "Partner of the Year," Procter & Gamble Blogs, https://us.pg.com/blogs/partner-of-the-year/; and "P&G Honors Suppliers Driving Excellence in Supply Chains," Procurement Magazine, https://procurementmag.com/sustainability/p-g-honours-suppliers-driving-excellence-in-supply-chains.

57. "Breaking Isolation," Facing History & Ourselves, https://www.facinghistory.org/resource-library/breaking-isolation.

58. Ibid.

59. "Marriage and Relationships," Los Angeles Times, November 9, 2005.

60. Susan Heitler, "Will Your Relationship Last? Let's Fight About It and See," Psychology Today, May 2016, https://www.psychologytoday.com/us/blog/up-close-and-personal/201605/will-your-relationship-last-lets-fight-about-it-and-see.

61. John Gottman, "How to Change Your Own Contempt," Gottman Institute Blog, https://www.gottman.com/blog/how-to-change your-own-contempt/.

Chapter 4

62. McKinsey & Company, "Organizational Culture and Performance," https://www.mckinsey.com/~/media/mckinsey/dotcom/client_service/Organization/PDFs/775084%20MM%20culture%202%2010.ashx.

63. David Ludden, "How Trust Transforms Relationships," Psychology To-

day, December 2024, https://www.psychologytoday.com/us/blog/relationship-emporium/202412/how-trust-transforms-relationships.

64. Stephen M. R. Covey, The SPEED of Trust: The One Thing That Changes Everything (New York: Free Press, 2006).

65. Edelman Trust Institute. 2026 Edelman Trust Barometer Global Report: Trust Amid Insularity. Edelman, 21 Jan. 2026. Global Report PDF.

66. Accenture, "Trust in Business," Accenture Insights, https://www.accenture.com/us-en/insights/strategy/trust-in-business.

67. Sandra J. Sucher and Shalene Gupta, "The High Cost of Lost Trust," Harvard Business Review, September 2002, https://hbr.org/2002/09/the-high-cost-of-lost-trust.

68. Kate Vitasek et al., Unpacking Trading Partner Trust in the Energy Industry (University of Tennessee white paper).

69. Contracting in the New Economy.

70. Deloitte, "Transparency in the Workplace," Human Capital Trends 2024, Deloitte Insights, https://www2.deloitte.com/us/en/insights/focus/human-capital-trends/2024/transparency-in-the-workplace.html.

71. There are several individuals and organizations that have made similar comparisons using a trust/transparency comparison, including Leadcase, "Trust and Transparency in Client Relationships," https://leadcase.net/topics/trust-and-transparency.

72. Paul Zak, "Proven Ways to Earn Your Employees' Trust," Harvard Business Review, June 2014, https://hbr.org/2014/06/proven-ways-to-earn-your-employees-trust.

73. McKinsey & Company, "The Dark Side of Transparency," https://www.mckinsey.com/capabilities/people-and-organizational-performance/our-insights/the-dark-side-of-transparency.

74. James Tamm and Ronald Luyet, Radical Collaboration (New York: HarperBusiness, 2005).

75. Kate Vitasek et al., RelianceCM Case Study (University of Tennessee Vested Case Study, February 22, 2019), https://www.vestedway.com/wp-content/uploads/2022/06/RelianceCM-Case-Study-Feb-22-2019-OK-to-distribute-v2.pdf.

76. Note: All of the quotes in this case study are from interviews conducted in August and September 2018.

Chapter 5

77. High Adventure Expeditions, "List of Mount Everest Climbers," https://haexpeditions.com/advice/list-of-mount-everest-climbers/.

78. Amir Goldberg, "Blurred Lines: How Collectivism Norms Operate

Through Perceived Group Boundaries," Stanford Graduate School of Business, https://www.gsb.stanford.edu/faculty-research/publications/blurred-lines-how-collectivism-norm-operates-through-perceived-group.

79. John Locke, Two Treatises of Government, Section II, Chapter II (London, 1689), https://oll-resources.s3.us-east-2.amazonaws.com/oll3/store/titles/2620/Smith_TMS-Languages1648_Bk.pdf.

80. USAFacts, "How Long Do Americans Stay at Their Jobs?" https://usafacts.org/articles/how-long-do-americans-stay-at-their-jobs/.

81. John F. Kennedy, "Address to a Joint Session of Congress on Urgent National Needs," May 25, 1961, John F. Kennedy Presidential Library and Museum, https://www.jfklibrary.org/learn/about-jfk/historic-speeches/address-to-joint-session-of-congress-may-25-1961.

82. "President Kennedy's Moon Speech," YouTube video, https://www.youtube.com/watch?v=LhoLuui9gX8.

83. Amy C. Edmondson, "Psychological Safety and Learning Behavior in Work Teams," Administrative Science Quarterly 44, no. 2 (1999): 350–383, https://web.mit.edu/curhan/www/docs/Articles/15341_Readings/Group_Performance/Edmondson%20Psychological%20safety.pdf.

84. Amy C. Edmondson, "Psychological Safety and Learning Behavior in Work Teams," Administrative Science Quarterly 44, no. 2 (1999): 350–383, https://www.jstor.org/stable/2634977.

85. Oliver E. Williamson, "Outsourcing: Transaction Cost Economics and Supply Chain Management," Journal of Supply Chain Management 44, no. 2 (2008): 5–16.

86. Damon E. Jones et al., "The Effects of Family Structure on Child Outcomes," Prevention Science 15 (2014), https://link.springer.com/article/10.1007/s11121-014-0480-4.

87. Society for Human Resource Management, "Office Romance and Honeymoons," HR Magazine, https://www.shrm.org/topics-tools/news/hr-magazine/honeymoons.

88. Oliver Hart, "Overcoming Contractual Incompleteness," October 2020, https://scholar.harvard.edu/files/hart/files/overcoming_october_2020.pdf.

89. Kate Vitasek et al., Preventing the Dispute Before It Begins: Proven Mechanisms for Fostering Better Business Relationships (Chicago: ABA Publishing, 2024).

Chapter 6

90. Jason Beaubien, "The Science Behind the Super Abilities of Sher-

pas," NPR, May 28, 2017, https://www.npr.org/sections/goatsandsoda/2017/05/28/530204187/the-science-behind-the-super-abilities-of-sherpas.

91. Gallup, "The Ultimate Guide to Micromanagers: Signs, Causes, and Solutions," https://www.gallup.com/workplace/315530/ultimate-guide-micromanagers-signs-causes-solutions.aspx.

92. PwC, "Why Autonomy Is the Key to Employee Engagement," https://www.pwc.com/gx/en/services/workforce/publications/provide-autonomy.html.

93. M. A. Abdallah et al., "Job Autonomy and Job Satisfaction: New Evidence," ResearchGate, https://www.researchgate.net/publication/5161837_Job_autonomy_and_job_satisfaction_new_evidence.

94. J. Block et al., "Autonomy and Entrepreneurial Performance," Small Business Economics 58 (2023), https://link.springer.com/article/10.1007/s11365-023-00834-9.

95. Stephen R. Covey, The 7 Habits of Highly Effective People (New York: Simon & Schuster, 2013).

96. Ibid.

97. Stephen M. R. Covey, interview by Anthony Orsini, "The SPEED of Trust with Stephen M. R. Covey," The Orsini Way podcast, https://theorsiniway.com/podcast/the-speed-of-trust-with-stephen-m-r-covey/.

98. Toyota Motor Corporation, "The Toyota Production System," https://global.toyota/en/company/vision-and-philosophy/production-system/.

99. "Toyota Production System Overview," Associated Press, August 3, 2007.

100. "Toyota Production System Explained," YouTube video, https://www.youtube.com/watch?v=0RQ3b-LQqyE.

101. Ibid.

102. Erin Golden, "School Bus Driver Shares Her Family's Story About the I-35W Bridge Collapse," KSTP News, https://kstp.com/kstp-news/local-news/school-bus-driver-shares-her-familys-story-about-i-35w-bridge-collapse/.

103. Curt Brown, "Lessons from the I-35W Bridge Collapse," Minneapolis Star Tribune, September 2007.

104. "Minneapolis Regional Chamber of Commerce and I-35W Bridge Collapse," Star Tribune, September 21, 2007, B3, https://www.newspapers.com/image/250708120/.

105. U.S. Department of Transportation, "Collapse of Interstate 35W Bridge over the Mississippi River," testimony, https://www.transportation.gov/testimony/collapse-interstate-35-west-bridge-over-mississippi-river.

106. A. Cho, "Mixing Social and Structural Skills; Leaders Guided Historic

Rebuild Project," Engineering News-Record, January 7, 2009, http://enr. construction.com/people/awards/2009/0107-Peter Sanderson.asp.

107. Society for Human Resource Management, "The Real Costs of Recruitment," https://www.shrm.org/topics-tools/news/talent-acquisition/real-costs-recruitment.

108. Kate Rogers, "Google's 20% Rule Shows Exactly How Much Time You Should Spend Learning New Skills," CNBC, December 16, 2021, https://www.cnbc.com/2021/12/16/google-20-percent-rule-shows-exactly-how-much-time-you-should-spend-learning-new-skills.html.

109. Interview with Seth, November 2025.

110. McKinsey & Company, "The Great Attrition Is Making Hiring Harder— Are You Searching the Right Talent Pools?" https://www.mckinsey.com/capabilities/people-and-organizational-performance/our-insights/the-great-attrition-is-making-hiring-harder-are-you-searching-the-right-talent-pools.

111. U.S. Department of Energy, "Rocky Flats Site: Colorado History and Documents," https://www.energy.gov/lm/articles/rocky-flats-site-colorado-history-documents.

112. U.S. Department of Energy, Rocky Flats Environmental Technology Site Large Area Fog-Nix Fix Report, https://lmpublicsearch.lm.doe.gov/NonEktron/1567-130-RFETS_Large_Area_FognFix.pdf.

113. U.S. Department of Energy, Rocky Flats Closure Legacy Report, https://lmpublicsearch.lm.doe.gov/LMSites/1702-Rocky%20Flats%20Closure%20Legacy%20Report.pdf.

Chapter 7

114. Peter F. Drucker, The Practice of Management (New York: Harper & Row, 1954).

115. Tom Peters, "What Gets Measured Gets Done," TomPeters.com, https://tompeters.com/columns/what-gets-measured-gets-done/.

116. George T. Doran, "There's a S.M.A.R.T. Way to Write Management's Goals and Objectives," Management Review 70, no. 11 (1981): 35–36.

117. Cary Greene, "Three Popular Goal-Setting Techniques Managers Should Avoid," Harvard Business Review, January 2017, https://hbr.org/2017/01/3-popular-goal-setting-techniques-managers-should-avoid.

118. Robert S. Kaplan and David P. Norton, "The Balanced Scorecard: Measures That Drive Performance," Harvard Business Review, January–February 1992, https://hbr.org/1992/01/the-balanced-scorecard-measures-that-drive-performance-2.

119. John Doerr, Measure What Matters (New York: Portfolio, 2018).

120. Major League Baseball, "MLB Standings—1997 Season," https://www.mlb.com/standings/mlb/1997.

121. The Baseball Cube, "MLB Payrolls—1998," https://www.thebaseballcube.com/content/payroll_year/1998/.

122. Major League Baseball, "MLB Standings—2000 Season," https://www.mlb.com/standings/mlb/2000.

123. National Aeronautics and Space Administration, "Mars Climate Orbiter Mishap Investigation Board Phase I Report," August 2009, https://sma.nasa.gov/docs/default-source/safety-messages/safetymessage-2009-08-01-themarsclimateorbitermishap.pdf.

124. National Space Science Data Center, "Mars Climate Orbiter," https://nssdc.gsfc.nasa.gov/nmc/spacecraft/display.action?id=1998-073A.

125. Oliver Hart and John Moore, "Contracts as Reference Points," Quarterly Journal of Economics 123, no. 1 (2008): 1–48.

126. Oliver Hart, "Overcoming Contractual Incompleteness," working paper, October 2020, https://scholar.harvard.edu/files/hart/files/overcoming_contractual_incompleteness_013122.pdf.

Chapter 8

127. Gallup, State of the Global Workplace (Washington, DC: Gallup), https://www.gallup.com/workplace/349484/state-of-the-global-workplace.aspx.

128. McKinsey & Company, "Experience-Led Growth: A New Way to Create Value," https://www.mckinsey.com/capabilities/growth-marketing-and-sales/our-insights/experience-led-growth-a-new-way-to-create-value.

129. Daniel Kahneman and Amos Tversky, "Prospect Theory: An Analysis of Decision under Risk," Econometrica 47, no. 2 (1979): 263–291, https://web.mit.edu/curhan/www/docs/Articles/15341_Readings/Behavioral_Decision_Theory/Kahneman_Tversky_1979_Prospect_theory.pdf.

130. Daniel Kahneman and Amos Tversky, "Prospect Theory: An Analysis of Decision under Risk," Econometrica 47, no. 2 (1979): 263–291, https://www.jstor.org/stable/41721919.

131. Adrian Gostick and Chester Elton, The Carrot Principle (New York: Free Press, 2007).

132. "Why You Feel Underappreciated at Work," Harvard Business Review, July 2024, https://hbr.org/2024/07/why-you-feel-underappreciated-at-work.

133. American Psychological Association, "Younger Workers Are More Stressed Than Ever," press release, June 2024, https://www.apa.org/news/press/releases/2024/06/younger-workers-stressed.

134. "Picocuries per Gram (pCi/g)," unit definition.

135. Jeffrey Mervis, "Science-Based Cleanup of Rocky Flats," Physics Today, https://physicstoday.aip.org/features/science-based-cleanup-of-rocky-flats.

136. Kathleen D. Vohs, Nicole L. Mead, and Miranda R. Goode, "The Psychological Consequences of Money," Science 314, no. 5802 (December 2006): 1154–1156.

137. Juanjuan Zhang et al., "Dynamic Pricing and Consumer Behavior," Management Science (2020), https://pubsonline.informs.org/doi/abs/10.1287/mnsc.2020.3721.

138. Joshua Dowling, "Uber Drivers Trigger Fake Surge Price Periods," Drive, https://www.drive.com.au/news/uber-drivers-trigger-fake-surge-price-periods/.

139. "Everyone Hates Uber's Surge Pricing—Here's How to Fix It," Harvard Business Review, December 2015, https://hbr.org/2015/12/everyone-hates-ubers-surge-pricing-heres-how-to-fix-it.

140. Emily Stewart, "Fast-Food Restaurants Are Testing Dynamic Pricing Algorithms," Vox, https://www.vox.com/money/24105250/fast-food-restaurants-dynamic-pricing-algorithm-wendys.

141. Paul Barshop, "Methods for Reducing Claims," in Reducing Construction Costs: Uses of Best Dispute Resolution Practices by Project Owners, Proceedings Report (Washington, DC: National Academies of Sciences, Engineering, and Medicine, 2007), 37–42, https://nap.nationalacademies.org/read/11846/chapter/9.

142. Ian O'Connor, "Smash His Own Records, but Nibbles at Them," New York Daily News, August 1, 1996, https://www.newspapers.com/image/492069125/.

143. To learn more about shading and shirking in contract, refer to the various works of Nobel laureate Oliver Hart— especially those after 2008.

144. Guardrails are the minimum and maximum economic thresholds mutually agreed by the parties. For example, a service provider may have a goal to have a profit margin of 10% and if the economics of the deal fall below 5% the parties agree to review the pricing model assumption and make adjustments.

Chapter 9

145. Kevin O'Leary, "Five Reasons Why Business Partnerships Fail," North One Blog, https://www.northone.com/blog/small-business/5-reasons-why-business-partnerships-fail.

146. Wendy Wang, "Divorce in Decline: About 40% of Today's Marriages Will End in Divorce," Institute for Family Studies, December 15, 2015, https://

ifstudies.org/blog/divorce-in-decline-about-40-of-todays-marriages-will-end-in-divorce.

147. Bain & Company, Engineering, Construction & Services Industry Report (2021), https://www.bain.com/globalassets/noindex/2021/bain_report_enr_report_2021.pdf.

148. Discovery Holdings, Discovery Health Medical Scheme Integrated Report 2024, https://www.discovery.co.za/assets/discoverycoza/corporate/investor-relations/2025/dhms-ir-2024.pdf.

149. Amanda Holpuch, "Sriracha Shortage Explained," Fortune, January 30, 2024, https://fortune.com/2024/01/30/sriracha-shortage-huy-fong-foods-tabasco-underwood-ranches/.

150. Jordan Valinsky, "What Really Caused the Sriracha Shortage," Yahoo Finance, https://finance.yahoo.com/news/really-caused-sriracha-shortage-2-110000803.html.

151. Rong-Gong Lin II, "Underwood Ranches Sues Huy Fong Foods over Sriracha," Los Angeles Times, July 12, 2019, https://www.latimes.com/local/lanow/la-me-ln-sriracha-lawsuit-underwood-ranches-20190712-story.html.

152. Reeves Wiedeman, "The Cellino & Barnes Breakup," New York Magazine, https://nymag.com/intelligencer/article/cellino-and-barnes-breakup.html.

153. Cellino v. Barnes, B303096 (Cal. Ct. App. 2021), https://law.justia.com/cases/california/court-of-appeal/2021/b303096.html.

154. Ming-Te Wang et al., "Parent–Child Estrangement and Psychological Adjustment," Journal of Child and Family Studies 28 (2019), https://link.springer.com/article/10.1007/s10826-018-1277-z.

155. McKinsey & Company, The Construction Productivity Imperative, https://www.mckinsey.com/~/media/McKinsey/Industries/Capital%20Projects%20and%20Infrastructure/Our%20Insights/The%20construction%20productivity%20imperative/The%20construction%20productivity%20imperative.pdf.

156. McKinsey Global Institute, Reinventing Construction: A Route to Higher Productivity, https://www.mckinsey.com/~/media/mckinsey/business%20functions/operations/our%20insights/reinventing%20construction%20through%20a%20productivity%20revolution/mgi-reinventing-construction-a-route-to-higher-productivity-full-report.pdf.

157. Minnesota Department of Transportation, From Tragedy to Triumph: How MnDOT Turned the I-35W Bridge Collapse into a Model of Recovery.

158. Michelle Hill, "10 Notable E. coli Outbreaks at U.S. Fast-Food Restau-

rants," UPI, December 31, 2015, https://www.upi.com/Health_News/2015/12/31/10-notable-E-coli-outbreaks-at-US-fast-food-restaurants/5781451489618/.

159. McDonald's, "Meet Our Suppliers: Lopez Foods," http://www.mcdonalds.com/us/en/food/food_quality/see_what_we_are_made_of/meet_our_suppliers/lopez_foods.html.

160. Nanci Hellmich, "New School Lunch Standards," USA Today, December 8, 2009, http://www.usatoday.com/news/education/2009-12-08-school-lunch-standards_N.htm.

161. U.S. Food and Drug Administration, "Outbreak Investigation of E. coli O157:H7 Infections Linked to Onions," October 2024, https://www.fda.gov/food/outbreaks-foodborne-illness/outbreak-investigation-e-coli-o157h7-onions-october-2024.

162. McDonald's, Moving Forward with Food Safety at the Center, October 27, 2024, https://corporate.mcdonalds.com/content/dam/sites/corp/nfl/pdf/Joe%20Erlinger%20Message_Transcript_10.27.24.pdf.

163. U.S. Food and Drug Administration, "Outbreak Investigation of E. coli O157:H7 Infections Linked to Onions," October 2024, https://www.fda.gov/food/outbreaks-foodborne-illness/outbreak-investigation-e-coli-o157h7-onions-october-2024.

164. Associated Press, "Boar's Head Recalls Products over Listeria Concerns," https://apnews.com/article/boars-head-listeria-recall-fcde06b66dca38d-53361c92495a7cfed.

165. Boar's Head, "Product Recall Information," 2024, https://boarshead.com/products-recall-2024.

166. Suzy Khimm, "USDA Documents Insects, Slime at Boar's Head Plants," NBC News, https://www.nbcnews.com/business/business-news/usda-documented-insects-slime-boars-head-plants-records-show-rcna187652.

167. Boar's Head, "Product Recall Information," 2024, https://boarshead.com/products-recall-2024.

168. "Boar's Head Recall Explained," YouTube video, https://www.youtube.com/watch?v=RZnkToMyi4Q.

Chapter 10

169. Russell L. Ackoff, "Systems Thinking," lecture.

170. Gartner, "Gartner Announces Rankings of the 2017 Supply Chain Top 25," May 25, 2017, https://www.gartner.com/en/newsroom/press-releases/2017-05-25-gartner-announces-rankings-of-the-2017-supply-chain-top-25.

171. "Corporate Collaboration Trends," Atlanta Constitution, August 11, 2006.

172. Stephanie Strom, "Coke and McDonald's, Working Hand in Hand Since 1955," New York Times, May 16, 2014, https://www.nytimes.com/2014/05/16/business/coke-and-mcdonalds-working-hand-in-hand-since-1955.html.

173. McDonald's, "Our Story," http://www.mcdonalds.com/us/en/our_story/our.

174. "Why Does Coca-Cola Taste So Good at McDonald's?" McDonald's FAQ, https://www.mcdonalds.com/us/en-us/faq/why-does-coca-cola-taste-so-good-at-mcdonald-s.html.

175. Ibid.

Index

www.ingramcontent.com/pod-product-compliance
Lightning Source LLC
Chambersburg PA
CBHW051243050726
47594CB00001B/285